The Spiritual, Mystical and Supernatural

Second Edition

Harold R. Eberle

Worldcast Publishing
Yakima, Washington, USA

The Spiritual, Mystical and Supernatural
Second Edition

© 2004 by Harold R. Eberle
© 2011 Second edition by Harold R. Eberle

Worldcast Publishing
P.O. Box 10653
Yakima, WA 98909-1653
www.worldcastpublishing.com
office@worldcastpublishing.com
509-248-5837

ISBN 978-1-882523-28-3
Cover by Lynette Brannan

Printed in the United States of America.

Credits and Thanks

Pastor James Leuschen of Spokane, Washington, helped me think through the many doctrinal issues and challenged me on numerous points. Also, I had input and editing advice from Pastor John Frady, Martha Brookhart, Pastor Peter Eisenmann, R. E. McMaster and Dennis Jacobson. James Bryson deserves special mention for extensive work restructuring and clarifying my thoughts. Tristan Kohl is my final editor. He is amazing!

However, I owe most to my staff who have given their time faithfully month by month and served in love over the years: Linda (my wife), Mike and Maria Clark, Mike and Maribel Pillsbury, Andy and Debby Breismeister, Frank and Jane Johnson, and R.D. and Patti Smith. I ask people who read these pages to pray for my staff, their marriages, children, lives and walks with God.

Table of Contents

Section 4: Powers and Activities of a Person's Spirit

Section 5: Spiritual Dynamics Between People

Introduction

I was so hungry for the spiritual and supernatural, I spent four years in prayer. All my life I have been a seeker of spiritual realities, but when I was 31 years old, I resigned from the church I was pastoring and entered into a lifestyle of Christian mysticism. On weekends I traveled and spoke in churches across North America, but most weekdays I prayed for several hours each day. I read every book I could find on the supernatural and spiritual dimension. I sought out Christian leaders who had experienced more of the supernatural than I had. I craved answers. I wanted to understand. I wanted to experience God's spiritual world and I wanted to see His power fully released into His Church.

It has been over 20 years since I spent those four years dedicated to prayer. Since then I have traveled the world. Much of my time has been spent in developing nations where the supernatural is more openly demonstrated. For several years I have traveled around Africa where I encountered spiritual phenomena and had to teach extensively on the related subjects. Today I still don't have all of the answers. I have experienced spiritual phenomena which I do not understand, but I am further down the road than I was when I began. And I am convinced that God wants His children stepping into greater manifestations of His power.

For this reason I write. I want to see the Church mature into all God has for Her. So in section 1 of this book, I will build a picture of how the spiritual and natural worlds interact and relate to one another. Then in section 2, I will present a view of human nature which helps us understand how we access and relate to the spiritual world. In section 3,

1

I will correct a common error among Christians who pursue spiritual things. Finally in sections 4 and 5, I will explain spiritual dynamics that take place between people.

I will be offering many examples from modern life, but our textbook will be the Bible. In Old Testament times there were "Schools of Prophets." Those with spiritual inclinations learned much about the workings of God and the invisible world. I hope this book will be of similar value. Let's call this the "School of the Spirit." Welcome to class!

Section 1

The Spiritual Realm and How We Access It

The spiritual world is very close. It is accessible. Let's investigate.

Developing a Picture of the Spiritual Realm

The prophet Elisha once prayed for his servant, saying, *"O Lord, I pray, open his eyes that he may see"* (II Kings 6:17). The servant's spiritual eyes were opened and he saw horses and chariots of fire on the mountain before him. God allowed Elisha's servant to see the world of the spirit and he was astonished.

What if we prayed and God opened our eyes? How would the spiritual world appear to us? If the walls disappeared and the ceiling vanished and we could see the entire invisible world surrounding us, what would we see? We can begin answering this by developing a picture of the spiritual world from what we see in Scripture.

Even though I refer to the spiritual and natural "worlds," we can also refer to them as "realms." In one sense this is more accurate because both realms exist in the one world which God created. Hebrews 11:3 tells us that the natural realm was made out of that which is invisible. Therefore, we know that the invisible spiritual realm existed before the natural realm. Whether we refer to these as "worlds" or "realms," it is best to envision the natural and spiritual as superimposed upon one another. The spiritual realm preexisted the natural realm and we may separate the two realms for discussion purposes, but we should keep in mind that they overlap and fill the same space.

The Spiritual Realm and the Natural Realm

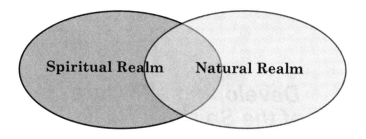

The spiritual realm is where angels exist and interact. Michael, the archangel, is revealed as a commander of God's angelic army. The Bible describes some beautiful angels (e.g., Is. 6:2; Ex. 25:20), but there are also spiritual creatures which are powerful and terrifying to humans. The prophet Ezekiel saw four living beings, each having four faces: that of a man, a lion, a bull and an eagle (Ez. 1:4-21). As these living beings moved together, lightning flashed round about them and the sight was terrifying to Ezekiel. Creatures such as these and others described in the Bible are not demons but spiritual creatures on God's side.

There is also an evil side, where Satan rules over his demons. Satan's realm is the dominion of darkness while God's kingdom is the kingdom of light. These two authorities are not on equal levels. We should not think of Satan as the opposite of God. Satan is merely a created being. It is more accurate to think of Satan as the counterpart of Michael. Furthermore, Satan's realm of darkness has been subjected to the kingdom of God. Jesus has been exalted *far* above all rule and authority (Eph. 1:20-22).

There are many things in the spiritual realm—not elements of physical substance, but things of spiritual substance, invisible to us but, indeed, real. In Ephesians 1:3, we

6

are told that God *"has blessed us with every spiritual blessing in the heavenly places in Christ."* God has prepared many blessings for those who love Him. Just as this realm has real things made of natural substances (rock, water, wood, etc.), so also the spiritual realm has things of spiritual substances. It is a realm full of unseen treasures.

It is equally important to realize that the laws which govern the spiritual realm are different than natural laws. In the natural realm there is a law of gravity. In the spiritual realm there is no such law; therefore, spirit entities can move about freely without physical limitations. Some have wrongly concluded that there is neither space nor distance in the spirit. It would be more accurate to say that there is space, but spirit entities are not limited by it, as we are in the natural realm. This point is vital for our later discussions so let's take a moment to confirm it.

We know there is space because Satan is not in all places at all times. In the book of Job, chapter 1, Satan tells God that he has been roaming about upon Earth. Satan does not fill Earth; rather, he is limited to one place at a time. The fact that Satan first had to go *into* the throne room of God in order to talk to the Lord implies that distance and location have some meaning in the spiritual realm.

Though distance and space are spiritual realities, the limits are not the same as on Earth. Consider Luke 8:26-39, when our Lord Jesus cast a legion of demons out of a certain man. In Bible times, a Roman legion consisted of anywhere from 2,000 to 6,000 soldiers. Since a legion of demons came out of one man, size and space in the spiritual realm must have different meanings than those to which we are accustomed in the natural realm.

There are spatial correlations between the spiritual and natural realms. When Elisha's servant saw the fiery chariots, those chariots were on the mountain (II Kings 6:17). Indeed, we see many such relationships in the Bible between natural mountains and spiritual positions of authority. For example, God met Moses on Mount Sinai. At another location Jacob saw a stairway upon which angels ascended and descended; Jacob placed a pillar in that place to mark the physical location corresponding to the spiritual vantage point (Gen. 28:10-22). Even the fact that demons seek to inhabit a human vessel implies their attachment to physical locations.

There are places of light and darkness both in the spiritual and natural realms. The spiritual realm is not a homogeneous mass. There are "hot spots" and "cold spots." There are holy places and desecrated places. The spiritual realm overlaps the natural realm and there are often correlations between events in the two realms.

Finally, we want to identify one other law and its significance in the spiritual realm. This law has to do with time. Do not make the mistake which some have made and assume that time does not exist in the spiritual realm. Some Christians have misunderstood Revelation 10:6, which says in the King James Version that *"there should be time no longer."* In reality, this verse is not making a statement about the existence of time. Rather it is in the context of God's coming judgments; the writer is saying there will be no more time before judgments fall.

There is time in the spiritual realm. If time did not exist, then Satan, who is a spiritual being, would exist throughout time and he would know all things beginning to end. One day God will throw Satan into the Lake of Fire, where he *"will be tormented day and night forever and ever"* (Rev. 20:10). If time restrictions were not imposed upon the spiritual realm, demons would simply escape God's judgment and move into another time period. Demons are limited in time, even though they exist in the spiritual realm.

It is also significant that things are changing in the spiritual realm. For example, 2,000 years ago Jesus ascended far above all rule and authority. Demons were rebelling at one point and then subjected to our Lord's authority at another point. If time did not exist in the spiritual realm, nothing could change.

We do not know whether time has always existed or whether it started *"in the beginning."* All we know for sure is that time exists now, both in the natural realm and in the spiritual realm. Having said that, we must point out that it is possible that God transcends both time and space. He is not limited as are created beings.

With this basic understanding, we can go on to study our relationship to the spiritual realm—how we influence it and how it influences us.

Our Contact with the Spiritual Realm

Christians believe that people have more to their beings than just a physical body. Each person has an invisible portion referred to as a spirit or soul. Section 2 of these studies is dedicated to explaining the nature and functions of the spirit and soul. Here I will simply refer to the invisible part of a person's being as the spirit.

The spirit of a person exists in the spiritual realm. Right now, while you are reading these words, you exist in two realms. Just as the body is in direct contact with the natural realm, the spirit is in direct contact with the spiritual realm. This is what the Christian faith declares, although many have not considered the implications.

You Exist in Two Realms

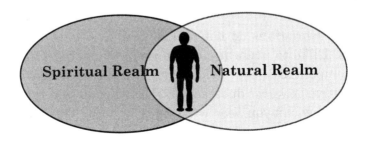

Spiritual Realm   Natural Realm

Christians and non-Christians experience the spiritual realm differently. Christians have access to the kingdom of God within the spiritual realm. Believers have been transferred from the domain of darkness into the kingdom of light (Col. 1:13). Non-Christians have a spirit in contact with the spiritual realm, and they can experience that realm, but not the fullness of God's blessing, because *"...unless one is born again he cannot see the kingdom of God"* (John 3:3). Both Christians and non-Christians are influenced by the spiritual realm, but believers can have access to God in a much fuller way.

Furthermore, when non-Christians "go into the spirit" (to be explained in the next chapter), they are exposing themselves to evil. Their spirits are an open door for demonic influences to work. In contrast, the Christian interacts with both God's kingdom and Satan's domain. We are told that whatever we bind or loose will be bound or loosed (Matt. 18:18-19). Of course, believers can be influenced by evil and tempted by the devil, but the believers also have access to God's power and blessings.

Let's identify how a person can sense things in the spiritual realm. Recall our earlier point: a person's spirit exists in the spiritual realm and is continually in contact with that realm. Everyone has spiritual senses. Just as they have physical senses (hearing, sight, touch, taste and smell) to perceive what is occurring in the natural realm, so also they have spiritual senses telling them what is happening in the spiritual realm.

Some Christians do not realize that they have spiritual senses. I like to make it clear to them by asking, "Are you ever tempted to do evil?" The obvious answer is always in the affirmative. My next question, "If it is a demon that is tempting you how can you *hear* what he is saying?" The devil and his demons exist in the spiritual realm. If you hear them, that means you have the ability to hear spiritual impressions, hence, you have spiritual ears.

The Bible reveals that every person has spiritual senses, but those senses are receptive to varying degrees. Consider Elisha when he prayed that his servant's spiritual eyes might be opened (II Kings 6:17); he did not pray that his servant would receive eyes, but rather that the eyes he had would be opened. Similarly, in the New Testament, Paul expressed his prayer that the eyes of the Christian's heart would be opened (Eph. 1:18). Many Bible passages talk about the "ears" of some people being open to God while the ears of others are closed. It is not the receiving of these spiritual senses but the quickening of them that people need.

The "quickening" of a person's spiritual senses can happen through the aid of good or evil spirit beings. In Acts 16:16-18, we read about a woman who could foretell the future through a spirit of divination. That spirit was a demon, which the apostle Paul later cast out.

There are also people whom God supernaturally has enabled to perceive things in the spiritual realm. Look what we are told about Daniel:

> *...an extraordinary spirit, knowledge and insight, interpretation of dreams, explanation of enigmas and solving of difficult problems were found in this Daniel....*
>
> (Dan. 5:12)

It was God's Spirit Who gifted Daniel in these ways. Similarly, the Holy Spirit enabled many in the New Testament to perceive and understand things in the spiritual realm.

It is not only those with special gifts who are able to perceive realities of the spirit. Of course, there are some with special enablements through either demonic or God's empowering, but every human being has a spirit with spiritual sensitivities. This "availability to all" is especially important for Christians, because the Holy Spirit desires to work in every believer's life, revealing the will of God and the realities of His kingdom (I Cor. 2:10-13). Receiving things from the Holy Spirit is not just a possibility for some Christians, but the privilege of all Christians.

Many Christians do not believe that God communicates directly with people. They believe that the devil inspires his thoughts in the minds and hearts of people, but they do not think God is doing the same thing. They have more faith in the activity of Satan than the work of God. This is foolish and tragic.

When God speaks to the Christian, it is not usually an audible voice from heaven. God can talk in that fashion, as He did several times in the Bible (e.g., Acts 9:4-7); however, He usually inspires His thoughts and desires upon one's conscious mind and heart through one's spirit. The apostle Paul explained it this way:

> *For to us God revealed them through the Spirit; for the Spirit searches all things, even the depths of God. For who among men knows the thoughts of a man except the spirit of the man, which is in him? Even so the thoughts of God no one knows except the Spirit of God. Now we have received, not the spirit of the world, but the Spirit who is from God, so that we might know the things freely given to us by God.*
>
> (I Cor. 2:10-12)

The will and thoughts of God are made known to us through the Holy Spirit revealing things to our spirits.

The communication which the Holy Spirit has with a person's spirit is not the same as communication on the natural level with other human beings. Paul explained that spiritual truths only can be relayed in spiritual terms (I Cor. 2:7-13). The language—and even the words we have developed to communicate with people in this world—are unable to convey spiritual realities. Our natural human thought patterns are not able to receive many of the spiritual truths God wants to communicate to us. For this reason, Paul explained in I Corinthians, chapter 2, that the naturally-minded person cannot receive the things of the Spirit. Spiritual thoughts can be communicated only to those who are spiritually-minded. Communication of spiritual realities must take place on the level of the spirit.

How, then, does the Holy Spirit communicate to our spirits? There are times when God uses words and thought patterns familiar to our natural reasoning, but primarily He uses *spiritual impressions.* The Holy Spirit reveals the will of God to us through stirrings, nudges, words, spiritual pictures, burdens and unctions. Ezekiel explained that the Spirit works within us, *"causing"* us to do the Father's will (Ez. 36:27). The apostle Paul wrote that the Christian's spirit is *"alive"* (Rom. 8:10), implying our spirits are responsive and sensitive to God. It is as if the Holy Spirit is brushing against us, silently pushing us from within according to the plans and purposes of God.

There is also a communication in the spirit which cannot be explained with human understanding. We call it revelation. A person simply "knows something." She does not know how she knows. She did not arrive at the understanding through experience, education or logical reasoning. As a light shining from a projector onto a screen, so is the direction of God revealed through the spirit and reflected upon the conscious mind. Some would call this intuition, but that term gives no credit to the role God's Spirit plays. I am not saying that all intuitive knowledge is from God, but there is a real transmission of information that takes place directly from the Holy Spirit to a person's spirit.

Spiritual communications all have qualities similar to a gentle breeze. Jesus explained:

> *"The wind blows where it wishes and you hear the sound of it, but do not know where it comes from and where it is going; so is everyone who is born of the Spirit."*

(John 3:8)

Like the blowing wind, so is the work of the Holy Spirit. Images, words, impressions, burdens, nudges, etc.—such are the workings of the Spirit as He acts upon and reveals things to the Christian's spirit.

Spiritual Communication Like the Breeze

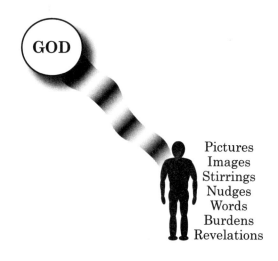

GOD

Pictures
Images
Stirrings
Nudges
Words
Burdens
Revelations

God also talks to people through other avenues, such as the written Word, other people, circumstances, events, etc. We must not limit our thinking to the spiritual, but our intentions in this book are to understand and open to the realm of the spirit.

How to Tune In to the Spirit

How can people tune in to the spirit? How can you and I access God and His blessings in the spiritual dimension? God has told us in several Bible verses that if we seek Him with our whole heart and soul, then we will find Him (e.g., Deut. 4:29). This discovering of God is not in the usual sense of God being with us every minute of every day. It is possible to seek God in a way that He actually will reveal Himself to us and make Himself more fully known.

How, then, can we find Him?

Remember our Lord's words, *"God is spirit and those who worship Him must worship in spirit and truth"* (John 4:24). Our Lord said this to a Samaritan woman who asked Jesus about different forms of worship—whether people should worship God on a specific mountain or some other location (John 4:20). She was focused upon natural aspects of worship. Jesus changed her focus from the natural to the spiritual, declaring that *"God is spirit"*—that is: He exists in the spiritual realm. When God states that He is *"spirit"* and that we must worship Him *"in spirit,"* He is taking the position that we must go into His realm to have contact with Him.

I can compare this with my relationship with you right now. I live in the state of Washington in the U.S.A. If I said,

"I am an American who lives in Washington," I would be stating my own residence. Then I could say, "If you want to talk to me, you will have to come to Washington." Of course, you can read the things I have written, but if you really want to talk to me, you will have to come to where I live. In similar fashion, God has stated that He is spirit. Those who want to worship Him must go into the spirit.

How, then, can we go there? God told us that if we seek Him with our whole being, then we will find Him. What a person must do is take his whole heart and aim it, direct it, focus it, point it, toward Him. The focus of one's entire heart, soul and mind is the requirement.

In the Old Testament we can read of King David going to *"inquire of the Lord."* In Psalm 131 we read of the attitude of David's heart when he approached God:

> *O Lord, my heart is not proud, nor my eyes haughty;*
> *Nor do I involve myself in great matters,*
> *Or in things too difficult for me.*
> *Surely I have composed and quieted my soul;*
> *Like a weaned child rests against his mother,*
> *My soul is like a weaned child within me.*
>
> (Ps. 131:1-2)

Notice, first and foremost, the calming of David's soul. David set aside all his natural concerns and took on an attitude of humility. In that state he approached God.

In the New Testament we are taught the same principles. James tells us that as we draw near to God, He draws near to us (4:8). He describes how we are to draw near by separating ourselves from the concerns of the world (vs. 1-4), humbling ourselves (vs. 5-6), submitting to Him (vs. 7), and then cleansing our hearts (vs. 8). James also tells us not to be *"double-minded"* when we come to God; we must be determined to encounter Him.

Now, some Christians may be confused by this teaching because they have been taught that God is always with them, and no process or steps are needed to approach Him. Of course, God receives His children on the basis of forgiveness and cleansing through Jesus Christ. God hears the prayers of His children and He always wants us to talk to Him. In addition, the human spirit always exists in the realm of the spirit. As I explained, God is always willing to communicate with us. However, it is also true that we must open ourselves to receive from Him, to encounter and experience Him in a fuller way. As Christians direct their attention toward God, they become more conscious of Him. Their souls come into agreement with Him. The body becomes filled with the nature of God as it fulfills its function as a temple of the Holy Spirit. The Spirit of God indwells the Christian at all times but God's presence is manifested to the entire being of the believer as he or she draws nearer to the Father.

Look again at the exhortation in James 4:1-10, concerning how we may draw near to God. After explaining how we must separate ourselves from this natural realm, put on humility and cleanse our souls, the writer says:

> *Be miserable and mourn and weep; let your laughter be turned into mourning, and your joy to gloom. Humble yourselves in the presence of the Lord, and He will exalt you.*
>
> (James 4:9-10)

The opening of the door to God's presence is preceded by instructions to *"be miserable and mourn and weep."* Why is this exhortation here?

In the modern-day Church we have so emphasized the elements of rejoicing and grace that many today cannot understand the significance of sadness in seeking God. Of course, the Christian life should be exciting and joyful, but pursuing God in the spirit is an entirely different issue.

Mourning produces a brokenness necessary for a person's heart to receive that which God wants to reveal. It positions the heart in humility before Him. The act of mourning causes a separation of one's being from everything clinging to it. The cares of the world and desires for other things exert a force upon people which holds them back from God. The person who is involved intensely in business may have a difficult time setting it all aside. The mother who is anxious about her children may have a hard time calming her soul enough to receive from God. The person whose soul is locked onto the natural realm will battle redirecting his or her attention. Mourning redirects the soul and allows it to break free (II Cor. 7:10-11). I like to compare mourning to a dog losing its hair. As the hair is shed, so also a person can shed attachments to the world.

The process of opening oneself to the spirit can be aided in several ways. Fasting (not eating food for a time) may help a person deny the desires of body and detach from the natural concerns of life. Music can benefit by creating a spiritual atmosphere in which a person can forget things and become at peace. The prophets in the Old Testament sometimes would call a minstrel, in order that they might be aided in hearing from God (II Kings 3:15). At other times people of God would separate themselves from others. In similar fashion, Christians may find themselves more able to receive from God during an extended time of isolation in a quiet place of prayer. Simply relaxing and calming the soul in a natural setting can open a person to the spirit.

Though outward conditions are beneficial, the real focus of our understanding must be upon the heart. When a person turns his heart away from the things of this world and directs it completely toward God, then God will reveal Himself. God declared that He is a jealous God (Ex. 20:5; see also James 4:5). He holds the greatest revelations of Himself for the one who seeks Him with *all* his heart. In that condition, a person may find himself losing interest in natural things and even "hating" them in a sense (Luke 14:26), as those natural things lose importance in comparison with finding God. As Moses cried out for God to reveal Himself, he said:

> *"If Your presence does not go with us, do not lead us up from here."*
>
> (Ex. 33:15)

Moses came to the point of not wanting even to go on unless God revealed Himself. In this sense, an individual may come to the point of wanting "nothing but God." Only when a person has come to such a focus has he or she completely turned away from other things and onto God.

At the start of seeking God, Christians may focus on all kinds of natural concerns, needs, desires and people. They have not turned their hearts completely toward God until all earthly things fade in significance. They have detached in heart when they no longer desire to go back to them. Gradually, and then suddenly, a change occurs as their hearts completely turn. Finally, they want to stay in the presence of God.

Although I am talking about encountering God and the kingdom of God, it is important to understand that our spiritual senses can open to the whole spiritual realm. God is not the only one out there. It is also the home of demons and the domain of which they are a part. So also the spirits of all people exist in that dimension. Forces which influence the future, along with an unlimited number of other spiritual "things" can be encountered. An entire spiritual world is out there.

In the book of Revelation, we read of how the apostle John was *"in the Spirit on the Lord's day"* (Rev. 1:10); hence, his spiritual eyes opened to see all the things that he described in the rest of the book. John wrote about angels, demons, future events, coming judgment and many other spiritual realities.

In the Book of Acts, we can read about the prophet Agabus who knew by the spirit what the future held in store for Paul (Acts 21:10-11). On another occasion, Paul's spirit sensed demonic influences over the city of Athens (Acts 17:16). When a person's spiritual senses are receptive, she may become aware of a multitude of things.

God may impart strength, extra grace, answers to prayers, physical healing, victory over sins and anointings. He may reveal His desires, the future, revelations or as Paul said, *"Things which eye has not seen and ear has not heard..."* (I Cor. 2:9-10). All these things may flow from the Holy Spirit through the spirit of the person seeking God. Most importantly, though, the believer may encounter God Himself in a very real, tangible sense.

Many Christians have never heard these truths. They may have experienced God in some measure during a worship service or a special time alone. Of course, we praise God for those encounters, but I am teaching a fuller revelation, available for everyone who will seek God with his or her whole being. Hidden in the cleft of the rock, Moses had the incredible experience of God's glory passing by. For us the potential is even greater. The curtain was torn through the death of Jesus Christ. Now all believers can go and see Him and know Him—to the degree they are willing.

How Evil Spiritists
Tap into the Spiritual Realm

I will discuss spiritual phenomena not only in Christians' lives, but also in the lives of ungodly men and women. The spiritual communication that witches, mediums, channellers, New Age disciples, etc., practice and experience, all come in the form of spiritual impressions, images and stirrings. In this sense, the communication they receive is very much the same as that which a Christian receives. The most obvious difference, however, is the source of that communication from within the spiritual world.

As I explain this, I am not giving credence to those who communicate with the dead or engage in spiritist activity apart from God. The Bible plainly warns us:

> *There shall not be found among you anyone...who uses divination, one who practices witchcraft, or one who interprets omens, or a sorcerer, or one who casts a spell, or a medium, or a spiritist, or one who calls up the dead. For whoever does these things is detestable to the Lord.*
>
> (Deut. 18:10-12a)

Make no mistake about God's attitude toward these spiritual

activities—He hates them.

When I refer to various evil spiritual exercises it is not to promote them. Instead, our goal is simply to answer questions in Christians' hearts. Many Christians have been exposed to various occult practices. The exposure may have occurred before they came to know Jesus personally, or they may simply have heard of evil activities and forms of witchcraft. Others are faced with related problems because in their personal ministries they deal with people who are involved in such practices. Many God-fearing parents are finding that their children are being exposed to witchcraft and other evil spiritual practices. We cannot hide from the needs around us. I do not want to glorify evil in any way, but believers must be equipped to set people free.

I also share examples of evil practices to help people understand what actually is taking place in the spiritual realm and how it relates to them. Satan counterfeits the truth. He perverts it. He did not create humankind nor the spiritual realm. He is merely usurping authority and using spiritual principles which God created and ordained. When I mention evil spiritual practices, it should stir in you an expectancy to see what God has that is greater.

Finally, I wish to expose the nakedness of all such evil. You see, there is developed around certain mystical experiences an air of power. Witches work hard to present an image of mystery and secrecy. New Age advocates project the image that they have some hidden truth that belongs only to their elite. Many Christians are threatened by these images. They wonder what witches can actually do. Not knowing how to tap into God's power, they feel inferior, at least in the spiritual dimension. Whether or not Christians admit it, many of them are fearful of the mystical air projected by occultists. Furthermore, they wonder whether they are missing out on something by being Christians who diligently and faithfully keep from even thinking about such evil practices.

I want Christians to know the truth. Being a Bible believing Christian who is aware of the spiritual dimension, I personally have found that the Holy Spirit desires to lead us far beyond—in glory and magnificence—anything that the occultists have. I am not just saying this by faith. I know it to be true. The Bible not only gives us more accurate information, but also a knowledge of the God Who created all. Because believers recognize that all authority comes from God, they do not need to suffer as witches typically do in their exercise of power (to be explained in later chapters). The Christian who truly taps into God's fullness has no less power nor authority. In fact, the Christian can far exceed that of which the evil workers partake.

Understanding this perspective, allow me to discuss briefly, now and in later chapters, some of the spiritual practices done by evil people.

Consider the witch who gazes into a crystal ball. Why does she do that? A witch does not see anything in the crystal ball; however, the large piece of glass serves as a focal point for her attention. As she stares into the glass she can fix her mind, detach from the natural world and begin to receive spiritual information. You have probably experienced a similar phenomenon when sitting by a campfire and staring into the open flame. Soon your mind fixates, the world around you is forgotten, and you are drifting in your imaginations. Some of those imaginations will arise from within yourself, but some others will be carried along by spiritual influences. It is in this fashion that a witch stares into her crystal ball, not because there is anything spiritual within it, but because it serves as a focal point.

Similarly, spiritists use small crystals. Staring into a crystal can cause their minds to detach from natural concerns. Having many crystals suspended on strings in a room can create an environment that seems mystical. Idols carved out of wood or stone may serve as objects upon which people can focus their attention. Indeed, as people sit quietly focused upon any such object, there is a feeling of detachment and their spirits may begin to receive spiritual information from the other world.

I share these things so that you may understand the spiritual principles involved. Witches go into the spirit and it requires a detachment from the natural world. They cannot experience the kingdom of God nor His blessings, however, they may tap into some spiritual influence. Christians may go into the spirit by seeking God with their whole souls and hearts. However, we do not use "illegal avenues of entrance" about which we will learn as we continue.

First, God does not want us having idols molded with hands or made in any spiritual image. God declared:

> *"You shall not make for yourself an idol, or any likeness of what is in heaven above or on the earth beneath or in the water under the earth. You shall not worship them or serve them; for I the Lord your God, am a jealous God...."*

(Ex. 20:4-5)

We must not put anything between us and God. It is Him alone we must seek and worship.

We can also talk about the use of rhythmic music, chanting or movement. Whenever a pattern is repeated over and over, the mind will tend to block out information coming in from the natural world. Yoga practitioners chant their mantras hour after hour. Mystics rock back and forth until their minds are drifting. New Agers listen to rhythmic music that causes their souls to quiet within them. Hypnotists may swing a pendulum in front of their patients.

Now Christians must not condemn categorically all rhythmic patterns, otherwise, we would reject the grandmother praying every night while relaxing in her rocking chair. We would also condemn the mother who sings to her baby while rocking the cradle. Rhythmic patterns are not evil. It is okay for Christians to sing songs during church services again and again until they have laid aside their natural concerns. Indeed, rhythmic music and movement help people focus their attention upon God.

However, Christians must recognize that rhythmic patterns can open one's spirit to receive spiritual influences that are not good. A hypnotized girl may be yielding her will to spirit entities or to the will of the hypnotist. The mantras that spiritual trainees repeat may be foreign words giving worship to false gods. Even people with whom we relax may impart spiritual influences into our being. It is not the rhythmic movement or rhythmic sounds that we should reject, but the opening of one's spirit without discernment or recognition of evil.

With a more critical eye, let's discuss the use of drugs for the purpose of entering the spiritual world. Common among primitive people are witch doctors and medicine men who put themselves into hallucinatory states with certain mushrooms or other plant materials. Having no knowledge of the true God, they open themselves to numerous evil spiritual influences.

The use of drugs, however, is not limited to primitive peoples. Some in modern society open their spirits to the spiritual dimension through the use of drugs or alcohol. Not all abuse results in spiritual experiences, but the possibility of detaching from the natural realm and yielding to the other side is powerfully enhanced by drugs.

In the blatantly evil practices of warlocks and witches, a mystical atmosphere is established during their black masses.

Incense captivates the sense of smell. Eerie music lures participants into a spiritual consciousness. Drugs further release them from this natural world. Mysterious rituals and alarming acts demand the full attention of those involved, and, hence, usher them corporately into the spiritual realm.

These exercises are disgusting and abominable in the sight of God.

Pain is also used by some spiritists as a path to enter the spiritual world. In inflicting or receiving pain, there may be a detachment of one's conscious mind from the natural realm. To escape from extreme pain, individuals may reach with all their strength into the spiritual dimension. Some of those involved in sadism, masochism and other forms of pain inducement find their pleasure in the pain itself. Others find it in the experience of power or some touch of the spiritual.

The Sun Dance, a ceremonial dance carried out years ago by certain indigenous groups of North America, provided the entrance of pain into the spiritual world. Hooks were driven through the pectoral muscles of willing men who were suspended by ropes attached to those hooks. During such torture, endorphins (natural painkillers) may have been released into their brains, inducing hallucinations. Some subjects may have escaped this natural world and touched spirit beings on the other side.

Sexual intercourse is another means of entrance into the spiritual realm. Those involved completely detach from this world for a moment in time and focus their entire beings. Every sexual encounter, even in marriage, is a spiritual experience.

There are other means people use to experience the spiritual realm, but what I want to make clear is the truth that whenever people focus their entire minds and hearts, detaching from the natural realm, they may be opening their spirits to the spiritual realm. I am not condemning categorically all experiences of the spiritual dimension. I am warning people that there are certain illegal avenues of entrance that will expose them to the powers of darkness.

What motivates people to experience the spiritual dimension? Some want to escape the pressures and trials of life. Others desire a certain pleasurable feeling. Those trained in evil spiritual practices may be attempting to contact a spirit being or to obtain spiritual power. However, most who seek the spiritual world are seeking the sense of purpose and meaning which it offers.

Consider that last statement carefully. Our inner being is anchored in the spiritual realm, therefore, to experience that realm is to get in touch with our roots. A heart in turmoil can be brought to rest with one glimpse of the spiritual realm. When an individual encounters that realm, he can be overwhelmed by a sense of meaning. In a natural realm filled with difficulties, a spiritual experience can restore to an individual a sense of sanity and purpose—even a sense of existence beyond this natural realm.

Remember, those having encounters apart from the true God can become terribly deceived. I am trying to explain why people hunger for spiritual contact. There are other reasons, but the desire for meaning is the single most powerful motivating force. The Bible tells us that God has placed eternity in the heart of every person (Eccl. 3:11). Every human being, no matter where she or he lives, has a desire for things beyond this natural realm. Spiritual hunger exists in everyone.

Let's summarize by saying that both the Christian and the non-Christian tap into the spiritual realm by focusing their minds and hearts. Christians and non-Christians encounter different aspects of the spiritual realm. There is only one spiritual realm, but in that realm both Satan's domain and God's kingdom exist. The spirits of all people exist in that realm, along with many other things about which we will learn. Concerning these spiritual realities, every human being has spiritual senses to perceive what his or her spirit contacts. Individuals are conscious of their spiritual sensitivities to the degree that their souls are directed. These are spiritual realities designed in the creation itself. It is how God made humankind.

How the Human Brain Is Affected

Now let's discuss the human brain and mind.

By *brain*, I mean the physical organ located in the head. The word *mind* is used in different ways in different contexts, but I will use the word to refer to the invisible part of our being which processes information and governs our thinking processes. To further clarify the distinction between the brain and the mind, we can say that the brain is the organ which provides the mind contact with the natural world. The brain also functions to keep the physical body operating properly. When we die, the brain ceases to function; however, the mind stays conscious in the spiritual realm. The mind is a part of a person's invisible side, while the brain is a part of the physical being.

The mind and the brain are interwoven in every aspect. Thought processes in the mind influence the brain and vice versa. There is an intimate correspondence between the two.

Many interesting studies have been done on the functions of the brain. The left side of the brain is most strongly activated when we are engaged in logical, analytical thinking. The right side of the brain becomes more active when we are in creative thought processes.

Associate these scientific observations with what we know about a human being's makeup. When the mind is directed to the natural realm with active, logical thoughts, the left side of the brain is most active. When the mind is pointed toward the spirit, the right side of the brain is most active. The focus of a person's mind influences the functioning of the brain.

We also know that when people are relaxing and thinking creatively, alpha brain waves flow through the brain. These are measured with instruments sensitive to tiny electrical impulses. When people are engaged in active, logically-oriented work, beta brain waves are predominant. Alpha brain waves are especially strong in artistic, inventive individuals. All people have alpha waves predominant when dreaming. People actually change the flow of electrical impulses from beta to alpha waves as they simplify their thoughts and focus on basic concepts of their lives.

When a person opens to the realm of the spirit, there is a measurable increase in alpha brain waves. As explained earlier, a person opens to the spirit by detaching from the natural world and focusing the mind. As a person does this, he may be allowing his own creativity to stir, or he may be opening to the spiritual dimension. Either way, spiritual energy is being released to flow. At the same time, the physical brain shows an increase in alpha brain waves.

Do not equate alpha or beta waves with spiritual energy. I am merely pointing out a correspondence between the spiritual part of a person and the natural. When a person is tapped into the spirit, the natural brain shows a change in the type of impulses flowing through it.

People require periods of both alpha and beta waves flowing through their brains to be healthy. People who spend their time in creative pursuits without a break, sooner or later find themselves in depression, sleeplessness, emotional extremes and physical illness. Others who spend extended periods with only beta waves predominant sooner or later experience a burnout and need a prolonged rest. Being healthy requires living as whole people—the way God created us to live.

There are many different conditions in which the mind can function, other than the two extremes involving only alpha or only beta waves. The range from the creative to the logic-controlled side is broad. People involved in various occult groups today use the terminology, "altered states of consciousness." Although Christians hesitate to use such vocabulary, we should not be threatened by mere words. If we change these mystical-sounding terms into ideas which are more familiar to us, perhaps they will not be as scary, and then we can see if there is any validity to the related concepts. The word "altered" simply means "changed." "Altered states of consciousness" refers to the changes in the mind which occur when people change the focus of their attentions. It is that simple.

From the biblical perspective, there is both good and evil in the related concepts. On the positive side, altered states of consciousness are a scientific reality. We experience many different states of mind in our daily lives. Whenever Christians seek God with any degree of seriousness, they are opening themselves to the spiritual realm and strong alpha waves are present. Their states of mind are definitely different (altered) from when they are working in their normal daily activities. The Bible encourages us to calm our souls and focus upon the things of God at specific times of our lives. In many passages, people are taught to meditate on the things of God, that is: thinking deeply on the nature of God and His Word. Our God laid out clear principles for taking time to work and rest; both of which produce altered conditions within our being.

There are also incidents in the Bible of godly people

experiencing radical extremes of altered states of consciousness. The most intense experience a human being can have is to encounter God's manifest presence. Make no mistake about this. When Paul was taken up to God, he did not know whether he was *"in the body or apart from the body"* (II Cor. 12:4). When Isaiah saw the Lord sitting on His throne (Is. 6:1-7), he was having "a way-out experience." When the apostle John beheld Jesus, as recorded in the Book of Revelation, he fell as a dead man (Rev. 1:17). Peter, James and John had no less of a radical shift in their conscious minds when they saw Jesus in His glory, standing with Moses and Elijah on the Mount of Transfiguration (Matt. 17:1-9). To these we could add the experiences of Moses seeing God, all the Jews before Mount Sinai, the priests in the Temple as the glory cloud fell, the disciples in the upper room and all of the early believers as they gathered in the building which began to shake as the Spirit came upon them.

We even read in the Bible about people going into trances. A trance occurs when the mind becomes so locked onto the spirit that consciousness of the natural world is completely severed. The apostle Peter went into a trance when God spoke to him as he was praying on the rooftop of Simon the tanner's house (Acts 10:9-16). Saul had a similar experience on the road to Damascus (Acts 9:3-8), as did Stephen when he was being stoned to death (Acts 7:55-56). In light of these and other such experiences, it seems quite foolish for any Christian today to deny the reality of altered states of the human mind and brain.

We need to include here the states of mind people experience when God talks to them in their sleep. Job 33:14-16, tells us:

> *Indeed God speaks once,*
> *Or twice, yet no one notices it.*

In a dream, a vision of the night,
When sound sleep falls on men,
While they slumber in their beds,
Then He opens the ears of men,
And seals their instructions.

Not every dream is God's communication, but while a person is asleep, he is detached from the natural realm and in an ideal state of mind to receive from God.

Finally, I must mention again the role that visions can play in the life of the Christian. I discussed these briefly in chapter 2, but it is worth mentioning again that a vision is the opening of a person's spiritual eyes to see into the realm of the spirit. By definition, a vision is an altered state of consciousness.

Almost every time the Bible reveals an instance when God supernaturally communicated with people, those individuals were not in a logic-oriented frame of mind. Recall how Jacob in his sleep beheld a stairway extending from heaven to Earth with angels ascending and descending upon it (Gen. 28:10-13). Think of Daniel how he fasted and prayed for days before interpreting dreams or angels came to him with answers to his questions (e.g., Dan. 9). In each case, the people involved were tapped into the spirit, either by their own attempts to seek God or by God's act of intervening in their lives.

Of course, God can communicate with people without changing the state of their minds. God does use our logical reasoning and He expects us to use it to our maximum potential. However, we must recognize the reality of how God created us. We were created with a wide range of conscious abilities.

We can close this discussion with a word of wisdom: the wise Christian does not make it his or her aim to have an altered state of consciousness; but rather to seek God, worship Him and receive from His nature. As the believer does these things, his or her state of mind may change. But the goal is to find God, not change the function of one's mind. As believers we can understand these principles, and, indeed, such understanding may aid us in approaching God. However, our goal is God, not mystical experiences.

Escaping into the Spirit

Some Christians emphasize only one side of their beings: the natural or the spiritual. Over-focusing on either side leads to problems.

Christians with an extreme emphasis on the rational and natural side of life tend to have a difficult time receiving anything from the Spirit. Some have been taught that the spiritual dimension is evil and so they remain detached from the spiritual side of their life. Other people are so programmed to natural, logical thought patterns that they are not conscious of the Holy Spirit speaking, leading or revealing anything to them.

At the other extreme are people who are more in tune with their spiritual senses than their natural senses. In some ways they are detached from the natural world.

People of this type have a difficult time functioning in everyday life. They can have their minds so fixed on the spirit that logical thought is difficult for them. Thinking about natural concerns, such as money, family responsibilities and employment seems out of reach to them. Their minds will not function along normal lines of thought. Some of the most spiritually sensitive people are so detached from the natural realm that they are described as "spaced out." I like the descriptive term, MEGO, referring to: "My Eyes Glazed Over!"

There are people who fixate on the spiritual side because of their belief systems. Eastern religious thought, in particular, promotes this lifestyle. The Buddhist religion teaches its followers to pursue "Nirvana" through meditation and various exercises. "Nirvana" is a condition of "total bliss" or "oneness with the cosmos." In reality, it is simply being completely detached from natural responsibilities and wide open to the spirit world. This philosophy is also promoted by many New Age teachers.

Tragically, this deception has crept into some Christian circles today. Even though they may not use Buddhist or New Age terminology, they stress the spiritual side to the exclusion of the natural. They start thinking and believing that God wants them to live every day and every minute with their minds entirely focused upon the spiritual dimension. Some Christians try to structure their lives doing only what they perceive from the spirit. They attempt to make all their decisions on the basis of visions, dreams, revelations and spiritual impressions. They deny their natural bodies and logical minds.

Initially, such a lifestyle may appear holy and right to some people. But, in fact, it is wrong. This is not what the Christian life is all about. Paul prayed that we may be sanctified entirely: body, soul and spirit (I Thes. 5:23). God never intended us to deny or reject a part of our nature. The message of the Gospel is redemption. That redemption is for one's entire being. God desires us to use our minds, emotions and all of our strength in serving Him. We can draw inspiration, purpose and divine direction from the spirit, but then it must be worked out in the natural. This is how God created us.

Of course, there will be occasions when Christians should set aside time to detach from the natural world in order to seek God with all of their hearts and souls. But for most of our lives we are called to function in this world. When hunger is felt in the physical body, it usually should be satisfied with food. If a Christian gets a flat tire on her car, she can use her head to get out and fix it without waiting for second-by-second instructions from the Holy Spirit. God designed us with the mechanism to live here successfully. That means being able to interact with this natural realm, evaluate the information we receive and make decisions with our own free wills. Of course, Christians should be open anytime to receive input from the Spirit, but that is not to be their sole conscious focus.

Look at John's words in Revelation 1:10: *"I was in the Spirit on the Lord's day...."* Saying he was in the Spirit *"on the Lord's day"* implies that he was not in it every day or constantly. The state of being completely conscious of that dimension was temporary.

The men and women in the Book of Acts lived similarly. Paul and Peter received visions and dreams, but also made very naturally-based decisions. In the fifteenth chapter of Acts, we see the early Church leaders discussing and debating—using their minds to make decisions about key issues for their times. The Holy Spirit was guiding them but note that they used more than spiritual input to govern their lives.

Some Christians say that Jesus made all of His decisions on the sole basis of guidance He received through His Spirit. Jesus did say that He did nothing on His own initiative, and that He only did what the Father showed Him (John 5:19, 30). However, this does not mean that He walked around with a glazed-over look in His eyes. On the contrary, Jesus was fully human, yet divine. He had a pure, untainted mind. His soul was holy. His body was not corrupted by sin. Therefore, for Him to do what seemed natural to Him would have always been the will of the Father. His motivations were perfect, and, therefore, the decisions He made by His free will always would have been in perfect agreement with the Father. In saying that He only did what the Father showed Him, He was not telling us that He walked around in a semi-conscious state. God just as easily could have shown Him things through His perfectly sanctified mind and even through His natural senses. The Father led the Son through His entire being.

What I am saying is that the spiritual realm should not become the sole focus in your life. I am concerned about this issue because the type of Christians most interested in reading a book such as this one, are the very ones with a strong drawing to the spiritual dimension.

There are numerous problems we see developing in the lives of Christians who are solely spirit-oriented. It is common for deceptions to enter into their thought patterns. When the mind is not grounded in the natural and logical realm, it may begin to "float and drift on the waves of spiritual energy." As a boat that is not anchored, so is the mind that is not in touch with natural reality. Christians floating in this manner often invent weird doctrines, fully convinced they are of God. The longer a person remains fixated only upon the spirit, the further he can be pulled off the path of reality and truth.

Excessively spirit-oriented people also tend to develop sexual and emotional problems. Because they detach from things of this world, they may cut themselves off emotionally or entirely from normal relationships. As a consequence, their own needs go unmet. They may try to deny those needs for a time, but sooner or later their unfulfilled needs will rise and take control (unless God has given them a special gift to deal with these needs, as mentioned in Matthew 19:11). Some of the most spirit-focused Christians develop compulsive behaviors, sexually perverted thoughts, unnatural views of marriage, uncontrolled fantasizing, overeating tendencies, groundless fears, loneliness and suicidal tendencies.

Because these Christians explain everything in terms of spiritual realities, they remain blind as to how to get free. If someone offers them the only real solution—that they have to change their lifestyle and get more naturally oriented— they reject the advice as evil and contrary to the leading of God in their lives. They would rather put all their energy into rebuking the devil, fasting and going deeper into the spirit. Typically, they experience temporary relief through such endeavors, but over the long run their problems only intensify. Some will only listen after months or years of seeing that their way of living does not work. It does not produce the victorious Christian lives which they have been seeking.

The Bible has much to say about the benefits of good, hard, honest work. Work is healing. So also proper relationships must be maintained if a Christian is to remain emotionally sound. The apostle Paul wrote to the early believers not to separate from their spouses for prayer for too long of a period, lest Satan come and find opportunity in their lives (I Cor. 7:5). Detachment is to be temporary for the purpose of seeking God. The overcoming Christian life is one of functioning and producing in very real, natural ways and maintaining healthy relationships both in marriage and with other believers.

The point is that Christians should live in touch with both the spiritual and the natural realms. Anyone who uses the spirit as an escape from natural responsibilities is wrong. They may be seriously earnest in their pursuits of God, but they are deceived if they think God is pleased with their lifestyles. The spiritual realm is not an escape route. It is the realm from which we receive inspiration, purpose and direction, but that which is received in the spirit must be worked out in the natural. To bring forth that which is received in the spirit requires healthy relationships, a sound mind, logical thinking, discipline and a strong body.

Doorways to the Spiritual Realm

We have been discussing our contact and interaction with the spiritual world. Now we can talk about how people can function as *doorways* for the spiritual world to influence the natural world. Every human being stands at the threshold between two worlds. We each possess the ability to release spiritual things into the natural world. It is the heart of a person which opens this doorway. Let me explain how this works.

When God created the world, He spoke over humankind and gave us dominion over Earth (Gen. 1:28). With that declaration, God imparted to us authority. Psalm 115:16 tells us:

> *The heavens are the heavens of the Lord;*
> *But the earth He has given to the sons of men.*

Since we have authority here, we decide what influences—good or evil—come into this world.

In reference to evil, we can consider how sin entered the world through Adam:

> *...through one man sin entered into the world, and*

death through sin, and so death spread to all men, because all sinned....

(Rom. 5:12)

Notice the entrance point for sin: a human being. Adam was the first doorway.

Every human being can bring evil into the world. The apostle James explained:

Then when lust has conceived, it gives birth to sin; and when sin is accomplished, it brings forth death.

(James 1:15)

From this passage we can see how evil longings within a person's heart actually draw within a person the evil substance of that which is desired. Those things are conceived or planted within as seeds. Eventually those seeds grow and bring forth sin and death.

Each Person Can Be a Doorway for Evil

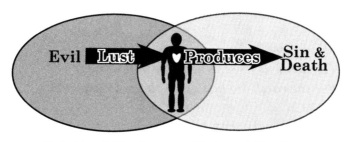

Spiritual Realm   Natural Realm

The heart of a person can draw in good or evil. Just as the physical heart in a person's body draws in food and oxygen, and then pumps those nutrients throughout a person's body, so also the inner heart of a person draws in spiritual substance and redistributes it throughout a person's entire life. It is through the heart that spiritual substance—good or evil—can pass from the spiritual world into this natural world.

Concerning good things we can say that every time we obey God we are giving Him access to this realm. Of course, God does not need our permission before acting in this world, however, He often chooses to work through yielded vessels. When we do His will, His will comes into this world.

There are other ways in which God and His blessings come into this world. Paul explained that the Holy Spirit manifests through His gifts.

> *But to each one is given the manifestation of the Spirit for the common good.*
>
> (I Cor. 12:7)

What is most interesting for our discussion is how the Holy Spirit manifests through Christians.

To see this, think of the word "manifest." This word refers to something in the spiritual realm revealing itself in the natural realm. For example, if there was an angel sitting next to you right now you could not see it or touch it. However, if that angel manifested, it would come out of its realm and reveal itself to you so that you could see it, touch it or in some way sense its presence. It is in this context that we talk about spiritual entities manifesting.

After Paul wrote that each person is given *"the manifestation of the Holy Spirit,"* he listed the nine gifts of the Holy Spirit through which He comes into this natural world. Paul tells us that the Holy Spirit gives gifts of tongues, prophecy and interpretation of tongues; when the Holy Spirit gives these gifts He speaks through believers so listeners can hear

Him. When gifts of healings, miracles and faith are given, the Holy Spirit comes out of His world and into this world to demonstrate His power, love and will. When a Christian receives from the Holy Spirit words of knowledge, words of wisdom or the gift of discerning of spirits, it is the Holy Spirit revealing to the person the thoughts of God. Each of these nine gifts is a way in which the Holy Spirit comes out of His realm and into this natural realm.

The Holy Spirit Manifests in Nine Spiritual Gifts

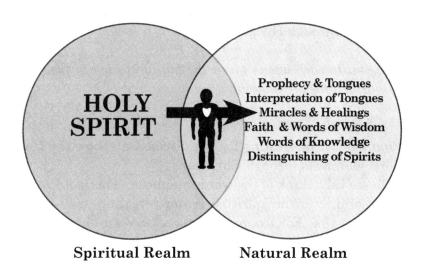

Prophecy & Tongues
Interpretation of Tongues
Miracles & Healings
Faith & Words of Wisdom
Words of Knowledge
Distinguishing of Spirits

HOLY SPIRIT

Spiritual Realm   Natural Realm

Non-Christians can also be doorways for spiritual things to enter the natural world. There are evil men and women who submit their lives to certain demonic powers and bring the related powers into this natural world. They, also, are acting as doorways. When God spoke that we will have dominion over Earth, He imparted that authority. Therefore, even ungodly people have the power to release spiritual things and influences into the natural world.

The important distinction between the Christian and the non-Christian is that we have the power and authority to access the kingdom of God and more of His blessings. Paul wrote that the kingdom of God consists of righteousness, peace, joy (Rom. 14:17), and power (I Corth. 4:20). The kingdom is all that God wills for us, including His provision, help, comfort, guidance and anointing.

God's Blessings Manifest in the Natural World

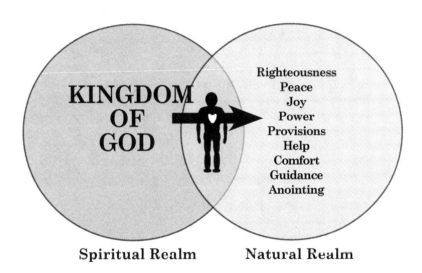

Spiritual Realm   Natural Realm

Finally, let's add to our understanding the fact that there are certain keys to releasing the spiritual realm into the natural. For many people, the spiritual realm seems to be a distant world into which we cannot tap—the door seems sealed. However, Jesus told us that He has given us the keys to the kingdom. Think of the keys that open the door to your house or start your car. Keys are very small items which unlock great power and give us access to previously closed areas.

What, then, are these keys which we have been given? In the next two chapters we will see.

Keys that Open the
Door to the Spiritual Realm

How things are released from one realm into the other is very similar to how people tune in to the spirit. I explained in chapters 3 and 4 how people can detach from the natural realm, focus their attention, and hence, open themselves to the spiritual realm. In that condition they are open not only to receive information, but also to release things from the spiritual realm into the natural, whether good or bad.

Consider our Lord's words in Matthew 6:22-23:

> *"The eye is the lamp of the body; so then if your eye is clear, your whole body will be full of light. But if your eye is bad, your whole body will be full of darkness. If then the light that is in you is darkness, how great is the darkness!"*

The light and darkness referred to here are spiritual in nature. Spiritual light or spiritual darkness fills a person, depending upon the focus of his or her eye.

The eye is the perspective of a person's life: the orientation of one's affections, desires and faith. In the verse preceding this one, Jesus said:

"for where your treasure is, there your heart will be also."

(Matt. 6:21)

Notice in this context the association Jesus made between singleness of eye and the direction of a person's heart. The eye, in this sense, refers to the basic orientation of a person's heart. Hence, the eye is oriented upon what the person believes and upon which one focuses one's life.

I hesitate using the word "focus" because too many people associate this term with a fixed mind-set—clinging to a certain set of thoughts in one's mind. I am not telling people to take on an intense, forceful frame of mind. It is the heart to which we are referring here. The characteristic of heart of which we are speaking has to do with a specific orientation. The proper orientation does not require an intense, serious demeanor. A person with singleness of eye may be joyful, relaxed, at peace, even laughing and having a great time. Emotions come and go. Thought patterns change. But a person who is single of eye has the orientation of his heart in one direction.

The proper focus for the Christian is, of course, toward God. This is more than going to church or having an occasional thought about Him. Rather, it is yielding to a loving, powerful, giving, concerned Father.

Read the context of Matthew 6. Jesus gave specific instructions concerning where one's eye should be set. He told the disciples to look at the birds of the air and the lilies of the field (Matt. 6:26-28). He explained how God provides for all these, and that certainly He will take care of us. The point is not simply for us to look at birds or lilies, but at a God Who is good, powerful and loving toward us. In contrast, Jesus also talked about the person who has his eye set upon needs and lack. The one whose heart is anxious, worried and greedy actually is bowing to mammon, rather than focusing on the goodness of God. He whose heart is at peace, knowing that God will provide, has the eye of his heart set in the proper place (Is. 26:3).

What happens to people who are single of eye? Depending on their focus, they will be filled with spiritual light or darkness. This light and darkness does not remain confined to the limits of their physical body. Jesus explained that whatever enters a person's heart flows out of the mouth and influences the person's entire life (Matt. 15:18-19; 12:33-35). Jesus said that the person whose eye is set on God and His goodness will have all things added to them (Matt. 6:33). In contrast, the one whose eye is set on problems, needs and lack (or has a concept of God being evil, harsh or cruel) will have a curse released over their life.

The focus of one's eye is the most important key to releasing spiritual power into this world.

Some of my readers may be disappointed at this point. In the previous chapter and this one, I have been leading you to discover keys that unlock tremendous power and spiritual blessings. Now I tell you that the focus of one's attention on God and His goodness is the key which will accomplish this very thing. Perhaps you expected to hear some hidden mystery. Maybe you wanted to read a secret method that will give you more power than warlocks and witches. Well, do not be disappointed. That is exactly what you have. Although it is no secret, the key of focusing one's life on God and His goodness will unlock tremendous powers. A lifestyle in which a Christian simply keeps his or her heart directed toward God will open a spiritual window from which consistent power will flow, greater than occultist or the most advanced warlock has ever discovered.

Let's apply the principle of the focused eye to specific areas. Sally worked as a secretary for a businessman I know.

She married late in life. Right after their wedding, her husband expressed great concern over a lump on her breast. She said the lump had been there for years and it was nothing about which to worry. However, because of his insistence, she had it checked by a doctor. When the news came back that the lump was cancerous, it consumed their thoughts. Immediately the cancer began to grow and spread rapidly. Approximately two months later Sally died.

Cases such as this are not infrequent. A person has a condition for years which is dormant, but as soon as a person's eyes become fixed upon it, the evil becomes activated. Now I am not implying that all cancer or sickness is the result of people's wrong focus. What I am saying is that in some cases, with some illnesses, the related problems seem to have been given power by the focus of the individual.

Everyone has experienced this to some degree. Consider the person who is nauseated from motion sickness or a common flu. If they focus on the sickening feeling, they quickly can yield to it and become overtaken by its influence. On the other hand, if they force themselves to think only about the work set before them, they can often overcome the weakness or illness.

Of course, most illnesses have a physical basis and should be treated with the best possible medical help. Yet, no matter what the illness, people can be strengthened by having the proper focus of their hearts. A person whose eye is clear will have greater spiritual strength, resulting in better physical health. A person whose eye is bad will be weakened spiritually and will more likely be subjected to physical ailments.

My main point here has to do with the focus of a person's eye and how it opens the door for light and darkness. We also can relate this truth to everyday temptations in our lives. If a woman is tempted, she will make a decision whether or not to listen to that temptation. If that evil thought is in line with her own lusts and evil desires, she will have a tendency to tune in and even yield her attention to it. Once her eye is focused upon the temptation, she releases its spiritual power into her life.

Consider Bill who focuses upon all his past failures and the negative attributes of his life. As he dwells upon these things, his spiritual strength is drained away. Bill then starts believing he is helpless and a failure. Soon Bill is in depression and is overcome by the circumstances around him.

Now consider the positive workings of this principle. Judy goes to church where the leaders believe in praying for the sick. She has been battling with cancer for several months. When the church elders pray for her, the focus of her life changes off the sickness and onto God. As the elders pray, they lay their hands upon her forehead and she yields to the authority and love expressed. Faith rises in her heart and for the first time she has hope that perhaps she will live through this trial. That time of prayer serves as a point of contact for her faith. Wherever she is, at home, driving her car or even in the doctor's office, she thinks back to the moment when the elders laid hands upon her and prayed. Because she changes her focus, spiritual light within her physical body increases and she is stronger in fighting the disease. Most importantly, she has opened the doorway to God so His healing power will flow into her.

Words spoken by a person of authority can also be points of focus for another's heart. For example, many churches believe in prophecy—the gift through which Christians speak out that which is stirring in their spirits by the Holy Spirit. As a believer speaks, others listen. Some listeners then fix their attention upon the message and continue to recall it in their minds. In this fashion, prophecy and other words can become keys which open the door to blessings.

Giving money can also serve as a focal point for one's faith—especially when a person has to sacrifice in order to give. In Old Testament times, people often would bring an offering to a prophet, which would release the prophet to hear God and give instructions. When Saul and his servant went to seek counsel from the prophet Samuel, the servant said:

> *"Behold, I have in my hand a fourth of a shekel of silver; I will give it to the man of God and he will tell us our way."*
>
> (I Sam. 9:8)

People often experience this truth in operation after giving when they are in need. They feel faith (light) rise in their hearts, bringing answers to the problems they face.

Many things can serve as points of focus. Some Christians latch onto the promises of God in the Bible, hence, releasing God's power. Others have the orientation of their hearts changed: at an anointed meeting, witnessing a miracle, at an ordination service or after being exposed to the needs of hurting people. Such events can fixate a person's attention and act as a key to open the spiritual realm.

On the negative side, there are shaking events which can captivate a person's heart, such as the death of a loved one, a car wreck, a harsh rebuke, the betrayal of a friend or a humiliating experience. Consider a war veteran who experienced overwhelming trials on the battlefront. His eye may have fixed—the orientation of his heart changed—and his spirit opened to the devastation he experienced. As a consequence, years later he may still have flashbacks of the tragedies he witnessed. These images can be so consuming that the vet cannot function in normal affairs of life.

In summary, we can say that the fixed orientation of a person's heart can open the world of the spirit, both its blessings and curses. Wise Christians will orient their hearts toward God and His goodness.

Open Doorways for Power to Flow

The extent to which a person serves as a doorway for spiritual things to enter the natural world is determined primarily by the agreement throughout his or her entire being. When the heart, mind and strength are oriented in the same direction, there can be a free flowing of spiritual substance through that person.

We can explain this same principle in terms of faith. Hebrews 11:1 (KJV) tells us:

> *Now faith is the substance of things hoped for, the evidence of things not seen.*

Notice that hope precedes faith. In this context, we see hope as the expectant desire of a person reaching out to God. The person's heart is literally drawing on God and His promises. Hope becomes faith, when the substance of that which is desired moves from the spiritual realm into the heart of the person. Faith is that substance.

Once spiritual substance has entered into the heart, it is only a matter of time until that which is believed begins to manifest in the natural realm. The heart is like soil, in which seeds grow. The spiritual substance of faith eventually grows to produce corresponding fruit.

Faith Is the Substance of What Was Hoped For

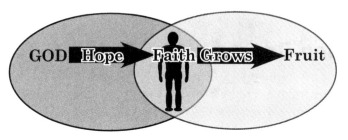

Spiritual Realm   Natural Realm

This process of spiritual substance passing from the spiritual realm into the natural is not always a slow process. In fact, the heart of a person can be fixed open to such a degree that spiritual substance flows unhindered. I call a person in this condition an "open doorway."

For example, certain worship leaders can open heaven so that the presence of God manifests in the atmosphere around a listening crowd. Many ministers have been used by God for conviction power and holiness to flow through them. During Charles Finney's ministry the convicting power of God would flow through him so strongly that people would cry out in anguish of soul. There were times in Leonard Ravenhill's ministry when the fear of God poured into the atmosphere, and everyone present came under its influence. Other Christians have been used to bring joy and laughter to God's people. Some leaders have been used by God as doorways for a spirit of liberality to come upon the people so that all present wanted to give away everything they owned to help others. I have been in meetings where heaven seemed to open and visions of the future manifested. In each case, God used a person at the front to open the windows of heaven to release an aspect of His nature into the natural world.

A doorway to the spiritual realm becomes locked open when a person comes into full and complete agreement. It is not just the casual believer who becomes an open doorway. Some people have such wholehearted belief throughout their beings, it's as if faith and confidence were given to them at birth. Others receive the ability as God touches them at some point during their lives. Most people pay a high price before attaining such a condition. Some have had to suffer or be put into extreme circumstances where they "had to believe." Others simply continued believing in some fashion for a long time and gradually their entire beings came into conformity. Pressure, trials, suffering, extended difficulties, continual exposure, etc., are often the environments through which a person is formed into an open doorway.

An open door may also be the result of a group dynamic where not just the leader opens the door to the spirit, but many people in agreement with that leader create the conditions. For example, James Steward was a powerfully anointed evangelist who ministered primarily in Western Europe. On one occasion, the presence of God descended upon a large congregation and a holy hush came over the meeting. At the end when everyone was dismissed, they left quietly without saying a word. So captivating was the presence that no one dared to start the motors in their automobiles, lest they violate the holy presence. All the people walked away that evening, leaving their cars in the parking lot.

What was going on behind the scenes of James Steward's meeting? A team of intercessors had gathered privately in another room and were reaching into the throne room of God through prayer and focused attention. They formed a united team for the nature of God to flow through James Steward and to the people. They were united with him in faith as an open doorway.

Relate these principles to the words of our Lord in Matthew 18:20:

"For where two or three have gathered together in My name, I am there in their midst."

In the context of this verse, Jesus was teaching His disciples about binding or loosing His power. Realize that binding and loosing involves a total agreement of people on one thing. It is not a casual prayer, nor does it happen in the normal gathering of Christians. Of course, God is present in spirit whenever Christians come together, but this verse promises us much more than His invisible, intangible presence. Jesus said He would actually and literally come—that is, manifest—whenever two or more believers come into full agreement. This is the open-door condition.

Those who come into agreement may be a team of prayer warriors or the listeners themselves. Some leaders can draw everyone present into unity of heart and mind. As people become captivated by the leader's words, they draw upon him or her to such an extent that they become the ones who open the door to the spirit. In another environment that leader could not function as a doorway for God's blessings to flow, but when people are longing with everything in their beings, then the individual in focus may become a door.

It is not only good things which can flow from the spiritual realm. There are also people have given themselves over to evil practices and beliefs to such a degree that they have become open doorways for evil to flow. Spiritual energy corresponding to Satan's desires flows through them, influencing other people in negative ways.

For example, there are people deeply involved in sexually

promiscuous lifestyles who believe 100% that what they are doing is right. Their thoughts, desires and entire beings have been conformed to the related evils. Those spiritual energies not only influence those individuals, but flow through them and "spill" out onto others. A prime example of people serving as open doorways is portrayed by some of those who walk on blistering hot coals without being burned. This practice has been carried on by several different groups around the world, some of which engage in trickery or simply in feats of mind-over-matter. Others, however, experience a truly spiritual phenomenon. For example, a tribe living in Suriname has an annual religious ceremony during which the men dance amidst flames reaching to their waists. During that dance, they are barefoot and have no protection from the heat. Afterwards they have absolutely no burns or blisters anywhere on their bodies. The spiritual part of this ceremony is evident as a woman of the tribe, called the virgin priestess, goes into a trance (under the influence of a demon). As long as she remains in this trance, the men continue dancing in the fire. When her trance-like state passes, the men immediately get out of the fire to avoid being burned.

In the book of Daniel, Shadrach, Meshach and Abed-nego were thrown into a blazing furnace. Even though the soldiers who threw them in were burned to death, the three men of God were unharmed while walking about in the midst of the flames (Dan. 3:19-30).

Open doors exist between the spiritual and natural world through evil mediums who contact the dead. Of course, there are imitators, pretenders, scam artists and hoaxes out there; however, there are also mediums who put themselves into trances and spirit entities flow through them, manifesting in the natural world.

Similarly, there are people used as channellers today.

Channellers are individuals who completely yield themselves so that those spirit entities may speak freely through
them. Channellers claim dead people or some wise spiritual
being is communicating. As Christians, however, we know
that such communication is demonic in origin and forbidden
(Deut. 18:10-12).

Contrast this with the Christian practice of prophesying.
When the Holy Spirit comes upon a Christian, he or she speaks
out a message from God. What makes this Christian practice
good and the channeller's practice evil is the source. Both
yield themselves to spirit beings, but God speaks through
the believer. Of course, not all prophesying is an open door.
When Christians prophesy, there are times when they yield
in full open-door fashion, but there are other times when a
more restricted flow moves through them.

Some people functioning as open doors go into trances.
Others maintain an awareness of everything going on but
seem uninvolved in the activity. Consider the ministry of
Kathryn Kuhlman. She would teach in her meetings for an
hour or so, and then the Holy Spirit would begin manifesting in such a way that people were healed physically. In the
most powerful services, she did not lay her hands on people
while praying for them. Instead, the power of God filled the
room, and she would simply watch the miracles happen and
point them out to the audience. In her own explanations, she
described how she felt uninvolved—as if she were standing
at a distance, watching herself move and act.

People used as open doorways often feel supernaturally
guided but I do not want to make this sound too controlling,
as if a person is unable to stop a spiritual manifestation.
That is usually not the case. In I Corinthians 14:32, Paul
explained that even the spirits of prophets remain subject to
the prophets. Any person being used powerfully by God could
stop it if they so choose. God usually does not force Himself

upon an individual. (There are some exceptions, because God is sovereign and can take control if He chooses: e.g., Luke 1:20-22). In contrast, an evil person may give himself over to Satan so often and to such a degree that he can no longer control himself. When speaking of God's power, we understand that Christians yield control rather than lose control. That distinction is important. Anyone can decide to stop if they so choose. However, they can also choose to continue to yield, and God strongly guides them.

Before closing our discussion of open doors, I should mention a characteristic seen in the lives of many powerful leaders. People used as open doorways are sometimes so focused in their particular fields of endeavor that they become unbalanced and extreme. In Church history, we read about certain leaders mightily used by God to accomplish great tasks, while at the same time being blind to other truths. Some missionaries have become fixated on visions of people going to hell and how they can lead the lost to Christ. Certain healing evangelists in the middle of the twentieth century seemed to consider healing the only thing important in the Christian experience. There have been many believers with a prophetic passion for some areas of ministry, and in their extreme emphasis, they were not balanced doctrinally, nor were they giving the whole biblical truth. In some cases it is their extreme nature which enabled them to be focused enough to accomplish what they did. Some of the most anointed individuals used to release spiritual power have had personal, marital or financial problems. They so focused their thoughts and affections on the fulfillment of one goal that they neglected other areas. Sooner or later, the neglected areas rise and destroy them.

This is neither necessary nor excusable. Believers can walk in power while maintaining Christian standards in all areas of their lives.

Discerning Spiritual Manifestations

The greatest challenge we face in our experience of the spiritual realm is discerning good from evil. In chapters that follow, we will discuss many supernatural and spiritual phenomena. We must do so with a biblical understanding of the spiritual realm. With that understanding we will be able to discern good from evil.

As various spiritual manifestations are brought forth, we must listen to the message being revealed. If indeed what is being spoken is from God, then it will agree with the written Word of God. Concerning the Bible we are told,

> *All Scripture is inspired by God and profitable for teaching, for reproof, for correction, for training in righteousness.*
>
> (II Tim. 3:16)

Since Scripture is inspired by God, it will always be in agreement with spiritual manifestations that are inspired by God. If any manifestation brings a message contrary to the inspired Word of God, then that manifestation is not from God.

In the Book of Isaiah, we read the exhortation from God through the prophet:

> *When they say to you, "Consult the mediums and the spiritists who whisper and mutter," should not a people consult their God? Should they consult the dead on behalf of the living? To the law and to the testimony! If they do not speak according to this word, it is because they have no dawn.*
>
> (Is. 8:19-20)

Our standard must always be the Word of God. We are never to consult mediums or spiritists. When any spiritual manifestation is brought before us, we must examine it to see if its message agrees or disagrees with the written Word that God has already given to us.

Our second basis for discernment of good from evil is to observe the results in individuals' lives. Our Lord Jesus taught us that there would be true and false prophets coming into the world and that we would be able to discern them by watching their fruit (Matt. 7:15-20). He said:

> *"A good tree cannot produce bad fruit, nor can a bad tree produce good fruit."*
>
> (Matt. 7:18)

As things are brought from the spiritual world into the natural, they will eventually produce visible effects in the lives of other people. Some of these effects may take time to reveal themselves, but if we watch patiently, the fruit will become evident.

Third and last, we must examine spiritual manifestations in respect to their exaltation of Jesus Christ as Lord. In I Corinthians 12:1-3, the apostle Paul tells us:

> *Now concerning spiritual gifts, brethren, I do not want you to be unaware. You know that when you*

were pagans, you were led astray to the mute idols, however you were led. Therefore I make known to you, that no one speaking by the Spirit of God says, "Jesus is accursed"; and no one can say, "Jesus is Lord," except by the Holy Spirit.

Paul is giving us a basis by which to judge so we will not be led astray. What is that basis? Whenever spiritual power or manifestations are evident, we must look to see who is being glorified. If the power being used is of God, then Jesus Christ will be exalted as Lord. If evil power is being released, then Jesus Christ will not be glorified.

This third test has been misunderstood by some people who are confused because they know of demonically possessed individuals who will say out of their mouths, "Jesus is Lord." However, the Jesus to whom they refer is not the One who came down from heaven to die for our sins and then resurrected from the grave. There are many people named Jesus (especially in Latin countries) who certainly are not Lord. When God's power is being used, "Jesus" refers to He Who died for our sins, resurrected and now sits at the right hand of God.

Confusion also comes when people combine various evil practices, while incorporating pictures of Jesus or words from the Bible. For example, some Filipino healers are known for carrying out mystical healing practices using the cross and other Christian symbols. Christian emblems or biblical terms do not necessarily mean the power is of God.

We must look for an actual belief and confession of Jesus as *Lord.* Lord means Number One, Master, Supreme over all. Sometimes the name of Jesus is used but not in the sense of His supreme lordship. He may be referred to as one of many great leaders or even gods. If Jesus is not recognized as the ultimate authority over all, then whatever spiritual phenomenon is being manifested, it is not from God.

One example I can give is from a community where approximately 4,000 people are presently living. The leader of this community is a woman who has at times been known to heal various kinds of diseases through the laying on of her hands. One time I was interviewing some people working at this center and I asked them point-blank, "Why did Jesus die on the cross?" I can remember the response of the first person: "I have no idea." That answer immediately tells us that the power at work among them is demonic rather than of God. Even though they talk about Jesus and think of Him as a great religious leader, they see Him as one of many "Ascended Masters," on a level equal with others such as Buddha or Mohammed. They do not see Jesus as Lord, above all others.

The more people get involved with demonic power, the more they will become confused concerning Who Jesus Christ is, and, in particular, concerning His supreme Lordship over all others.

Jesus gave an interesting lesson to His disciples. They came to Him complaining that another man not associated with them was healing people using the name of Jesus. Our Lord's response was surprising to the disciples. He said:

"Do not hinder him; for he who is not against you is for you."

(Luke 9:50)

Notice that spiritual power is either for God or against Him. As people use the name of Jesus and truly see His power, they will become more and more convinced of Who Jesus truly is. On the other hand, whenever people use demonic power, they become progressively confused about His Lordship.

Fix these fundaments for discernment in your mind and heart:

1. agreement with the written Word of God,
2. good fruit,
3. the exaltation of Jesus Christ as Lord.

It is vital that Christians embrace, understand and apply these if they are going to examine spiritual and supernatural phenomena.

Conclusion

In section 1, we have identified an invisible spiritual realm where both good and evil exist. I explained how people can tune in and receive information from the spiritual realm. We saw how they can act as doorways for spiritual things to enter this natural world. Finally, I laid out a biblical basis for discernment. With this basic understanding, let's continue our investigation.

Section 2

The Breath of God in Us

In section 2, we turn our attention to the nature of humanity and its relationship with the spiritual world. Only as we have an accurate understanding of a person's spirit, soul and body can we give clear explanations for the spiritual and supernatural phenomena seen in the world around us.

The Origin of a Person's Spirit and Soul

In the book of Genesis we read how God created Adam:

And the Lord God formed man of the dust of the ground, and breathed into his nostrils the breath of life; and man became a living soul.

(Gen. 2:7 KJV)

Identify three elements involved in Adam's being: the body formed from dust, the breath released from God and the soul which was created.

God Breathed into Adam

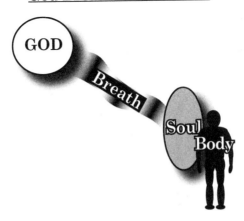

Some Christian teachers say that the soul of Adam was fashioned out of the spiritual breath of God, much as the dust of the earth was used to form the physical body. If that is true, then Adam had only two parts to his nature: a soul and a body. This view is called *dichotomous*, meaning two parts.

The Dichotomous View of a Person's Nature

Soul Body

Other Bible teachers say that the breath of God went into Adam, yet remained separate from the soul. God's breath is said to form the spirit within Adam. Indeed, the Hebrew word for "breath" is *ruah* and this word can also be interpreted as "spirit." This way of thinking leads us to understand that Adam consisted of three parts: a spirit, a soul and a body. This three-part view is called *trichotomous*.

The Trichotomous View of a Person's Nature

Spirit Soul Body

We really do not know in what way the breath of God was used to bring the soul into existence; however, to help us understand the nature of humanity, we have numerous Bible passages which talk about the various activities and functions of a person's being. There are some verses in the Bible which refer to persons having three parts and other verses which seem to indicate an individual has only two parts. For example, trichotomous teachers like to quote I Thessalonians 5:23, where Paul wrote:

> *Now may the God of peace Himself sanctify you*
> *entirely; and may your spirit and soul and body*
> *be preserved complete, without blame at the com-*
> *ing of our Lord Jesus Christ.*

This verse mentions three parts of a person's being: spirit, soul and body. In contrast, teachers who favor the dichotomous view like to focus on Bible verses which mention only two parts, a natural part and a spiritual part (e.g., I Cor. 7:34; Matt. 26:41).

I do not want to make this seem complicated, but I must acknowledge the fact that the Bible has some verses speaking from the trichotomous view and others from the dichotomous view. That is the reason some Christian teachers today teach one way, while others take the other perspective. If we are going to be true to the biblical revelation, we must see people as being both dichotomous and trichotomous.

An excellent way to explain this is by thinking of electricity flowing into a light bulb and causing a light to shine. The spirit is seen as the electric energy and the resulting light is seen as the soul. With this comparison we can see how the soul is completely dependent upon the spirit for its existence.

The Soul Is Dependent Upon the Spirit as the Light from a Light Bulb Is Dependent Upon Electricity

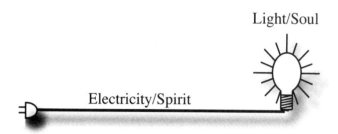

Light/Soul

Electricity/Spirit

In one sense, a person is a two-part being, because the spiritual substance of God's breath was used in some fashion to actually bring the soul into existence. Furthermore, the spirit and the soul are so intertwined that in many ways they are one.

At the same time, we can talk about the spirit as being separate from the soul. For example, we separate the two when talking about their origins—the spirit coming from God's breath and the soul being created. Because the spirit came from God, we later will see how this "God stuff" within us has certain characteristics not associated with the created soul.

We also must separate them when talking from God's perspective, because several verses mention how God could withdraw His breath from people if He chose to do so. For example Job 34:14-15 tells us:

> "If He [God] should determine to do so,
> If He should gather to Himself His spirit and His
>   breath,
> All flesh would perish together,

And man would return to dust."

Because God can withdraw the spirit from humanity, we must recognize the spirit as separate from the soul when looking from His viewpoint. In the following pages, when I talk about the spirit as an entity apart from the soul, I am speaking of that spiritual energy or life-energy which originated from the breath of God, yet now is resident within a person. When I speak of the spirit/soul, I am talking about the two elements which function together as one. When I talk about the soul only, I am doing this for the purpose of understanding; but please keep in mind that the soul does not exist independently of the spirit which sustains it.

12

Every Person Has the Breath of God

We can understand that God breathed life into Adam, but how does His breath actually get into all other human beings?

With the breath released into Adam, God fathered not just Adam, but all of humanity. Consider the power in that first breath. Compare it with God's other creative acts, such as when He spoke into existence the plant life. In God's spoken words, *"Let the earth sprout vegetation"* (Gen. 1:11), there was enough power to give life to all plants for the duration of this world. In a corresponding way, there was enough power in the divine breath released into Adam to give life to all the generations which would follow him.

The Breath of God Released into All Humanity

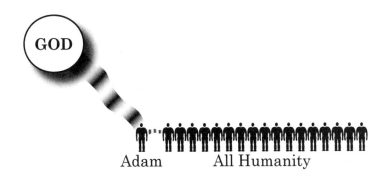

GOD

Adam   All Humanity

In the Bible, the Lord is referred to as the *"God of the spirits of all flesh"* (Num. 16:22; 27:16) and the *"Father of spirits"* (Heb. 12:9). God is the Originator, the Source, the starting point for all of life. The spiritual substance which God released into Adam became the substance of life which energized all people.

It is important to recognize that God began the entire human race through Adam. The apostle Paul explained,

> *"The God who made the world...He Himself gives to all people life and breath and all things; and <u>He made from one man</u> every nation of mankind to live on all the face of the earth...."*
> (Acts 17:24-26; emphasis added)

The spiritual substance of life originated with the breath of God, and it is passed on through the generational lines. Even today, the spirit which sustains life in a newborn baby originated with that first breath released into Adam.

At this point some Christians have a misconception. They imagine God releasing spiritual life into the womb of a mother each time there is conception or at some point during the gestation period. That is a common misunderstanding, and we need to establish the fact here that the spirit-substance of life itself is passed through the generational lines.

Evidence of this truth can be seen when we study the account concerning Abraham and Levi in Hebrews 7:9-10. We are told that when Abraham brought his offering to God, Levi was *"in the loins"* of Abraham. Levi was not born until four generations later, but notice his location when Abraham was alive. The Bible tells us that he was in the loins of his great-great-grandfather. When Levi was conceived, he did not come down to Earth from heaven and then enter the womb of his mother. The spiritual substance was resident in his forefather.

I am not saying that Levi fully existed before his conception, but the spiritual substance existed within Abraham. Levi's soul—the created element—would not have come into existence until the spiritual substance came in contact with the physical substance in the womb of his mother. Both the genetic code and the spirit (or what we can call the "spark of life") are passed through the generational lines.

Think again of our comparison with electricity flowing though wires to a light bulb. This time the wires represent the generational lines and the light bulb is at the point where a new person comes into existence.

Spirit-Energy Passed Through the Generational Lines

When does human life begin? Notice what King David said as he praised God:

For You formed my inward parts;
You wove me in my mother's womb.
I will give thanks to You, for I am fearfully and
*   wonderfully made;*

And my soul knows it very well.

(Ps. 139:13-14)

The soul of a person comes into existence simultaneously as the body is formed within the womb of the mother.

I can summarize this by saying that all human beings depend upon the breath of God to sustain their lives. That breath originated from the first breath released into Adam. Through Adam, God fathered all of humanity. The breath is passed through the generational lines just as the genetic code is. When the spirit and the genetic code are activated within the womb of the mother, a new soul comes into existence.

The only exception to this was the birth of Jesus. He was born of the Holy Spirit as the Spirit came upon the virgin Mary (Luke 1:26-35). He descended directly from heaven as the Word became flesh (John 1:14; 6:46-51; 8:23, 42). Jesus was the *"only begotten Son"* of God (John 3:16). In contrast, all the rest of humanity has been born of Adam.

13

The Nature of a Person's Spirit and Soul

If you could see a person's soul, what would it look like? How about the spirit of a person? As I answer these questions, keep in mind that every human being—Christian and non-Christian—has a soul and a spirit. Later, I will explain how the spirit of a Christian is different from the spirit of a non-Christian. Here we will consider the basic structure of the soul and spirit.

The soul (in contrast to the spirit) has a definite shape and size. It is structured as the human body. There are several reasons to believe this.

First, the Bible associates the soul with the blood. This is seen in several Bible passages, although some translators interpret the Hebrew word *nephesh* as "life," rather than "soul."

> *"For the life* [soul] *of the flesh is in the blood...*
> (Lev. 17:11; see also Gen. 9:4; Deut. 12:23)

As the blood saturates every part of a person's physical body, the soul does also. The soul is not existing physically in the blood, but it is an invisible, spiritual entity corresponding to the blood. Therefore, it is best to think of the soul as filling the body just as the blood does.

We can also see the structure and shape of the soul as we study biblical passages which describe the human soul after it has left the body due to death. For example, in I Samuel 28:8-19, we read the story of how King Saul had a medium conjure up the prophet Samuel from the dead. This is an evil exercise forbidden by God, but note from this Bible account how the prophet Samuel appeared in the form of an old man (vs. 13-14). He was even recognizable.

We can also see the "recognizable soul" in Luke 16:19-31, where our Lord told a story of Lazarus and a rich man who had died. In this passage, He referred to the finger of Lazarus and the tongue of the rich man, even though their physical bodies were decaying in the grave. The two were able to recognize each other. We can conclude from such accounts that if we were able to see the soul with our natural eyes, it would appear as the body, having arms, legs, head and facial features.

The Soul Is Shaped Similar to the Body

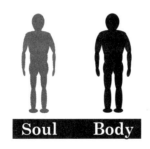

At times I will diagram the soul as being separate from the body (as above), but keep in mind that the soul is actually superimposed over and filling the same location as the physical body (until separation after death).

Contrast this with the spirit of a person. If I were to talk about the spirit independently of the soul, I would not describe it as having shape or size. Of course, the spirit fills and gives life to the soul and body, but it comes from the breath of God. As such, it is the "God stuff" in each of us. Because it is divine in origin, it is wrong to define a person's spirit in natural terms of shape or size.

It is helpful to think of the spirit as energy or light. In deed, the Bible describes attributes of the spirit as both of these. Since the spirit is the energy which sustain a person's existence I will draw the spirit as a spark of energy or a burst of light.

The Spirit Is the God Stuff In Each of Us

We must not limit our understanding of the spirit to energy or light, nor to any other natural comparison that we can make. Comparisons can help us understand some of the functions of the spirit, but they can never give us the whole picture. Energy, for example, is something which functions in this natural world according to natural laws. The spirit is of the spiritual world. Since it is the God stuff resident in each of us, it does not function according to the natural laws which govern this world. As we continue, we will see that the spirit of a person is not limited in space and that, indeed, it can reach beyond the physical body (sections 4 and 5). Therefore, in order to understand this spiritual substance resident in a person, we must not limit ourselves to natural comparisons.

Next we need to identify the flowing nature of the spirit within a person. The spirit is not a stagnant structure. It is more accurate to think of it as moving energy, flowing from within a person's innermost being. The book of Proverbs talks about this energy, explaining that from the heart *"flow the springs of life"* (Prov. 4:23).

The Flowing Nature of the Spirit

Finally, let's examine the difference between the spirit of the Christian and the spirit of the non-Christian. The apostle Paul explained:

> *If Christ is in you...the spirit is alive because of righteousness.*
>
> (Rom. 8:10)

This quality of being "alive" is unique to the spirit of the Christian.

Jesus explained that he who believes in Him would have rivers of *living water* flowing from his innermost being (John 7:38). Both Christians and non-Christians have a spirit which sustains their lives and flows within them, but the rivers within the believer consist of *living* water. In another Bible passage, our Lord explained that those who came to Him would have a *"well of water springing up to eternal life"* (John 4:14). Again, we see life as springing forth from within the Christian.

When we submit our lives to Jesus Christ, we are born into the family of God. The life within us provides us with eternal life and it causes our spirit to be responsive and alive unto God. We identify the introduction of new spiritual life as the experience of being "born again."

In summary, we can say that both Christians and non-Christians have a soul and spirit. The soul is structured as the human body. The spirit is the flowing, moving energy which sustains life. The spirit within the believer has a quality of life related to its association with God.

The Whole Person: Emotions and Thoughts

I have introduced the terms dichotomist and trichotomist in reference to the differing views of a person's nature. Unfortunately, if we embrace either one of these labels, we tend to form images in our minds of a person being divided into the corresponding parts. Those images are misleading because each person functions as a unit.

A Human Being Is a Unit

Spirit/Soul/Body

We should not divide a person into two or three parts, thinking that any one of those parts functions independently of the other parts. Whatever happens to the spirit influences the soul and the body. What happens to the soul affects the spirit and the body. And what influences the body influences the spirit and the soul.

Some Christians miss this truth. They tend to over-compartmentalize the various functions of a person's being. Concluding that humans are three-part beings, they try to assign various functions to just the body, just the soul or just the spirit. One erroneous teaching common among Christians today is that the soul consists of the mind, the will and the emotions.[1] Such compartmentalization can easily be proven as untrue.

First, consider a person's emotions. Some have tried to assign human emotions only to the soul. But in the Bible we can see verses which attribute emotions to both the soul and the spirit. For instance, Psalm 42:11 tells us of emotional turmoil within the soul, while I Kings 21:5 speaks of sadness of spirit. Luke 1:47 tells us of joy coming from a person's spirit, while Psalms 94:19 and 103:1-2 speak of joy within the soul. In John 13:21 we are told that our Lord Jesus was troubled in spirit, while Matthew 26:38 tells us He was grieved deeply in His soul. From these and many other verses in both the Old and New Testaments, we have to conclude that emotions cannot be assigned to only to the soul.

Furthermore, we know that the physical body plays a role in emotions. Various physiological changes and biochemical reactions are evident whenever emotions rise or fall. Scientists can measure the related changes in bodily functions.

This feature of a person's emotional existence in the physical body is even more interesting when we consider certain physical stimuli. For example, when depressant drugs are injected into the bloodstream of an individual, her entire being is affected. There are other drugs which can cause the sexual passions to be aroused. Electrical impulses on certain

---

1 The profound impact ancient philosophers such as Plato and Aristotle have had on Western Christianity has led to the over-compartmentalization of a person's nature. For more teaching on this subject see my book entitled: *Christianity Unshackled.*

parts of the nervous system can trigger many different emotional responses.

Emotions and feelings can also be stirred from the other side. By this I mean that spiritual influences acting upon a person's spirit may cause responses in the soul and physical body. For example, as God's Spirit comes upon a person, he may feel it physically. The devil may come to a man or woman causing physiological changes to occur, as well as causing an emotional reaction of fear, bitterness, anger, etc. The point is that emotions exist throughout a person's entire being, and whatever happens in one part influences all.

Emotions Exist Throughout a Person's Entire Being

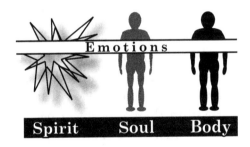

In the same way, we can identify thought processes occurring on all three levels. First, consider how the spirit of a person is involved in thought processes. The apostle Paul posed the question:

> *For who among men knows the thoughts of a man*
> *except the spirit of the man which is in him?*
> (I Cor. 2:11a)

The obvious answer to this question is, "No one." It is the

spirit within a person which illuminates his being and reveals thoughts. It is helpful to see the spirit in this sense, as a light shining within a person, illuminating the mind.

The Spirit of a Person Illuminates Thoughts

Spirit　　　Soul　　　Body

Once we identify the role which the spirit plays in helping a person to think, we can note a fundamental difference between Christians and non-Christians. The spirits within believers have been made alive unto God. Therefore, the energy flowing from within their innermost beings will cause their thoughts to come more and more into alignment with God's thoughts. Paul explained that the natural man cannot understand the things of God, because his spirit has not been changed within (I Cor. 2:10-14). However, Christians have the ongoing work of the Holy Spirit within their spirits to reveal the thoughts of God (I Cor. 2:9-10). In the book of Proverbs we read that *"The spirit of man is the lamp of the Lord"* (Prov. 20:27a). It is through the spirit that God shines His light, revealing His thoughts.

However, thought processes also take place in the soul and body. When we talk about thought processes within the soul, we are usually referring to the more conscious decisions we make. As explained in section 1, the word *mind* is usually used when speaking of the location of our thought processes within our soul. In the body each person has a physical brain that also processes information, makes decisions and sends millions of electrical impulses coursing through the nervous system throughout each day. The brain decides how warm to keep the body, how much food to digest, where to send more blood, etc. Millions of thoughts are processed every minute.

The main point is that thought processes occur throughout one's entire being, spirit, soul and body.

Thought Processes Involve a Person's Entire Being

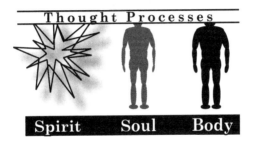

As we come to understand these truths we can see how wrong it is to try compartmentalize a person's being placing certain functions just in the spirit, just in the soul or just in the body. Furthermore, it is wrong to say that the soul is the mind, will and emotions. We have seen how emotions and thought processes involve the whole person. Now let's discover how the will of a person involves their spirit, soul and body.

Identifying the Will of a Person

Where is a person's will located?

Some people have taught that the will is within the soul. Others try to locate it in the spirit. And those who see an individual as merely a physical being usually conclude that a person's will is within his brain.

What is the truth?

The will of a person permeates the entire being. To see this, first identify the decisions made at the level of the body. There are hundreds of biochemical processes going on inside of you right now, all governed by the dictates of your brain. You can influence some of the natural processes from a deeper level within your being. For example, you can make a conscious decision at the level of your spirit/soul not to sleep. However, the demands of the physical body eventually will overrule your conscious mind.

Consider the control of your breathing. You are capable of making a conscious decision right now to stop breathing. In that case, your spirit/soul to some degree is ruling over the natural governing processes of your body. However, you cannot hold your breath indefinitely. In just a short time, you will lose consciousness and your physical body will "overrule" your inner being. So, we see that your conscious mind has some degree of authority over your body, but your physical body has some degree of control over your conscious decisions.

The truth is that many things about your life are decided at the level of your body, and you do not have the willpower in your spirit/soul to overpower them. This is true of many physical desires and needs, most of which you are not even conscious.

Decisions made within the body go beyond physical functions. Paul explained that the body is actually involved in moral decisions, and that the body may have within it the desire to sin:

> *For I joyfully concur with the law of God in the inner man, but I see a different law in the members of my body, waging war against the law of my mind and making me a prisoner of the law of sin which is in my members. Wretched man that I am! Who will set me free from the body of this death?*
>
> (Rom. 7:22-24)

Notice that the will is located in both the inner man and in the body. In the experience Paul described in these verses, the will of the body was greater than the will of the inner man. We must conclude that the will of a person to sin or not to sin is located in part within the physical body.

As we discuss the struggle between the inner person and the outer person, we are assuming that the will, in part, resides in the spirit/soul. Most Christians accept the role the spirit/soul plays in determining a person's decisions, so I will not spend much time proving the will's existence on the deeper levels, except to point out the following.

I explained how the spirit gives a person the energy to live and think. If a woman does not have enough spiritual strength, she will be ruled by that lack and be incapable of acting in the way she desires. It is enlightening for us also to see how God can influence people's decisions through their spirits. For example, we read how *"...the Lord stirred up the spirit of Cyrus king of Persia..."* (Ezra 1:1). Consider also the words of Isaiah spoken to those under God's judgment:

> *For the Lord has poured over you a spirit of deep sleep,*
> *He has shut your eyes....*
>
> (Is. 29:10)

The people under such a spiritual influence were incapable of acting independently of the spiritual influence enveloping them.

The devil, too, may tempt or inspire a person to make certain decisions. An evil spirit may have such a hold on a certain woman's life that her behavior is actually controlled. So then, the spirit or entities working through the spirit of a person, do show some influence upon the will of that person.

Finally, consider the soul. In some cases the soul of a person has authority to make a decision—even over the person's spirit. To see this, look at the following verses:

> *...the spirits of the prophets are subject to prophets.*
> (I Cor. 14:32)

> *Like a city that is broken into and without walls*
> *Is a man who has no control over his spirit.*
> (Prov. 25:28)

Notice that people can exercise authority over their own spirits. (In chapter 26, I will explain when and why this is necessary.)

The point is that the entire being is involved in making decisions. The will of a person permeates their entire being.

The Will Involves a Person's Entire Being

To see a real-life example of how the will involves the entire person, consider Clarence, a man who gave himself to a sexually promiscuous lifestyle for many years before becoming a Christian. Because of evil lusts, Clarence drew within himself spiritual influences related to sexual perversions, and, as a result, his spirit was defiled. His soul became bonded to others and his thoughts conformed to perverted ways of thinking. As he repeatedly submitted himself to sinful behaviors, his physical body developed cravings for increased sexual satisfaction.

When Clarence became a Christian, freedom came only after a cleansing of his entire being. He repented and asked God to forgive him; however, his body continued to crave unnatural sexual pleasures. He had many thought patterns that he had to renew according to God's Word and God's desires. Clarence did not become entirely free until there had been a sanctification—spirit, soul and body.

With this in mind, note again the blessing Paul spoke over the early Christians:

> *Now may the God of peace Himself sanctify you entirely; and may your spirit and soul and body*

be preserved complete, without blame....

(I Thess. 5:23)

A blessing such as this for sanctification only makes sense if one's entire being is susceptible to sin. What we conclude, then, is that the will of individuals involves and permeates their whole being, spirit, soul and body.

Identifying the Heart of a Person

We are created as whole persons, not divided into three parts. The soul fills the body. The spirit fills the soul. All three parts are integrated and superimposed one upon the other. It is helpful to think of the body as the physical expression of our invisible existence. What the body has, the soul has. What the soul has, the spirit has. The various parts of our nature were not fashioned by different makers. God created all three parts after the same image. They fit together in one package.

Let's see this correlation by locating the "heart" and seeing how it exists on all three levels of a person's being.

Of course, there is a physical organ pumping blood which we call the heart. However, we must see the heart as existing throughout the core of a person's being. The Greek word for heart, *kardia,* also means the core or the center. In our everyday conversation we can talk about the heart of an issue or the core of a specific item, such as the core of an apple. It is in this sense that we can also talk about the heart of a man being at his deepest center. At the center of his body is the heart; at the center of his soul is also the heart; and finally at the core of a person's spirit is also his heart.

The Heart Is the Core of a Person's Being

What then is the heart? It is the fountainhead of a person's life. Proverbs 4:23 tells us:

Watch over your heart with all diligence,
For from it flow the springs of life.

This shows us that the heart is the focal point of one's being. It is the seat of desires (Matt. 5:28), faith (Rom. 10:10), and purpose (Acts 11:23; II Cor. 9:7). Just as the physical heart pumps blood, so also the heart within our spirit/soul circulates the springs of life. The physical heart draws in oxygen through the lungs and food from the stomach. In a corresponding way, the invisible heart draws in good through holy desires and evil through lusts. That which is received grows and flows outward. The heart, then, is the core of a person's being, while at the same time serving as the fountainhead of life.

The Heart Is the Fountainhead of One's Being

Spirit/Soul/Body

This point cannot be emphasized enough for our future understanding. Wherever the heart of a person is pointed, their life will follow. From the heart, do, indeed, flow the springs of life.

Finally, let us put together the overall picture we have developed of a person's nature. In our attempt to see the individual as a whole person, we have dispelled the misconception that the various functions of a person are limited to only the spirit, soul or body. Earlier, we saw how a person's emotions, thought processes and will involve the entire person. Now we see how the heart also exists throughout one's being and it functions as the fountainhead of life.

Born of Incorruptible Seed

Now let's identify more clearly what happens within individuals when they become Christians.

Through the work of Jesus Christ, people find forgiveness of sin and God does a cleansing work within them (Acts 15:9; Titus 3:5). God breathes new spiritual life into the person and that life gives them eternal life (I John 5:11-12). Their spirit comes alive unto God (Rom. 8:10). They are *"born of God"* (I John 5:1). They become members of the family of God (John 1:12).

God Breathes Eternal Life into the Believer

Some Christians teach that much more happens through the born again experience. They add that the entire spirit of the Christian is transformed: that the Christian's spirit is instantly made perfect and recreated totally in the image and glory of God. They say that the spirit of the Christian cannot be corrupted, hurt or in any way improved. This is the "perfect-spirit doctrine."

The Perfect-Spirit Doctrine

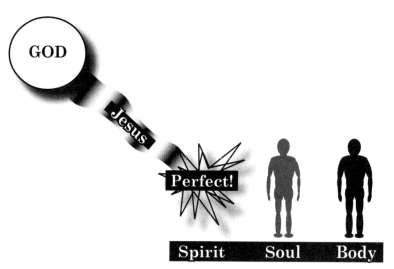

In Romans 8:10 we are told that the Christian's spirit is *"alive because of righteousness."* But the term *alive* is not a synonym for the word *perfect*. The perfect-spirit teachers miss this point. They develop their doctrine by reading the Bible through an extremely trichotomous view of humanity. Rather than think of a person as a unit with the spirit, soul and body totally integrated, they envision the spirit of a person as something which can be made perfect without simultaneously transforming the soul and body of the Christian. That over-compartmentalized understanding of a person's nature leads to some subtle, yet destructive misunderstandings. Several errors will be mentioned here, but more will become evident in section 3.

I will be teaching from the more commonly accepted view that when people become Christians, God plants new life into them: spirit, soul and body. More specifically, we can say that Jesus comes to dwell within the Christian's heart.

> *Because you are sons, God has sent forth the Spirit*
> *of His Son into our hearts, crying, "Abba! Father!"*
> (Gal. 4:6)

As we have seen, the heart exists throughout a person's spirit, soul and body. Therefore, the whole person is influenced when he or she becomes a Christian. We can emphasize this point by noting how the Bible tells us that the *body* of the Christian is a temple for the Holy Spirit. Yes, even the physical body is a temple for God to indwell.

Jesus Comes into the Heart of the Believer

109

There is an aspect of the Christian's being which is perfect. Peter wrote how we are born of the perfect and incorruptible seed (I Peter 1:23). That perfect seed is planted in the heart, which is the core of the spirit, the core of the soul and the core of the body. So we see that the perfect seed is in the spirit (as well as in the soul and body), but there is no verse in the Bible which states or implies that the Christian's entire spirit is instantaneously made perfect.

The perfect-spirit doctrine typically is developed from two verses in the Bible which are misinterpreted. Hebrews 12:23 refers to *"the spirits of the righteous made perfect."* The perfect-spirit teachers like to include present-day Christians in this description, but in reality, this verse refers to those who have died and are already living in the presence of God. Furthermore, the verse tells us that those people who have died have been *"made perfect"*—not just their spirits, but they themselves have been made perfect. Indeed, those now fully with Jesus have been transformed into His image, but Christians who are alive on Earth are not yet in that group.

The other verse that is sometime misinterpreted is the King James translation of II Corinthians 5:17, which says:

> *Therefore if any man be in Christ, he is a new creature: old things are passed away; behold, all things are become new.*

Using this verse, the perfect-spirit teachers stress the word "all" and then assume that the writer was referring to all the Christian's spirit when he said "all things." Yet, the context of this verse in no way indicates that the things being made new refer to the spirit of the Christian. The passage is primarily speaking of the change in our relationship to God, our perspective of life and how we live—these things have become new.

Furthermore, we can study II Corinthians 5:17 in the original Greek language, and we find that the word "all" is not there. It was added by the translators of the King James Version. A more accurate translation is from the New American Standard which says:

Therefore if anyone is in Christ, he is a new creature; the old things passed away; behold new things have come.

(II Cor. 5:17)

Yes, new things have come, but the Bible does not say that all things in the Christian's spirit have become perfect.

To see that Paul was not teaching the perfect-spirit doctrine in II Corinthians 5:17, all one has to do is read 23 verses later where Paul went on to tell the Corinthian Christians:

Therefore, having these promises, beloved, let us cleanse ourselves from all defilement of flesh and spirit, perfecting holiness in the fear of God.

(II Cor. 7:1)

The perfect-spirit teachers must ignore this verse in order to continue holding to their doctrine. Since Paul talks about the Christian's spirit being defiled and needing cleansing, he obviously was not teaching 23 verses earlier that the Christian's spirit is already perfect.

It is important that we note that in the verse we just quoted, Paul was speaking to Christians: to *"beloved"* who have the promises of God. He also includes himself in this exhortation: *"let us cleanse ourselves of all defilement of flesh and spirit."* Obviously, the Christian's spirit can be defiled.

This issue has so many far-reaching implications and is so critical for topics which will follow, that it is worth our

111

time to glance at a few other Bible passages which contradict the perfect-spirit doctrine. Consider Paul's exhortations for Christians to stay *"in one spirit,"* that is in Greek, *en heis pneumatos* (Phil. 1:27; see also Eph. 4:3). If Christians already had a perfect spirit, they would always be perfectly united in spirit, and Paul's exhortation would be foolish and wrong. That would be similar to telling a person, "Do not sin," while at the same time believing that they could not sin. Obviously, Christians can sin and they can be spiritually disunited.

Several Bible verses talk about things being added to the Christian's spirit. For example, Paul wrote to the Philippians, *"The grace of the Lord Jesus Christ be with your spirit"* (Phil. 4:23). Paul used similar terminology in his letters to the Galatians (Gal. 6:18) and his letter to Philemon (Philemon 1:25). This truth that things can be added to the Christian's spirit is contrary to the perfect-spirit doctrine.

Peter exhorted the Christian women to have *"a gentle and quiet spirit"* (I Peter 3:4), a teaching which would be misleading if the Christian's spirit were perfect.

In Romans 12:11, Paul exhorted all believers to serve the Lord, being *"fervent in spirit."* Similarly, he commanded the unmarried women to dedicate themselves to the Lord that they *"may be holy both in body and spirit"* (I Cor. 7:34). Such terminology would be in error if the Christian's spirit was perfect in holiness simply because of the new-birth experience.

In II Corinthians 7:13, we read Paul's words to the Corinthians concerning Titus: "...*because his spirit has been refreshed by you all.*" A perfect spirit would not need refreshing, and it would have been wrong for Paul to speak in these terms, if, indeed, the Christian's spirit was already perfect.

More than one Bible passage refers to a broken, crushed or wounded spirit. For example:

The spirit of a man can endure his sickness,
But a broken spirit who can bear it?

(Prov. 18:14)

A soothing tongue is a tree of life,
But perversion in it crushes the spirit.

(Prov. 15:4)

And again:

A joyful heart is good medicine,
But a broken spirit dries up the bones.

(Prov. 17:22)

King David often spoke of pressures to which his spirit was subjected:

When my spirit was overwhelmed within me....

(Ps. 142:3)

Answer me quickly, O Lord, my spirit fails....

(Ps. 143:7)

Other references talk about being *"oppressed in spirit"* (e.g., I Sam. 1:15). Isaiah prophesied:

"Then the spirit of the Egyptians will be demoralized within them...."

(Is. 19:3)

Such Scripture passages which refer to negative effects upon the spirit of a person are numerous.

Although the references in the last paragraph are taken from the Old Testament, the verses which I gave you preceding those are all recorded in the New Testament, and all of them are speaking about Christians. In the Old Testament, numerous verses talk about a person's spirit being broken, crushed, bruised, overwhelmed, failing, demoralized, etc. In the New Testament, different verses talk about the Christian's spirit being defiled, refreshed, having grace added to it, being in unity or disunity with other believers, etc. As we acknowledge these Scriptural truths, we cannot accept the perfect-spirit doctrine.

Throughout this book, I will be teaching from the view that when a person becomes a Christian, the perfect seed of God is planted within his or her heart. Indeed, that seed is perfect and incorruptible (I Peter 1:23), but it must grow and mature. It is not an instantaneous work of perfection throughout the Christian's spirit accomplished at the new birth. Rather, it is a progressive work which begins at that time. Once a person has been begotten of God, he or she progressively matures into a greater and greater manifestation of God's nature—spirit, soul and body.

God's Spirit and the Christian's Spirit

How is God's Spirit related to the Christian's spirit? As I answer this, realize that God's Spirit is the same as the Holy Spirit. It is the relationship between the Holy Spirit and the Christian's spirit which we will now examine.

The Christian's spirit, even though it is alive unto God, is still an entity separate from the Holy Spirit. Romans 8:16 tells us:

> *The Spirit Himself testifies with our spirit that we are children of God.*

Notice that there is an agreement between the Holy Spirit and the Christian's spirit, but they are still distinct entities.

This distinction can be identified when we discuss how the Christian's spirit is subject to the Christian. Paul explained that even prophets must exercise authority over their spirits:

> *...and the spirits of prophets are subject to prophets.*
> (I Cor. 14:32)

In contrast, we know that the Holy Spirit is always subject to God, the Father (John 16:13-15).

When people become Christians, they become temples for the Holy Spirit to indwell (I Cor. 6:19). Christians, therefore, have both their own spirits and the Holy Spirit present within. However, we must not think of the entirety of the Holy Spirit dwelling within the Christian. To state this simply: "God is big!" When the Jews in the Old Testament times started to think that God was dwelling exclusively within their temple, God declared from heaven that Earth is His footstool (Is. 66:1). It is true that God's presence manifested at times in the Jewish temple, but not "all of God" was contained within it.

We can also learn from a passage in Malachi 2, where God rebukes people who broke their marriage covenants, declaring that none of them have a "remnant" or a "residue" of the Spirit left (Mal. 2:15). Such terminology implies that the measure of the Spirit within a person can change. Only Jesus Christ had the complete fullness of the Spirit while on Earth. We, as Christians, have the first fruits (Rom. 8:23), or the down payment of His fullness (II Cor. 1:21-22). Of course, it is the purity and wholeness of the Godhead, but it is still only a measure of God's Spirit.

To further understand our relationship with the Holy Spirit we must not think of Him as a force or impersonal power. He is a Person. He can be grieved (Eph. 4:30) or quenched (I Thess. 5:19). God, the Father, is jealous over the Holy Spirit:

> *Or do you think that the Scripture speaks to no purpose: "He jealously desires the Spirit which He has made to dwell in us"?*
>
> (James 4:5)

God's jealously concerning His Spirit means He guards and does not allow the Holy Spirit to be abused. In the context of this verse, James says that as we draw near to God, He draws near to us. It is true that God will not abandon us, but it is also true that He fills our temples and reveals Himself to us in various ways, depending upon our heart attitude toward Him.

As Christians yield their lives to the Father, the Holy Spirit becomes a more powerful influence in their lives. Paul wrote:

> *But the one who joins himself to the Lord is one spirit with Him.*
>
> (I Cor. 6:17)

The context of this verse is making a comparison with two people who are having sexual relations. As two become one through bonding in sexual intercourse, so also the Holy Spirit and the Christian's spirit become one as the Christian joins himself to the Lord.

Notice that this understanding portrays the Christian's spirit as not always one with the Holy Spirit. The relationship between the Holy Spirit and the Christian's spirit changes from time to time. Compare the relationship to a marriage. Two people who are married live together, have a covenant relationship and bond between them. However, they are not always in total agreement and unity. At times they may be in harmony as their hearts agree with one another. At that time they are "one" in a much deeper sense of the word.

In similar fashion, we understand that the Christian's spirit and the Holy Spirit are bonded and exist in the same dimension; there is a covenant relationship which God has established. As the believer yields his or her will to the Lord, the Holy Spirit and the Christian's spirit "become one."

This oneness is not automatic; otherwise the apostle Paul would not have exhorted the Corinthian Christians to "join" themselves to the Lord. If we were always one with Him, it would not make sense for James to tell us that as we draw near to Him, He draws near to us (James 4:5). Such exhortations can only be understood as we realize that the Holy Spirit is a Person separate from the Christian's spirit, yet willing to unite as we fully yield to Him.

God's Spirit and the Christian's Spirit

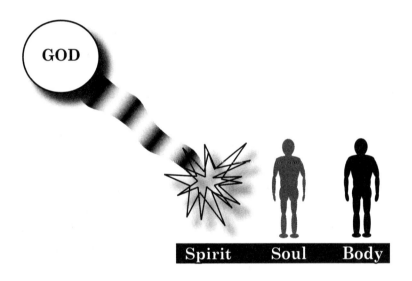

GOD

Spirit   Soul   Body

I can offer a beautiful comparison by telling you about one group of people indigenous to the North American continent who express their love for each other, not by kissing each other, but by standing very close to each other and inhaling each other's breath. This symbolizes an exchange of life between them. In similar fashion, God draws near to His people, and there is an exchange of spiritual substance, Spirit to spirit.

The Greek word used in the original Bible writings and interpreted *inspire*, literally means *to breathe into*. When we speak of God inspiring something, we are saying that God has breathed in His life, energy, thoughts, authority and nature.

As we develop this understanding, keep in mind that a person is a whole person. God does not just breathe into the spirit of the Christian without influencing the soul and body. As I have emphasized, it is impossible to touch the spirit without touching the soul and the body at the same time. The Holy Spirit cannot dwell within the spirit of the Christian without simultaneously dwelling within the soul and body of the Christian. Again, we see the importance of recognizing how the Christian's body is the temple in which the Spirit dwells (I Cor. 3:16-17).

Can Evil Reside Within a Christian?

Can evil be inside a Christian who has both the Holy Spirit and a personal spirit which has been made alive by God? Can both good and evil exist within the same vessel?

Read Paul's words about his own struggles:

> *I find then the principle that evil is present in me, the one who wants to do good.*
>
> (Rom. 7:21)

In the context of this verse, Paul explained that evil dwelt within his body while his inner man wanted to please God. Even though evil and good lodged in different places, both were present within his own being.

We can also consider again, Paul's exhortation in II Corinthians 7:1:

> *Therefore, having these promises, beloved, let us cleanse ourselves from all defilement of flesh and spirit, perfecting holiness in the fear of God.*

Notice that the Christian's spirit and flesh can be defiled— that is, stained and influenced by evil.

This is easy to see when we consider James' explanation

of how lust conceives evil within a person (James 1:14-15). People—even Christians—can lust; that is, turn their hearts to desire things from an evil motivation. That lust actually conceives evil within.

Recognizing these realities, we must conclude that evil spiritual influences can be brought into a person. This is true even in the life of the Christian, but we must be careful to understand that the life of God is resident within the believer. Light and darkness oppose each other.

Because of this opposition, some Christian teachers argue that Christians who are filled with the Holy Spirit cannot have a demon within their being. I would agree that a Christian who is "filled completely" with the life of God could not have a demon, but I doubt that any Christians are filled completely at all times. As I explained in the previous chapter, we have the first fruits of the Holy Spirit and we can grieve Him.

Some Christians have a difficult time understanding how both good and evil spiritual influences active within a Christian, because they are thinking from a natural perspective of limited space. In chapter 1, I explained how space has a different meaning in the spiritual dimension. I pointed out that a legion of demons, meaning one thousand or more demons, existed within a single person (Luke 8:30). This implies that spiritual space is not limited as we understand physical space.

To see this more clearly, we can ask the question, "Can the Holy Spirit and the devil be in the same city, together?" The answer is obviously, "Yes." Can they be in the same building together? Yes, because the devil even came into the presence of Jesus to tempt Him (Matt. 4:3-11). Can they be in the same room together? Yes, because the Book of Job describes how Satan goes into the very throne room of God (Job 1:6). Next, answer this: "Is there more space inside a room than there is inside a person's spirit?" It is difficult to answer this, but the sequence of questions challenges us to think of the spiritual dimension in terms that are not so limiting as the natural dimension.

I do mean not to say or even give the impression that demons can fill or control Christians. It is more accurate to think of Christians as having light shining within them and that light radiates outward. Demons hate the light. They are weak in the presence of the light. They flee from the light. However, there may be times when a demon has found access to the believer through that believer's lusts and continued sinful activity. Still, most negative thoughts which a Christian experiences are simply his or her own fleshly thoughts. Whether it is the result of a demon tempting or the person being carried away by lusts, the believer has authority from God to resist. We are promised that if we resist the devil he will flee from us (James 4:7). Greater is He who is in us than he who is in the world (I John 4:4).

Releasing the Holy Spirit

Becoming completely one with God—this should be our goal as Christians. Jesus was able to say, *"I and the Father are one"* (John 10:30). His will and the Father's will were in perfect harmony. Our Lord prayed for us, saying:

> *"...that they may all be one; even as You, Father, are in Me and I in You, that they also may be in Us...."*
> (John 17:21)

We have not yet attained to this perfect oneness with each other, nor with the Father, but we are *"being transformed into the same image from glory to glory"* (II Cor. 3:18). We are progressing toward that goal.

In this process, the union of the Holy Spirit and the Christian's spirit is not just a mixing of two entities; rather, they "become one." The believer's spirit then becomes inseparable from the Holy Spirit. They are indistinguishable. We then no longer can talk about the Christian's spirit and the Holy Spirit as separate entities. Consider Paul's words again:

> *But the one who joins himself to the Lord is one spirit with Him.*
> (I Cor. 6:17)

When a Christian's will is in total union with God's will, then the Holy Spirit and the Christian's spirit are no longer two, but are made into one entity.

Consider the implications of this. When the Christian woman, who is one with the Father, releases the human spirit within her, she is also releasing the Holy Spirit to flow out. When she yields to the spiritual urging within her, she is yielding to God. When words come out of her mouth, they are the words of God. When she uses her authority, she is using God's authority. If, indeed, a Christian were totally one with the Father, her spirit, words, thoughts and authority would be God's Spirit, words, thoughts and authority.

Sometime people will ask, "Are we releasing the Holy Spirit or the human spirit?" If a Christian's heart is in harmony with God's heart, then the Holy Spirit and her spirit are one; therefore, to release the human spirit is to release the Holy Spirit.

In contrast, when a man is not in harmony with God, he may release his own spirit, separate from the Holy Spirit. In the Old Testament we read the warning concerning prophets who prophesy from their own inspiration and their own spirit, rather than from the Spirit of God (Ezek. 13:23). Jesus explained that he who seeks his own glory speaks from himself (John 7:18). Notice that the heart of a person determines what spirit is motivating him.

Apply this truth to various ministry situations. Many Christians wonder how they can see God's glory manifest in the world and in the midst of the Church. The answer is to become one with God and release that which is within them. If a certain minister desires to release the Spirit of God as he preaches, then he must release the human spirit which is within him. If a worship leader wants the presence of God to manifest in the midst of the congregation, he must let his own spirit fill the building. When a Christian desires to release healing power for the physically ill, he must release the spirit abiding within. If Christians hesitate in releasing the spirit within them, then they are holding back the workings of the Holy Spirit of God. To the degree they allow a free flowing of the spiritual energy within them, to that same degree they are releasing the Spirit of God which is one with their spirits.

Dr. David Yonggi Cho, who leads the largest church in the world, has an interesting teaching which is helpful to note at this point. When asked by the pastors under his care how they could bring the presence of God to their meetings, he responded by saying, "You bring His presence by your words." This is a profound statement because it implies that releasing or bringing in the presence of God is dependent upon us and what we do.

Jesus said that we have the authority to bind or loose. He said the Holy Spirit will flow from *our* innermost being (John 7:37-39). Of course, God can and does move sovereignly by His Spirit in this world, but believers must also realize that the moving of God's Spirit is dependent upon our willingness to release the human spirits within our beings. Where our spirits go, the Holy Spirit goes. Of course, this is only true to the extent that we have joined ourselves to the Lord.

This truth of our spirits being one with God's Spirit reveals one reason why the Holy Spirit flows out of people differently. Though we are one, we still have our individual personalities. God uses our unique personalities as He moves through our lives. Compare this with the marriage relationship. When two people join in marriage and they are becoming one in heart, they maintain their distinct personalities. Though their desires melt together and complement one another, they still act as unique persons. In similar fashion, a Christian woman will not lose her personality when she makes herself one with the Lord. Fleshly desires and selfish goals disappear, but personhood remains a part of what flows out.

I like to compare this flow with the enjoyment we experienced as children when we purchased Pixy Sticks from the local candy store. Pixy Sticks were straws filled with sweet-flavored powder. Children could pour the sweet powder into their mouths or suck water through the straw, so the water would come out with a delightful flavor. You and I are similar to Pixy Sticks. When the Holy Spirit flows through our lives He comes out in our flavor. When the Holy Spirit flows through your life He comes out in a different flavor than when He flows through my life. This is how God works in our lives—not to eliminate our personalities, but to bring them to life.

Finally, we need to realize that even though our goal as Christians should be to be one with the Father, it is a serious error to lose sight of His distinct and separate existence from us. Sometime Christians, in learning about the Holy Spirit Who dwells within, begin to focus all their attention upon that which God is doing in their innermost beings. They start perceiving God as a force Who moves within them, rather than as a Person separate from them. They live their lives waiting to yield to that which is within, and they lose sight of a God Who is in heaven. Then they become confused concerning whether they should pray to God or simply wait for Him to move within them.

Only if we see God as a separate Person, greater than ourselves, will we have a proper relationship with Him. Jesus taught us to pray to the Father, *"Who is in heaven."* As we keep our minds focused upon a personal God above, He becomes one with us within.

Compare again our relationship to the Father with a marriage relationship. When a husband focuses his heart and mind upon his wife, there arises within him desires and thoughts of how to please her. It is as they focus upon one another in love that they become one. In the same way, as Christians turn their hearts toward God, there rises from within them desires centered on pleasing Him.

What I want you to see is that the focus for Christians should be upon God, the Father, Who is in heaven and Who is a separate Person from ourselves. Nowhere in the Bible are we told to focus upon the human spirit within, but many Bible verses exhort us to set our minds upon God Who is in heaven. Colossians 3:1-2, for example, tells us to:

> ...*keep seeking the things above, where Christ is, seated at the right hand of God. Set your mind on the things above, not on the things that are on earth.*

Even though God comes to dwell within the believers, our focus is not to be inward—but upward. The inward indwelling is the result of the upward focus.

Conclusion

The single most profound truth we have discovered in this section is that God's breath resides in us. We each have a deposit of this divinely-originated substance, and it provides us with the energy necessary to live. It energizes our being and allows us to think. It is also the part of our nature with which God makes Himself one. As Christians become one with the Lord, their entire souls and bodies become saturated with God's Spirit, and they become temples in which God dwells.

We have also introduced the concept that spiritual energy can flow from out of a person and influence the world. This foundational truth gives us a key to understanding many mystical experiences, demonstrations of supernatural power, paranormal experiences, spiritual dynamics between people, and other phenomena which we will examine in sections 4 and 5.

Section 3

Escaping Dualism

In this section, we will uproot some false teachings concerning the nature of humanity. All Christians, whether or not they realize it, have been influenced by these crippling doctrines. When they see the truth, their eyes are opened and they realize why they have not been experiencing the freedom that God promised. As we expose these false teachings, I hope to show you a more biblical view of humanity, one that helps Christians live more successfully in this world, using the authority and provisions of God. It is also essential to understand these truths before we further discuss how the spiritual and natural realms can be influenced by human beings.

21
Correctly Dividing Asunder

In much of the Body of Christ today there is a doctrinal error which begins with a misinterpretation of Hebrews 4:12. The King James Version of the Bible states this verse as follows:

> *For the word of God is quick, and powerful, and sharper than any twoedged sword, piercing even to the dividing asunder of soul and spirit, and of the joints and marrow, and is a discerner of the thoughts and intents of the heart.*

From this verse a teaching is sometimes brought forth which shows the sword (which is the Word of God) being dropped between the soul and the spirit of a person, dividing these two parts of a person's being one from the other.

This is a "dualistic" mind-set. The word dualistic simply means "two-sided" or "two-folded."

Dualism leads to errors and confusion when Christians not only separate the spirit from the soul, but when they go on to think of the spirit as good, while thinking negatively about the soul and/or body.

The Error of Dualism

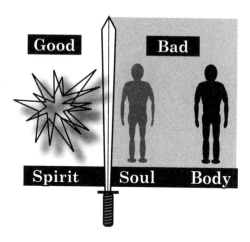

Dualism may sound reasonable to many of my readers at this point, but I hope you will follow with me to see how subtly destructive this way of thinking becomes. Many Christians today have been indoctrinated completely into this philosophy, while others have been pulled in gradually without considering the implications. Some have been taught dualistic perspectives, even though Hebrews 4:12 was never used as the specific Scripture to promote it.

To whatever extent a person has embraced dualistic patterns of thought, I want you to see some of the negative results in people's lives. But first I must show you how it has no basis in Scripture.

To cut at the very heart of this false doctrine, we need to see what the original manuscripts of the New Testament (most of which were written in the Greek language) literally say in Hebrews 4:12. Where we are told that the Word of God pierces, even unto the dividing asunder of soul and spirit, the Greek word for "spirit" here is *pneumatos*. The first half of this word, *pneuma*, means "spirit." The ending on this Greek word is *atos,* which indicates possession. Therefore, the word *pneumatos,* should not to be translated "spirit," but rather "of the spirit."

This small distinction, which was overlooked by the translators of the King James Bible and a few other versions, has profound implications when we consider exactly how the Word of God divides. The correct interpretation of Hebrews 4:12 must indicate that the Word of God pierces even to the dividing asunder *"of the soul"* and *"of the spirit."* The passage does not say that the soul and spirit are divided one from another. It says that both of them are divided.

The soul is divided and the spirit is divided.

In our diagram of a person's three-part nature, the sword must cut horizontally into a person, rather than vertically between the soul and spirit. The Greek literally tells us in Hebrews 4:12, that the Word of God pierces even to the depth of souls and to the depth of spirits in such a way that they themselves are divided.

Correct Understanding of Hebrews 4:12

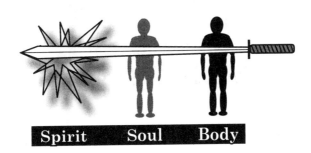

Spirit   Soul   Body

Studies in the original Greek Bible will confirm this. Let me quote from the Greek New Testament scholar Wuest in his *Word Studies in the Greek New Testament:*

Piercing is the translation of *"diikneomai"* which means "to go through". The words "the dividing asunder of soul and spirit" do not mean, "the dividing asunder of the soul from spirit". Nor is it "the dividing asunder of the joints from the marrow". The case in Greek is the genitive of description, defining the action in the verb in this case. It is a going through the soul, a going through the spirit.

This understanding of Hebrews 4:12, which sees the soul and spirit being pierced within rather than divided from one another, is consistent with the rest of the Bible. Consider when Peter preached on Pentecost Day, we are told that the word *"pierced to the heart"* (Acts 2:37).

The Word of God Pierces the Heart

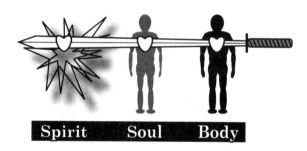

This becomes more obvious once a person thinks about the implications. The Word of God has to penetrate *into* the spirit and *into* the soul of the non-Christian; otherwise, the seed could never be planted within and salvation would be impossible. Even in the Christian's life there must be an ongoing planting of the Word of God within the spirit and soul.

We must, therefore, think of the Sword of God going into the person rather than dividing him or her in half. Nowhere in the Bible is there any passage which indicates that the soul and the spirit should be divided one from the other. The role of the Word of God in the ongoing Christian walk is not to be separating the spirit from the soul. It is the Word of God which is able to pierce into our beings, removing anything that is not in line with the nature of God. We must see the Word as piercing us in shish kebab fashion. As we allow the Word of God to come into us, it pierces our hearts and penetrates our entire beings.

Why is this so important? In the following chapters I will show you implications that dramatically shift the way Christians live.

Knowing God's Will

One major area of confusion in the life of dualistic Christians pertains to knowing God's will. Because dualists think of the soul and body as evil, and the spirit as good, they wrongly conclude that God only leads through a person's spirit. At the same time, dualists try to deny the soul and body, thinking that all desires arising from within the soul and body are fleshly or from the devil.

Dualistic Thinking Concerning God's Will

There is some truth to recognizing how God's will can be made known through the spirit of a person. The Bible tells us:

The spirit of man is the lamp of the Lord....
(Prov. 20:27)

God communicates with people through their spirits.

However, God's can also make His will known through a person's soul and body. For example, a mother who has very natural desires to care for her children is doing God's will by yielding to those desires. Natural motherly instincts are God-instilled.

Think of the physical desires to eat. These are not evil. Of course, these desires can be corrupted, but God placed hunger within people to motivate them to survive. We also can talk about the natural desires for sexual relations. The normal physical passions that a husband and wife have for each other are good (I Tim. 4:3-4).

I am not saying that *all* natural desires are good. Rather, I am stating that *some* natural desires are good. Of course, we know there are also some bad natural desires. I can state this truth by saying that some desires arising in the soul are good and some are bad. Some desires in the body are good and some are bad. We must discern. Our sword to judge what is right and what is wrong must be pierced horizontally through the desires that arise within our soul and body.

The same can be said for our thoughts and emotions. We should not think of all the thoughts and emotions arising in our soul and body as evil. On the contrary, the ability to think is God-given. We were created with emotions to stir us to action and help us succeed in life. God does not want us to deny these aspects of our nature, but rather to discern and yield to those which are good.

Correctly Dividing Desires, Thoughts and Emotions

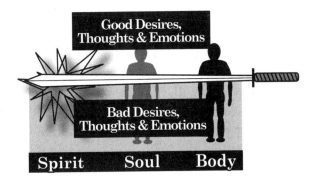

Notice in the diagram above, that I dropped the sword even through the spirit. In chapters 14 and 15, I explained that the spirit is involved with desires, thoughts and emotions. Later I will explain why it is important that we extend the sword through the spirit and hence, discern good from evil in the spirit. For now, I hope you can avoid making the dualists' mistake in thinking that everything coming from the soul and body are evil.

These truths are most profound when we consider the leading of God in the life of the Christian. God can lead a person through their natural desires, thoughts and emotions. In fact, God is actively working in the Christian constantly sanctifying the soul and body. Therefore, the longer a person is walking with God, the more their desires, thoughts and emotions are the same as God's desires, thoughts and emotions.

In fact, God makes His will known primarily in and through the life of the believer. Do you want to know what God's desire is for a certain situation? Ask God's people what their desires are for that situation. For example, most Christians want for their cities peace, love, joy, revival, young people walking with God, prosperity and the salvation of souls.

That is also what God wants. The two are not in conflict with each other, but the same.

Dualists have a difficult time accepting this truth. They tend to think of God's will and their own will as enemies. It is common to hear dualists say things, such as:

> "I want God's will, not my will."
> "I want God's thoughts, not my thoughts."
> "I do not want to act out of my emotions,
> but by the leading of the Holy Spirit."

No matter how holy such statements may sound, they are based on a misunderstanding of how God leads His children. Notice they assume that the person's will, thoughts and emotions are contrary to God's will, thoughts and emotions. That way of thinking is wrong.

Of course, there are times when we must reject certain desires, thoughts and emotions. Jesus Himself prayed in the Garden of Gethsemane that the Father's will be done and not His own will (Luke 22:42). Indeed, there can be times when the human will must be conquered and brought into submission to the will of God. But that is not the norm. Jesus did not live in the Garden of Gethsemane, constantly fighting His own will. In fact, He came to Earth to do the will of the Father and His will was the Father's will. In similar fashion, God is causing our desires, thoughts and emotions to conform to His desires, thoughts and emotions.

How, then, can a Christian know the will of God for his or her life? By looking at the desires and thoughts within his or her own being. Do you want to know what God wants you to do in life? Then ask yourself, "What do *I* want to do in life?" This includes both naturally-oriented desires and those related to more spiritual issues. A mother who has desires to spend time with her children is doing God's will by spending time with her children. God's will is not contrary to her will. It is, in fact, the same. The man who wants to provide financially for his family is doing God's will by doing what he wants to do. Even in spiritual areas this is true. The believer who desires to pray is doing God's will by praying. The woman who passionately desires to go overseas and preach the gospel as a missionary is being obedient to God by doing what she most wants to do.

I am not giving credence to every evil lust and thought one has. We must drop the sword within our own beings and separate the carnal from the good. Remember, that sword is dropped within our own beings. The good thoughts and desires of God are not outside of us. They are there, arising within our own minds, hearts and entire beings.

Of course, I could talk here about the many other ways that God leads us, such as through the Bible, through other people, through circumstances, etc. God also communicates with people, giving spiritual impressions, dreams and visions. I have much to say about all that in coming chapters. But here I am settling foundational issues. Our main point is that God is in each of us—spirit, soul and body. Dualists never fully embrace this truth.

Fulfilling God's Will

Not every Christian who drops the sword between the spirit and soul falls into the errors which I am describing. Many Christians have been taught the dualistic interpretation of Hebrews 4:12, but they have the wisdom to avoid the pitfalls. However, if we get our theology correct from the start, we may help those less fortunate.

Dropping the sword wrongly leads some dualistic Christians to divide the entire spiritual realm from the natural. In their thinking, they have dropped a sword which separates the two realms, and then they think about the spiritual things as good and the natural as bad.

Dualistic Error: Dividing the Spiritual from the Natural

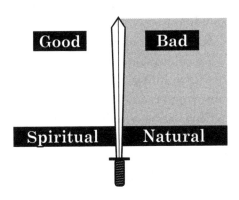

This way of thinking tends to make people feel as if they are doing God's will only while they are engaged in spiritual activities. For example, the mother who has to care for little children may feel condemned because she is not praying all the time. The man who works 40 to 60 hours a week may feel inferior to the one who sits at home trying to tap into the spirit. Sometimes an entire church congregation will have embraced this dualistic mind-set, and whenever anyone engages in naturally-oriented labors, they are made to feel as if they are failing God and are out of His will.

Every dualist needs to meditate on this: Jesus was no less in the will of the Father as a carpenter than He was during the last three years of His ministry. If this thought shakes you, then you have dualistic thinking.

Dualists tend to judge themselves and others wrongly. They examine how successful people have been at detaching from the natural world. Those who are extreme dualists either consciously or subconsciously feel best about themselves when they are doing something which either they do not like to do and/or when they are unsuccessful in natural affairs. This may sound strange, but it is common to find a person who has fully embraced dualistic thinking to be financially hurting, owning nothing of value, not involved in anything significant in society and suffering rejection by other people. I have known some dualistic people who have gone through a divorce, and they view it as a "price they had to pay for God" when in reality, it was a price they paid due to their inability to function in the natural realm. Of course, most dualists do not show their errors so obviously, but the errors manifest in underlying feelings and beliefs throughout their own persons and experiences.

In contrast, Christians who have the proper biblical view evaluate their own lives on the basis of fruit. They look at their own lives and see how successful they have been in walking out their Christian beliefs. For them the vital questions are,

"Is our Christianity actually working in our marriages, in our homes and with our children? Are we successful at paying our bills and blessing others? Are our lives impacting and changing society in some substantial way?" Healthy Christians have a realistic view of their lives, in which they honestly look to see what tangible results are coming forth from their labors. Positive results are the proof of their faith.

In making their division between the spiritual realm and the natural, dualists often misinterpret several key Bible passages. There is a line in their field of vision that divides everything in half, and often that division line falls in the wrong place.

For example, dualists commonly misinterpret Matthew 6:24 (KJV), where we are told:

You cannot serve God and mammon.

Dualists love to use verses such as this one, because they can align their own division between the spiritual and the natural along the line of division between serving God and serving mammon.

Dualistic Error Concerning Serving God or Mammon

When serving mammon is equated with doing natural activities, the dualist can justify not giving much energy to naturally-oriented tasks. Working a job is contrasted with serving God. Cleaning the house is equated with being a slave to natural things. In their mind, taking care of possessions is the same as seeking natural things, rather than the kingdom of God. In reality, serving God may mean working 40 to 60 hours a week. Pleasing God has absolutely nothing to do with the line between the spiritual and the natural realms.

What we must do is rotate the dualist's sword by 90 degrees. Some natural things we do are pleasing to the Father. Other natural things are not pleasing to Him. Some spiritual activities are pleasing to God. Other spiritual activities are not pleasing to Him.

Biblical Truth Concerning Serving God or Mammon

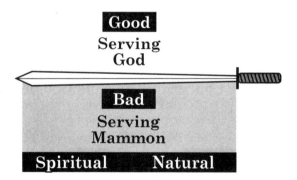

When we talk about pleasing God, we must not think in terms of spiritual versus natural. We must ultimately develop a picture from His throne of judgment. Consider the parable Jesus told of the three men who received certain talents (Matt. 25:14-30). The two men who used their talents received great rewards, while the one who hid his talent was punished. Of course, we know that all people will be judged, first and foremost, on their acceptance or rejection of Jesus Christ. However, beyond that, there will be different rewards given to believers, depending upon how they have used the gifts given to them.

Do you want to fulfill God's will for your life? Then take a realistic look at your own talents, gifts, abilities, assets and opportunities. Use them for God. Do not think God's will for your life is some mystical formula written in the world of the spirit. It is right there around you and within you now. When you use what you have been given to the best of your ability, then you are fulfilling God's will for your life.

Serve God with Your Whole Soul

Now let us look more carefully at the soul and its function in the ongoing daily life of the Christian. In developing this understanding, it will be helpful for us to draw a few more contrasts between the dualistic view and the biblical perspective. Our goal is to see when and how the soul is to be involved in our daily lives and in our relationships to the spiritual realm.

The dualistic mind-set has produced many misconceptions concerning the value and function of the soul. Advocates over the years have coined certain words, such as "soulical" and "soulish." You may or may not be familiar with these terms, but I hope you can see that the deception in such words lies in placing the soul of a person in a negative context.

The basic commission from God to His people is:

> *"...to serve the Lord your God with all your heart
> and with all your soul."*
>
> (Deut. 10:12)

"All your soul" means *"all your soul."* Dualists have a difficult time with this. They would rather sentence the soul to death than see it resurrected to life. The true biblical ideal is that Christians are not living their fullest for God until "everything"

153

in their souls is being used for God.

There are New Testament verses just as clear on this subject, however, some modern English Bible versions mistranslate the Greek word, *psuche,* as "heart" rather than what it actually means, "soul." For example, Ephesians 6:6 tells Christians that they should be *"doing the will of God from the heart."* This last word *heart* is mistranslated from the Greek word, *psuche.* Therefore, what we are actually being told to do in this verse is to serve God from our soul.

Colossians 3:23 similarly exhorts us:

> *Whatever you do, do your work heartily, as for the Lord rather than for men.*

The word translated *heartily* in this verse is from the Greek words *ek psuche*, meaning, *"from the soul."* It is clear that our labors should be performed with our entire soul involved.

Consider now what we would call natural talents and abilities, such as logical thinking, organizational skills and planning. Dualists tend to associate these with the soul of a person, and therefore—consciously or subconsciously—reject them. If they do not condemn outrightly the associated abilities, they tend to view them as "lower functions of life" in contrast to the more "spiritually-oriented" activities. Upon the natural abilities of a person, the dualists would apply their negative label, "soulish."

Let me give you an example of how dualists may misjudge a specific situation based on their rejection of the soul. If we were to talk about some well-known minister used by God to evangelize thousands of people, Christians generally would be supportive. If that minister were to speak in a stadium and huge crowds gathered to hear the Word of God, we probably would rejoice to hear of the event.

Now if we discuss how much work went into such an

event, some people's views may change. Instead of focusing on the single minister being used by God, let's note how many ushers are there keeping the crowd orderly. Then let's talk about the custodians who clean the toilets and the stadium afterward. And how about the financial experts who budget, plan and organize? Then there are the advertising experts, artists, sound people, lighting crew, engineers, parking lot attendants, etc. Managing each area is an administrator using all of her or his planning and organizational skills. Hundreds of people are working together, even though the viewers' eyes will all be focused on the single preacher standing on the platform.

Dualists like to recognize the anointing upon the leader, and they may give credit also to the prayer warriors behind the scenes, but they would hesitate in admitting that the administrators, advertisers, engineers, financial managers, etc., are equally as important. If they are considered important, it will be with a subconscious attitude that all those "natural gifts and talents" are necessary burdens. The naturally-oriented activities are never valued as highly as the spiritual.

In contrast, the Christian with a healthy, biblical view sees the financial administration and the planning board just as glorifying to God and essential as the minister in front. The spiritual activities are no more pleasing to God than the natural. That which is associated with the soul is not of lesser value than what some would label as "belonging to the spirit."

The concept of humanity that we are developing here is that all of one's being can be sanctified and used for God's glory. "Whole Christians" may obtain authority from God and inspiration through the spirit, but they use their minds, emotions, organizational skills and everything else within their being to walk out God's plan for their lives. They serve

God with their whole souls and with all of their strength.

Once we embrace the proper role of the soul we can discuss what dualists call "soul ties." This term is used to refer to the bonding between two individual souls. The dualist almost always uses this term in the negative sense (because, again, dualists see the soul as evil), and Christians, therefore, are exhorted to break all soul ties between themselves and others.

In contrast, several Bible passages talk in a positive way about the people of God becoming of one heart and one soul (e.g., Acts 4:32). The apostle Paul talked about Timothy who was of kindred soul to him (Phil. 2:20; original Greek: *iso-psuchos*). Paul specifically told all Christians that they should endeavor to be one in soul (Phil. 2:2; original Greek: *sum psuchoi*). Each of these bondings involving people's souls is spoken of as good.

Of course, not every relationship between people is according to God's will. I am challenging the dualistic mentality that categorically rejects anything pertaining to the soul. Christians must, by an act of their wills, choose with whom they will be bonded. We must discern which relationships are of God. Some soul ties good and some are bad.

Biblical Truth Concerning Soul Ties

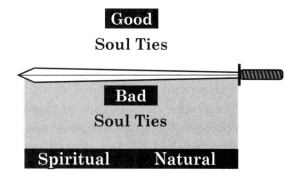

Good
Soul Ties

Bad
Soul Ties

Spiritual   **Natural**

To whatever degree Christians have embraced dualistic thinking, they will be helped by reconsidering the related issues. Let this one fact now be established: Christians should use their souls, and in fact, can only fulfill God's command by serving Him with all of their strength and with all of their souls.

Soul Power

I have been talking about the implications of wrongly dividing the soul from the spirit. And although I am discussing these implications, do not lose sight of my earlier discussion, where I showed that the foundational thinking of dividing the soul from the spirit originated from a misinterpretation of Hebrews 4:12. The entire concept of dropping a sword between the two is contrary to what the Bible really teaches. I am spending all this time unraveling a confused mass of teachings, all stemming from a misinterpretation of one verse in the Bible.

Different Christian groups have been influenced in varying degrees by dualistic thought. Perhaps the strongest dualistic teacher during the twentieth century was a man named Watchman Nee. Watchman Nee was an amazing Christian leader, greatly used to establish the home church movement in China. He paid a high price for his Christian stand in a country then very antagonistic toward the gospel. However, he was also dualistic in his theology, and he wrote several books promoting that way of thinking. Those books have influenced millions of Christians throughout the world.

Watchman Nee and other dualists take their strongest stand when it comes to what they call "soul power." When dualists talk about soul power, they are referring to a power which comes out of the soul of person, in the form personal charisma, confidence, a strong sense of identity and the forces which flow out of these attributes to influence other people. Strict dualists condemn all such soul power as evil. At the same time, dualists claim that all energy coming forth from the spirit of the Christian is good.

Realize that the reason they call soul power evil is because they have already decided doctrinally that the soul is evil. They wrongly have dropped a sword between the spirit and the soul, and sentenced everything in the soul to their negative judgment. As a consequence, any power coming from the soul must also be evil.

Dualistic Deception Concerning Soul Power

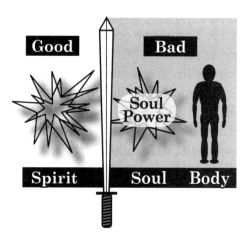

In order to sort out truth from error, let's first discuss strength of soul. Dualists tend to reject anything of the soul and, therefore, they immediately have to conclude that strength of soul is bad.

Such thinking is wrong. King David, for example, praised God, saying:

You made me bold with strength in my soul.
                                    (Ps. 138:3b)

Strength of soul here is a characteristic to be desired. King David was referring to his own level of confidence and leadership strength. God gave him strength of soul.

There are numerous other Bible passages talking about restoration, health, blessings or prosperity of soul; for example:

The Lord is my shepherd...
He restores my soul.
                                    (Ps. 23:1-3a)

But the soul of the diligent is made fat.
                                    (Prov. 13:4b)

Beloved, I pray that in all respects you may prosper
and be in good health, just as your soul prospers.
                                    (III John 2)

In Acts 14:22 we read how Paul went from one group of Christians to another, *"strengthening the souls of the disciples."* It is God's will for Christians to be strong of soul. It was John's prayer that they may prosper within their souls. When the Holy Spirit floods Christians, their souls are made vibrant and bold. This is a work of God in our lives. Strength and health of soul are good.

For a comparison I can talk about the strength and health of the human body. We know that each of us should serve God with all of our strength. It is a good thing when a woman on the mission field uses her physical strength to reach people in remote regions with the gospel. Also, the man using his strength to feed the poor in his city may be fulfilling

God's calling on his life. The strength and health of the human body is a good thing which every Christian should be using for God's glory.

Dualists do not understand this fully. In reference to strength of the body or of the soul, they may say, "I want God's strength, not my strength!" A dualist tries to separate the two. That is foolish and wrong. For the Christian trying to serve God, his strength is God's strength. The two must not be separated. God may increase the strength of a person supernaturally, and God often does use weak people. However, we must not fall for the dualistic deception which sees one's own strength as evil. The truth is that God rejoices in the strength of His people.

I have been trying to impact you with the fundamental truth that we should serve God with all of our strength. This includes not only our bodies, but the great commandment specifically tells us to serve Him with our entire soul. We now need to see that this includes soul power or any other energy that comes from the soul of the Christian.

In section 2, I explained how the soul of a person is a created entity, limited in size and shape. The soul does not emanate out of the body, as the spirit may. In other words, it does not flow from out of the body in the form of energy. Therefore, the label "soul power" is a misnomer, and that is why it is nowhere in the Bible. When the dualists talk about soul power or soul energy, they are confusing this with spiritual energy. The soul can and does act as a doorway for energy to flow from the spirit of the person or from the spiritual world into the natural. However, even the idea that the soul flows out as energy is questionable.

We do know that spiritual energy can flow through the soul of a person. Some of that spiritual energy may be evil. Therefore, the Christian must use discernment. That discernment is not the same as the dualist's trying to divide between the soul and spirit. Rather, we must look more deeply at the spiritual energy being released.

The sword which divides must be rotated 90 degrees, separating both the entire person and the spiritual world. People have some power within their own being, and there may be evil elements within the soul of a person needing sanctification. But the real issue when talking about spiritual power is in discerning that which comes from God and that which comes from Satan.

Biblical Discernment of Spiritual Energy

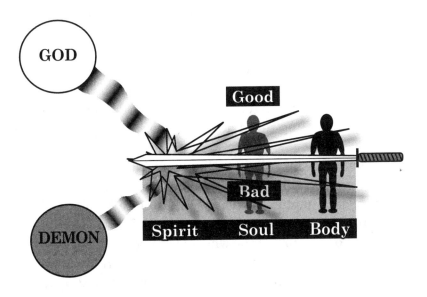

Notice how different this way of thinking is from the dualist's. The dualist tries to separate energy coming forth from the spirit of a person from energy coming forth from the soul. The biblical perspective looks to see if spiritual energy is flowing from God or from Satan's realm. Whether or not the soul is involved is irrelevant.

Now, let's compare the discernment of a dualist with the discernment of a Christian with a biblical view. Consider a preacher who attracts crowds easily. This preacher I will call Pete. When Preacher Pete speaks, he is very dramatic, and the audience seems to become caught up in all that he is saying. If he has an altar call at the end of his meeting, many people usually respond. Pete has come to expect these results. Dualists sitting in the midst of the congregation will tend to judge the preacher, either consciously or subconsciously, by trying to divide spirit from soul. They may be skeptical of Preacher Pete because he seems too emotional. Depending upon the skeptics' type of dualistic thinking, they may focus on how the audience seems to be mesmerized. Our dualistic friends may then reject Preacher Pete's ministry because Pete expects results, which, in the dualists' minds, implies that evil soul power is being used. Finally, the dualistic observers may identify any other elements which they have defined as belonging to the soul, and then leave the meeting concluding that Satan's power was at work, rather than God's.

In contrast, Christians with a more biblical understanding will evaluate Preacher Pete's ministry on an entirely different basis (chapter 10). They will listen to Pete's teaching to see if it agrees with the written Word of God. They will be sensitive to the spirit of the whole meeting to see if it glorifies Jesus Christ. And they will observe the fruit. If many people are being drawn to Jesus and the teaching is according to the Word of God, then God's power is at work.

Allow me to repeat: The question of soul power versus spirit power is irrelevant. To think in those categories is deceptive and unbiblical. What is important is to discern between the Spirit of God and evil spirits.

This issue is important. Some ministers have become enslaved by a dualistic doctrine which has kept them from being effective. One well-known evangelist was used while just a young man to lead thousands of people to God, but then a strict dualist pulled him aside and filled his mind with all kinds of false, unbiblical ideas about the soul being evil. This evangelist then became filled with doubts. He stopped his evangelistic work for fear that he might release this evil soul power. When he did try preaching again, he battled to keep himself from showing any emotion or directing any energy toward those to whom he was speaking. As a result, he was never again used to bring large numbers of people to Jesus.

The preacher in the example I just gave you was Evan Roberts, who led the revival in the country of Wales. That revival was one of the most dramatic movings of God's power seen in any nation in history. After a series of intense meetings, young Evan Roberts was exhausted, so a little-known minister named Jesse Penn-Lewis invited Evan to stay at her place for a period of rest. During that rest period, Jesse Penn-Lewis convinced Evan that he had been using soul power throughout the revival. After two years of some of the most effective preaching the world ever has seen, Roberts stopped his preaching ministry. One the central reasons was his fear that he might again use this evil soul power. A short time later, he coauthored a book with Jesse Penn-Lewis, entitled, *War On the Saints*. This book has been revised and reprinted several times, but the earlier versions clearly show Evan and Jesse renouncing much of the revival which Evan had been used to stir.

In history we also find Jesse Penn-Lewis as the one who had a profound influence on Watchman Nee—of whose writings I have already warned you.

The example of Evan Roberts ending his preaching ministry may seem extreme, but I hope you see its implications within your own life. The Bible teaches us to do whatever we do "wholeheartedly"—that is, in Greek, with all our souls

(Col. 3:23). Christians should not be bound with fears that evil soul power is resident within them. They need not hold back from showing emotions or releasing all that is within their souls. On the contrary, believers should direct their lives to serve God confidently with all of their souls and all of their strengths. Of course, evil may be released through a person and we must be sensitive and able to discern this (as we will teach in the next chapter), but the question of soul power versus spirit power must not be the focus of our judgment.

One more area of application we can mention here is intercessions and prayers. Some Christians are afraid to put any energy or force behind their prayers because they do not want the evil soul power to be released. As a consequence, their prayers are always weak and without passion. To see the truth, all we need to do is consider our Lord praying in the Garden of Gethsemane; there He fell on His face and prayed with such fervency that His sweat became as drops of blood (Luke 22:44). At that time He also said to His disciples, *"My soul is deeply grieved, to the point of death; remain here and keep watch with Me"* (Matt. 26:38b). Effective prayer sometimes incorporates the entire being of a person, and attempts at subduing the soul are foolish.

To think and judge with a dualistic mind-set is to look with blinded eyes. Years ago when I was attending a university, I had a roommate who was color-blind. Laundry day for him was a terrible ordeal, because he could not match his socks properly one to the other. Since he could not see the obvious color differences, he would carefully examine differences in size, texture and amount of wear on each sock. Unfortunately, even with his most careful examinations, he still made some rather comical mistakes, wearing different colored socks at the same time. In a corresponding fashion, dualists tend to be "color-blind." Their minds are doctrinally trained to look for that which they associate with the soul, and to reject accordingly. Such a trained mind-set leads to serious misjudgments. If people are programmed by their doctrine to look for certain natural aspects, they often will miss the obvious identification marks of God's work—marks which the Bible clearly teaches are the true bases by which to judge.

What I am asking you to do is to judge spiritual things on the basis of their agreement with the Word of God, their exaltation of Jesus Christ and the fruit produced. This will open your eyes to see and free you to serve God with your whole heart, soul and mind.

Discerning the Flow of Spiritual Energy

I have explained the error of dualism in its attempt to divide the spirit from the soul. I have shown how dualists' negative view of the soul is wrong. Now let's turn our focus toward the spirit and the spiritual energy that can flow through a person. The dualist sees the Christian's spirit as good and incapable of error. This, we will see, is a serious mistake.

Most dualists believe that the Christian's spirit has been made perfect through the born-again experience. In chapter 17, I explained why this perfect-spirit doctrine is contrary to what the Bible teaches. I will not repeat that discussion, but I will briefly mention the key points.

When a person becomes a Christian, God breathes new life into his or her spirit. However, the person's whole spirit is not made perfect instantaneously. There is an ongoing sanctification process that must take place, and the Word will grow to produce fruit. The Holy Spirit may give additional anointings, empowerings, gifts and grace. For Scriptural references of these truths, I refer you back to chapter 17.

The Christian's spirit may also be wounded, oppressed, broken or defiled. This last characteristic is key and worth mentioning again. The apostle Paul wrote concerning how a Christian's spirit can be *"defiled."*

> *Therefore, having these promises, beloved, let us*
> *cleanse ourselves from all defilement of flesh and*
> *spirit, perfecting holiness in the fear of God.*
>
> (II Cor. 7:1)

Notice that Paul is talking to Christians, *"beloved,"* who have the promises of God. To brothers and sisters in Christ, Paul writes that they are to cleanse themselves from defilement of flesh and spirit.

It is important for us to see that evil spiritual substance can be brought into the life and being of a Christian. Earlier I explained how the heart is the pivotal point in a person's being. From the heart flow all the issues of life (Prov. 4:23), and into it flows spiritual energy. Just as the physical heart draws in blood and then forces it out throughout the entire body, so also the heart of the inner person receives and emanates spiritual energy. Both good and evil can be drawn within. The heart is as soil receiving the good things of God (Matt. 13:19-23). Evil, too, may be "conceived" within the heart. James wrote that when we lust for things, we actually conceive that evil within ourselves. In time, the evil conceived will grow as seeds to give birth to sin (James 1:14-15).

Consider George, a Christian man who loves God, but was hurt emotionally in a church split. As George meditates on how unjustly he was treated, he draws within himself seeds of bitterness. Then one day George speaks out in a church service, and, at first, what he says seems very inspired by God, and everyone is greatly blessed. But then George makes a few comments that reveal the hurt in his heart; bitterness pours out for a minute or two. Both good and evil come out of George's mouth. We must discern between the two.

In James 3:9-11, we are told about the human tongue.

> *With it we bless our Lord and Father; and with it*
> *we curse men, who have been made in the likeness*
> *of God; from the same mouth come both blessing*
> *and cursing. My brethren, these things ought not*
> *to be this way. Does a fountain send out from the*
> *same opening both fresh and bitter water?*

The human being is compared with a fountain here and a contrast is made. The fountain does not release both good and evil at the same time, but a human being often does.

Sometimes that mixed flow is the result of a person's own bad heart motivations. Other times it is the result of the devil finding a foothold in the person's life. The devil is trying to deceive everyone, and at times we all submit to his temptations. At that moment we are allowing his evil nature to flow through us.

We can see this in several incidents in the Bible. For example, the disciples reacted wrongly when Jesus was rejected by a certain Samaritan village. In indignation they asked:

> *"Lord, do You want us to command fire to come*
> *down from heaven and consume them?"*
> (Luke 9:54b)

Jesus responded, rebuking them and saying:

> *"You do not know what kind of spirit you are of...."*
> (Luke 9:55b)

The disciples, for a moment, were being motivated and inspired by a spirit contrary to God's nature.

We can see a similar phenomenon in Peter's life. In Matthew 16:13-16, Peter made the great declaration of our Lord

171

being the Son of God. Jesus responded by telling Peter that the Father revealed, that is, inspired this truth in him. But just six verses later, we find Peter taking Jesus aside and trying to discourage Him from His mission. Jesus responds by saying to Peter, *"Get behind Me, Satan!"* (Matt. 16:23). We see, then, the first words Peter spoke were inspired by God, and the second were inspired by the devil.

We can also read in the Bible how other evil spiritual influences came upon people. For example, Isaiah rebuked the leadership of Egypt and declared that God had sent a *"spirit of distortion"* upon them.

> *The Lord has mixed within her a spirit of distortion;*
> *They have led Egypt astray in all that it does,*
> *As a drunken man staggers in his vomit.*
>
> (Is. 19:14)

Notice that this deceiving spirit was *"mixed"* within them. As a consequence, some of the things they were inspired to do were right and some were wrong.

When there is a mixed flow, we still recognize the spiritual energy moving through a person. However, it is as if those rivers have become polluted.

Why is all this so important? I am showing you how evil spiritual influences can work through any person. This is important because it demands that we, therefore, judge the spiritual flow through every person—even Christians. The strict dualists will not allow judgment of the spiritual things received. Because they believe the Christian's spirit is good and perfect, they see no basis for even trying to discern that which flows out. Dualistic doctrine, in fact, forbids it.

Repeatedly in Church history, various groups have drifted into error because they did not allow any judgment of the spiritual things flowing through their leaders. In such groups, Christians were taught that the spirit in their leader is perfect, and, therefore, no one should judge what comes forth through inspiration or revelation. Then, if deception creeps in, there is no defense, nor even the ability to discern. Anyone who disagrees with the leader is pushed aside. Even thoughts within the leader's mind that question his own activities are forcefully rejected.

Sometimes the deceived leader will go so far as to say that everything he does while under the anointing is right from God's throne, and it must not be judged in any way. Then, if the leader gradually gets pushed away from biblical truth, strong deception takes over. The people involved continue to follow their leader without question because they have been trained never to judge the "anointing." Sooner or later, history repeats itself as destruction sweeps in and devastates the lives of those involved. The Bible is very clear about judging all spiritual impressions, revelations, manifestations, etc. The apostle Paul gave instructions to the Corinthian believers.

> *When you assemble, each one has a psalm, has a teaching, has a revelation, has a tongue, has an interpretation...let two or three prophets speak, and let the others pass judgment.*
> (I Cor. 14:26b-29)

Notice the clear instructions to judge that which comes forth by inspiration. Judgment only makes sense if, indeed, there is the possibility for error. Obviously, there is.

Hence, we see the need to drop the sword, as we are instructed, through the whole of a person's being, even unto the dividing asunder *"of the spirit,"* that is, in Greek, *pneumatos.*

173

Biblical Discernment of Spiritual Energy

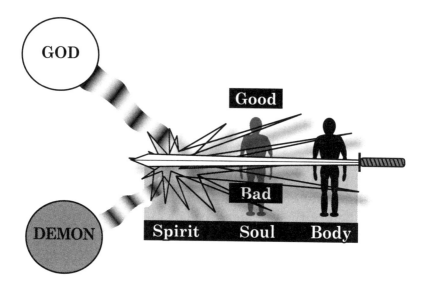

Allow me to give you a few examples from present-life situations. Consider Carol, a Christian woman who is discipling a small group of new believers. She is doing an excellent work, as far as teaching the Word of God and making her students solid in their faith. However, in her heart there is also a hidden anger toward the whole church and a bitterness because of problems which she experienced several years earlier. Although Carol tries not to let out the dark side of her feelings, it does come upon her listeners and is actually imparted into their lives. Soon her disciples are having similar thoughts and feelings of anger toward the church.

Not only bitterness, but other evil spiritual influences can also be transmitted from one person to another. Paul warned the Corinthian Christians about a sexually perverted man in their midst. He explained that if they allowed him to continue, the evil would spread to the rest of the church, just as leaven leavens a whole lump of dough (I Cor. 5:1-7).

I know of one minister who was traveling from church to church, teaching and praying for people. As he laid hands upon them and prayed, many received help and real healings in their bodies. However, some also began having various marriage problems immediately after their spiritual encounter. When this minister was investigated by some other Christian leaders, it was discovered that he had serious problems in his own marriage. He was transmitting, through the laying on of hands, not only healing power but also a destructive influence.

I dare say that every minister and every Christian has a "mixed flow." That is the very reason we are told to judge the spiritual manifestations. Every time a certain preacher speaks before her congregation, she speaks from out of that which fills her heart. Hopefully, the minister is spiritually strong and in close communion with God; but within the heart of every person there remains open doors for the devil to find access. Until we have been completely sanctified—spirit, soul and body—as Paul prayed (I Thess. 5:23), there remains the possibility for error and the necessity, therefore, for discernment.

The Christian must not be deceived. Even the most powerful leaders can have a mixed flow. King Saul, we are told, led the nation of Israel by the anointing of God (I Sam. 10:6-7). But then later in his life his heart became corrupted, and an evil spirit started to work upon and through him (I Sam. 16:14). We must not be overwhelmed by the anointing upon any man or woman, to the degree that we abandon discernment.

The sword must fall not only across the words, actions and soul of a person, but also through his or her spirit. The spiritual impressions, revelations and inspirations all must be judged (I Thess. 5:21).

Dualism: Seedbed for Sexual Perversion

In addition to the problems already discussed, dualism is a seedbed for sexual perversions. As I explain this, we must expand our thinking of dualistic thought. It is not limited to small Christian circles which misinterpret Hebrews 4:12. To some extent dualism has influenced our entire Western culture. It was the ancient Greek philosophers who spoke strongly in terms of dividing the spiritual world from the natural. Most prominently Plato (c. 427-347 BC) taught that only the spiritual things are significant and good; whatever is done in the natural, he said, is insignificant. This ancient Greek way of thinking is at the foundation of our Western society today. It has influenced the Church and the entire Western world.

Plato took the division made between the spiritual and natural realms and applied it to the nature of humanity. He viewed the invisible, spiritual side of a person as the true person. He thought of the body as an insignificant, temporary container. This dualistic concept of humanity infiltrated the ancient Greek culture.

The logical conclusions of this philosophy led the Greeks into many problems, including sexual perversions. Because the spirit/soul was considered the real person, the physical body was completely separated with regard to moral responsibility.

Therefore, many Greek philosophers taught that in the physical realm all forms of sexual perversion could be practiced and that any participant could still be good and spiritually pure.

Dualistic thinking pervaded most of the Greek and Roman intellectual worlds during the first two centuries. It became introduced into the Church primarily through leaders such as Augustine and Origen. These two men accomplished much good for Christianity, and they were each great defenders of the faith. However, they were both dualistic in their thinking, and hence, helped introduce the related thought patterns into theology.

Augustine was perhaps the most influential along these lines. He lived from 354 to 430 AD, during the time when the Roman government was embracing Christianity as its primary religion. Because the Roman government was at the height of its power, what the Emperor decreed on spiritual matters influenced the entire empire. Augustine was the most prominent theologian of the day and was able to spread his understanding quickly and effectively throughout the known world.

Before becoming a Christian, Augustine was a student of Greek philosophy. Being trained with a strong dualistic worldview and continuing to deal with the intellectual world of his day, he kept the spiritual world separate from the natural world in his understanding.

This way of thinking added to serious personal problems in Augustine's own life. Before he was a Christian, he had given himself over to many sexual perversions. In line with Greek thought, it did not matter. After he became a Christian it did matter, but he was unable to overcome sexual temptations until late in life. In his own writings he describes the constant battles he had, along with the related sins.

All of this added to his negative view of life in this natural realm. In developing his theology, he took Greek thought a step further into dualism. The ancient Greeks thought of the natural as insignificant. He concluded that it was corrupt. Origen (ca. 185-254) had similar thinking which he brought to the Church. To see the dualistic mind-set he had, I can mention that he lived much of his life denying himself of natural pleasures and doing things such as sleeping on bare boards. His negative view toward sex is evident by the fact that he made himself a eunuch by crushing his testicles with two bricks.

In history or in modern life, when people have embraced dualistic thinking, they will follow one of two paths during their lives: licentiousness or asceticism. Licentiousness is simply the loose, carefree living which says, "If it feels good do it." This is based on the satisfaction of all natural desires, denying morality and guilt. It is down this road that we find many of those who were raised in strict, moral, yet dualistic environments. They were unable to live up to the demands of dualism, so they eventually gave up and decided to yield to their perverted lusts.

Asceticism is the other extreme where a person sees the natural world as evil, and, therefore, tries to withdraw as much as possible from the natural affairs of life. Escape, rules, laws and stronger controls are the answers for which they must reach—none of which produce a victorious lifestyle (Col. 2:20-23).

The conclusion we can draw from history is that dualism produces bad fruit.

On a more personal level, we can say that individuals with a dualistic mind-set consciously and/or subconsciously see other people as divided. They tend to think the real person standing in front of them is the invisible part, while the visible, physical body is just a container. At first this may seem acceptable to many readers, but please follow with me here to learn how destructive and wrong this way of viewing others truly is.

When a sexually perverted man rapes a woman, he must make this division in his mind. He does not allow himself to see the victim as a person with friends, feelings, responsibilities, goals, etc. It is common for a rapist to embrace an attitude of seeing a female victim as "a slut," "a bitch," or simply as insignificant. He either must hate or be totally unfeeling toward her. Of course, he may not have this attitude before or after the violation, but during the act, he, in almost every case, must take on this dualistic frame of mind.

A man who looks at pornographic pictures is similarly divided in his thinking. He is not seeing the real people behind the images. The viewer has no thoughts or concerns about the individuals themselves. He is not experiencing sadness because of the photographed person's situation in life, nor is he concerned about that person's financial or relationship struggles. Instead, he is looking through eyes which have distanced the person away from the physical body. He sees the body as merely an object to be enjoyed.

Similarly, when a man abuses a child, he already has separated in his mind that child from real feelings, future activities, thoughts—personhood. Only as he thinks of that child as an object to be used, can he carry on with his evil behavior.

I want you to see how the soil in which sexual problems grow is very commonly dualistic thinking. Of course, I could point to sin and fleshly lusts as the root, but I am identifying the anchoring place for such lusts. The dualistic mind is a seedbed in which sexual problems can develop. I am not saying that dualism is the source of evil. There is a real devil and people have lustful thoughts within themselves. However, the truth is that the person who sees others as whole people will be healthier and freer of sexual problems.

Dualism: Seedbed for Sexual Perversion

Most of the negative fruits of dualism are much more subtle than acts of violence, rape or sexual molestation. When children tease the homely boy at school, they are not seeing him as a person, but an object. When a husband looks condescendingly upon his overweight wife, in his mind he is separating her body from her as a person. When a male boss sexually harasses his secretary, he is denying her as a person. Racial prejudice which separates the body from the person also has dualistic thinking at its root.

Tragically, some of the most spiritually-gifted Christians have embraced dualistic mind-sets. In their endeavor to please God, they have sought a separation of themselves from the world. Teachings concerning the denial of self have captivated their consciousness. Then, when they find themselves unable to resist sin, they place stronger and stronger laws upon themselves. An entire system of thought and doctrine gradually takes over their minds. Many devoted, sincere Christians have traveled down this road and became enslaved to sexual perversions, crushed under the weight of their own broken rules.

Most people enslaved to sexual sins will not get free until they retrain their minds to see others as whole people. The man whose eyes compulsively jump from one pretty girl to another needs to tell himself that the girls he is watching are real individuals with homes, families, friends, problems, goals, feelings, etc. He will be helped by directing his attention toward their personhoods and wondering for a brief moment what responsibilities and burdens they each are carrying. For the fellow who is having difficulty in keeping his eyes off a certain woman, he may, when possible and appropriate, approach her and ask her, for example, how her day is going. As she speaks, he actually needs to listen for her to express who she is. As he tunes in to the person behind the face, he is actively healing the division in his mind and breaking dualistic thought.

I do not want to make the attaining of freedom seem so easy that no effort is involved here. The Bible tells us that we do fight against a real devil (Eph. 6:12). Any person who is struggling in these areas should seek both counseling and the help of other Christians to stand with him or her. Troubled individuals may be benefited by a wide range of ministries, and they should obtain whatever help is available. However, they also must abandon dualistic ways of thinking. Healing of the dualistic mind comes with the discovery that every person upon whom one's eyes fall is a real person. The solution is not to isolate oneself from other people, but actually to engage them as people. With that revelation, a person can begin developing a biblical, whole view of people.

The Biblical View of the Physical Body

Now let's consider the proper attitude for a Christian to have toward the physical body.

When Adam and Eve were created, they were created in the image of God. The whole person—spirit, soul and body—was created in His image. Even the physical body bears the image of God. When God finished fashioning Adam and Eve, He declared over His work that *"it was very good"* (Gen. 1:31). This concept that the entire person—including the human body—is good by God's design, is the correct biblical view.

Biblical View of the Human Body

Of course, we know that sin has had a corrupting influence on humanity. Yet, we are still created in God's image.

With this in mind, we need to value correctly the physical body. Most dualists focus on the spiritual side of a person's nature and diminish the significance of the physical body. They tend to see it as a mere vessel or container for the spirit/soul to indwell. Dualistic Christians often quote the words of the apostle Paul in II Corinthians 5:1-4, where he referred to the body as an *"earthly tent."* They also emphasize that our physical body will be eliminated someday.

In reality the body is much more than a tent. In order to discover the importance of a person's body, we need to read the entire passage where Paul refers to our body as a tent.

> *For we know that if the earthly tent which is our house is torn down, we have a building from God, a house not made with hands, eternal in the heavens. For indeed in this house we groan, longing to be clothed with our dwelling from heaven; inasmuch as we, having put it on, will not be found naked. For indeed while we are in this tent, we groan, being burdened, because we do not want to be unclothed but to be clothed, so that what is mortal will be swallowed up by life.*
>
> (II Cor. 5:1-4)

Paul describes how we will feel when we leave this body at death: *"naked"* and *"unclothed."* We will be groaning and longing to be clothed with a new body. It will be uncomfortable for us to have no body.

Our body is not just a useless container of which we hope to dispense. That is not what Paul was teaching when he called it a *"tent."* On the contrary, our body is a vital part of our being, and it will be difficult for us to be without it.

Furthermore, the body is an intrinsic part of our nature. In chapter 15, I explained how the physical body is actually

184

involved in the daily decisions we make. I will not repeat that earlier discussion, but I can point out again that the will of a person is, in part, located within the physical body. This means that the body is not just a useless, flexible shell, but rather a part of who we are.

Next, we need to see that the physical body is temporary only in the sense of it someday being transformed into a new body. Paul explains in another passage (I Cor. 15:35-55) that when the final trumpet blows, our physical bodies, which have decayed in the ground, will resurrect. As the residue arises, it will be transformed into imperishable substance, and we shall receive new immortal bodies. God originally created people as three-part beings, and we will be three-part beings (including a body) for eternity.

This concept has escaped many Christians. They wrongly envision a bodiless eternity. They think they will be floating around on clouds, with a smile on their face, in a mystical, spiritual state forever. That idea is foreign to the Bible. The idea of a disembodied eternity came from the influence of ancient Greek thought. Remember how the Greek philosophers separated the spiritual world from the natural, and then thought negatively about the natural? Those who embraced that way of thinking looked forward to a day when they could escape this natural world and leave their physical bodies behind. That was the Greek concept of the afterlife, before Christianity was brought to that society. None of our early Christian writings (from the first century) teach a disembodied eternity. That way of thinking gradually developed in the Church during the Third and Fourth Centuries, as Greek philosophy began influencing the Church. As a result, the established Church at that time embraced the disembodied view of eternity, and many Christians even today still have a mental picture of heaven as a place in the clouds for smiling, ghost-like people.

What the Bible teaches is quite different. All believers in Jesus will receive new, immortal bodies. Then they will be walking around on a new Earth. We will exist for eternity as three-part beings with an imperishable body.

To see this more clearly, we can look at the nature of our Lord Jesus. *"And the Word became flesh..."* (John 1:14). He did not come to Earth and dwell in flesh. No. The Word *became* flesh. He took on human nature. After Jesus died on the cross, He arose on the third day. He came forth in His body. That body was transformed and glorified. It was not discarded, but changed. The grave in which He was placed is empty today. The substance of His body was used. Today, Jesus is sitting in heaven on a throne at the right hand of the Father. Someday He will return to Earth. When we get to see Him, we will look at a real face and a real body. He did not take on a body for just a short period of time. The Word became flesh and He has chosen to dwell among us forever. He is not in some mystical, spiritual form. He has body as people do, yet glorified.

When the apostles first saw Jesus after His resurrection, they made the mistake of thinking that He was *"a spirit."* Luke reported:

> *But they were startled and frightened and thought that they were seeing a spirit.*
>
> (Luke 24:37)

Jesus corrected their thinking and reassured them, saying:

> *"See My hands and My feet, that it is I Myself; touch Me and see, for a spirit does not have flesh and bones as you see that I have."*
>
> (Luke 24:39)

Notice that Jesus specifically denied the thinking that He was *"a spirit."* Today Jesus has hands and feet. Of course, His body has been transformed into a spiritual state, but it is important to note that He still has a spirit, a soul and a body.

Look carefully at the transformation that Jesus experienced after His resurrection. The corruptible body He had while on Earth was transformed into an incorruptible one. Paul explained in I Corinthians 15:34-58 that after death, the perishable body is changed into an imperishable body (15:42). This transformation someday will happen to all believers in Christ (I Cor. 15:51-54), but here it is important to note that Jesus already went through that process. He was the *"firstborn"* of many brethren. As such, He has a body made not of corruptible material from Earth, but of incorruptible substance from heaven.

In regard to this transformation, the apostle Paul made an interesting comparison between Adam and Jesus. He wrote:

> *So also is the resurrection of the dead. It is sown a perishable body, it is raised an imperishable body; it is sown in dishonor, it is raised in glory; it is sown in weakness, it is raised in power; it is sown a natural body, it is raised a spiritual body. If there is a natural body, there is also a spiritual body. So also it is written, "The first man, Adam, became a living soul." The last Adam became a life-giving spirit.*
>
> (I Cor. 15:42-45)

Notice that the words *"spiritual"* and *"natural"* are being contrasted throughout these verses. In referring to Jesus as a life-giving spirit, Paul is not calling Jesus "a spirit." Rather, Paul was explaining that Jesus has a "spiritual body"—a body that is made of immortal, heavenly material. As Adam's body was formed from the dust of the Earth, Jesus' new body was formed from the substance of heaven. Here we see the use of the word "spirit" to mean spiritual in nature. The main point of the text is that Jesus still has a body; that body, however, has been transformed from its natural existence into a spiritual state.

The apostle Paul wrote these words in I Corinthians in order to encourage the Christians and let them know that they, too, someday would receive spiritual bodies.

> ...in a moment, in the twinkling of an eye, at the last trumpet; for the trumpet will sound, and the dead will be raised imperishable, and we will be changed. For this perishable must put on the imperishable, and this mortal must put on immortality.
>
> (I Cor. 15:52-53)

On that transformation day, we still will be three-part beings, but our resurrected bodies will take on a spiritual nature.

After the final judgment, those whose names are written in the Lamb's book of life will live on the new Earth (Rev. 21). They will have real bodies which are not subject to disease nor pain, but incorruptible. We will not spend eternity in suspended animation just praising God. We will have definite positions and responsibilities throughout eternity. We will have jobs and real tasks to accomplish. There will not be any curse upon the new Earth, but we will be active and our labors will flourish.

We do not know all that is in store for us, but we do know that the future will be glorious. This biblical view of eternity helps people hold a proper view of their bodies today. The dualistic or Greek view is wrong. Seeing that our bodies will play a role in our eternal existence elevates our understanding of their role in our present existence. We were created as three-part beings and we will have three parts for eternity. Now while we are alive on Earth, we must accept our bodies as a part of our beings. It is, in fact, a beautiful part of Creation. It is the means by which we can live and accomplish God's will in this natural world. The natural realm itself is good, as God declared it to be. We live here. We have three wonderful parts to our nature. We must live as whole human beings. We must think of ourselves as whole individuals.

Embrace Your Life on Earth

At the root of dualism is a negative view of the world, life and self. The people most prone to dualistic ways of thinking are those living in difficult circumstances who would enjoy thoughts of escaping this natural realm.

It is enlightening to know the circumstances surrounding some of the major proponents of dualism such as Augustine and Watchman Nee. Until late in life Augustine was unable to conquer his sexual passions, and he lived in disgust of his own physical weakness. Watchman Nee also lived under tremendous physical stress. He completed his best-known book, *The Spiritual Man* (sometimes published in three volumes), at the age of 25, while suffering with tuberculosis on what was thought to be his deathbed. Although he recovered over time, he continued under heavy persecution during most of his life.

There are many people who have lived in difficult circumstances physically, emotionally or spiritually. They are the ones most prone to interpret life and the Bible with a perspective of rejection pertaining to the natural things. They seek refuge in the spiritual realm. There is, of course, benefit in finding refuge in God, but the negative basis for such a pursuit leads to subtle deceptions.

A Bible verse often misunderstood by dualists is John

12:25, where Jesus said:

> *He who loves his life loses it, and he who hates his life in this world will keep it to life eternal.*

Sometimes dualist take this verse and teach that we actually and literally should hate being alive. The Greek word for *"life"* in the first part of this verse is *psuche*, and, therefore, the dualist can further justify his rejection of his natural existence by saying we are not to love our *psuche-life*, that is our soul-life.

In reality, this verse is not teaching what filters into the dualist's mind. The same exhortation from our Lord can be found in the other three gospels, however, the reference to hating one's soul-life is followed by these words:

> *"For what will it profit a man if he gains the whole world and forfeits his soul? Or what will a man give in exchange for his soul?"*
>
> (Matt. 16:26)
> [Mark 8:36-37 and Luke 9:25 read similarly.]

Notice that this verse gives us a contextual understanding of how we are to look at our soul. The truth is that our soul is the most valuable thing we possess. What could one ever give in exchange for it? The obvious answer is, "Nothing."

This conclusion is exactly the opposite of that at which the dualist arrives. After isolating John 12:25 from its context, the dualist concludes that we should hate our soul or our soul-life. But really, our soul is what we are told to treasure above all else.

What does it mean, then, to *"hate our life in this world"*? The emphasis is on the phrase, *"in this world."* We are to hate the thought of losing our soul in this world.

To confirm this, consider our Lord's words in Matthew 6:24.

"No one can serve two masters; for either he will hate the one and love the other, or he will be devoted to one and despise the other. You cannot serve God and wealth."

According to this verse, every man will give his life to God or to wealth. It is in this sense that we lose our soul-lives. Christians are not supposed to hate their lives. Nor do we hate this world. What we must hate is the losing of our souls to this world. That thought should be despicable to us. Our souls are the most treasured things we have. We must love our souls and lose them, that is "place them" in the care of God.

This understanding is completely different from the dualists'. They want to justify their hate, both for this world and for their own lives.

Much of the confusion about hating this world stems from differing uses of the term "world." The Bible uses this term in at least three different ways. In John 3:16 we are told, *"For God so loved the world...."* Here we understand that the word *"world"* refers to the people who live on Earth. In other passages it refers to the natural creation—the mountains, trees, oceans and everything we can see around us (e.g., Acts 17:24). This natural world has been affected negatively by the sin of humanity, but it is good in its original design. A third definition focuses upon the evil system over which Satan rules. The Bible tells us that Satan is the ruler of this world (John 14:30); as such, the world is our enemy (John 15:19; I Cor. 2:12). Since all three of these definitions of the term *"world"* are used in the Bible, we must be careful how we use these terms as we communicate with each other. As Christians, we should love the world as God does when speaking of the people who inhabit Earth. We should also love the natural world because of the beauty in which it was created. However, we must not love the world of Satan's domain and his work here (I John 2:15-16; James 4:4).

With this understanding, we can embrace the proper view of our lives here on this planet. Dualists tend to hate their existence within this natural world, and that is wrong. Not only is it wrong, but it causes dualists to waste much of the lifetime they have been given here. Allow me to explain.

Dualists, consciously or subconsciously, think of the world (the general population) around them as evil, so they ultimately try to live in isolation. Rather than being a light to the world, they tend to withdraw and never influence, in any significant way, anyone outside their circle of Christian friends.

Dualists who do get involved with efforts to change society are ineffective for several reasons. The attitude of isolationism tends to breed an evil suspicion toward others. As a consequence, they keep themselves aloof and are rarely able to develop the working relationships with people that are necessary to accomplish significant change. They set out from the perspective, "It's us versus them; the good guys against the bad guys." At the very start, they believe in their hearts that everyone is against them, and, therefore, they make enemies and create unnecessary resistance. Even evangelism is difficult, because when Christians have judgments within their hearts against the people to whom they are talking, the listeners can sense it and they respond negatively.

In addition, the statement, "you cannot change what you hate," proves true again and again in the life of the dualist. Members of dualistic groups, whether or not they realize it, tend to breed a hatred toward society and anything which does not conform to their ideals. It is common to hear sarcastic remarks being passed around such groups pertaining to the evils of our government, how our educational system is corrupt, etc. These statements may have some truth in them, but attitudes of hate toward others, not wanting to be involved or thinking that the problems are too big to change, are contrary to the nature of God and His commission to believers.

When a group of Christians develops dualistic concepts, it tends to draw within itself and become very ingrown and stagnant. Its members may form into some type of separatist community or they may remain living in society but have their defenses so hardened against outsiders that no one from outside their own group can enter.

There are some positive aspects to the bonding together of Christians in a community fashion, however, the dualistic mentality too easily leads to a pride in which those involved start to think of themselves as more holy than outsiders. It is common for dualists to talk about the "select few," "the true believers" or "the remnant." Deception commonly creeps into such groups, and in time they experience terrible destruction.

Another problem which dualism promotes is legalism. Because the natural world is viewed as evil, there typically develops a *"do not touch, do not taste"* attitude, against which we are warned in the Bible (Col. 2:21-23). The proper Christian view toward food is that *"...everything created by God is good..."* (I Tim. 4:4). In contrast, dualists often exalt fasting and denounce the enjoyment of food in an unbiblical fashion. Similarly, the pleasures within marriage are sometimes looked down upon as unholy. In addition, such things as newspapers, sports activities, radio, business, technological advancements and medicine are sometimes condemned categorically. Of course, every Christian should exercise wisdom with regard to his or her involvements, but it is legalism in these areas about which I am warning. The mind-set of viewing everything that is natural as less than God's best, develops into an endless number of rules and regulations which keep a person from enjoying what God has created for us.

We also see Christians who embrace dualistic ideas becoming unable to function successfully in this natural world. Because they consciously or subconsciously think of the natural things as evil, they have less and less energy to do what needs to be done. The importance of working at a job diminishes. Fixing the house or the car may be viewed as unnecessary and too temporal. Caring for one's own appearance and physical body can seem vain. Dualistic individuals often find themselves losing interest in accomplishing anything significant in this natural world. As a consequence of not putting time and energy into that which needs their attention, they gradually slip into poverty, physical ailments and marriage problems. Dualists commonly have difficulties in one or more of these areas.

When individuals hate this world in their hearts, they emanate spiritual energy which forbids them full access to it. Dualists do not consider their possessions as gifts from God, but rather as "junk" or just "stuff weighing them down." Subconsciously, they may have judgments against people who are financially blessed, thinking of them as being less pleasing to God than those who are poor. Work is viewed not as a privilege, but a necessary evil. This leads to frustration because dualists try desperately to live according to what they believe, but their lifestyle simply does not produce victory nor abundance. People can neither receive nor enjoy the blessings of God if they are rejecting those very things in their hearts.

In addition, dualists find relationships with people hindered. I already mentioned the suspicion that is bred toward outsiders, but even those who should be insiders suffer. Because the dualists' hearts are directed toward the spiritual side, they cannot give themselves fully to their spouses in marriage relationships. Children may grow up unable to ever fully touch the heart of a dualistic parent. Because that parent is detached and uninvolved, the children very often begin rebelling against anything associated with the Church. Bonding is almost impossible, because the dualist constructs an invisible wall within his heart toward natural attachments.

In today's world, there are some Christians who develop attitudes about faith that lead to dualistic lifestyles. Some confuse faith with denial of reality and eventually detach from the natural world. James explained in the Bible that faith which does not produce works is dead (James 2:14-26). True faith leads people to face their problems with confidence, rather than deny them.

Although I am pointing out all of these negative tendencies in dualistic Christians, I also acknowledge a seriousness and earnestness often seen in their walks with God. Because they separate themselves from society, responsibilities and the concerns of the world, they frequently appear very intense and committed to God. Indeed, many of them dedicate more time to prayer and worship because their interests are not divided among people and natural concerns. I have met several Christian leaders whom I have greatly admired, in spite of the fact that they had dualistic tendencies. Having said that, I believe that we can all be zealous in our walks with God, while at the same time holding to a healthier form of Christianity.

To develop a proper Bible-based perspective, we must perceive of the natural realm not as evil, but as redeemable. We must lose our lives to God, which means that we will do His will in this world. Our gifts and abilities are the means by which we are to work out in this natural world that which God has given us to do. The natural world is not something from which we must escape, but rather the realm in which we are to demonstrate and establish the kingdom of God.

Simply put, Earth is where we live. And it is not a bad place to live. After God finished each of His creative acts, He declared, *"It is good."* Yes, sin has had its effect upon this world, but nature is still abundant and glorious (I Cor. 15:40-41). People who think that their natural lives are evil will have a difficult time experiencing the beauty of a mountain, the colors of a flower, the laughter of a child, the love of a spouse or the blessings with which God is trying to surround them. When these principles are explained clearly to people who have been dualistic, they begin enjoying more fully the simple pleasures, such as eating a good meal and spending time relaxing with others. Strict dualists rarely allow themselves to experience these joys. Mild dualists enjoy these things from time to time, but feel a little guilty about it. You need not be among either group. God wants you to be happy.

You Are a Human Being

Dualism is a lie in people's minds and hearts that can usher them into blindness and slavery. I have discussed the resulting bondages related to sexual perversions, legalism, defeated lifestyles, isolationism, poverty, broken relationships and false spiritual influences. Here I want to deal a final deathblow to dualism and declare a truth that will set people free. I am offering you a more biblical view of how people were created, and, therefore, how we must function in this world. I want to answer the basic question, "What is a human being?"

The easiest way to answer this is to challenge one more dualistic deception. This one pertains to another false doctrine which dualists sometimes develop from a mistranslation of John 4:24. This verse records a statement made by Jesus, one which has been translated from the original language differently in different Bible translations. The King James Version of this verse says:

> "God is a Spirit: and they that worship him must worship him in spirit and in truth."

Dualists like to use this translation of John 4:24 and emphasize how God is said to be *"a spirit."* From this point the dualists' develop the following argument:

1. God is a spirit,
2. Man is created in the image of God,
3. Therefore, man is a spirit.

The last point here is presented as a logically deduced conclusion. The teaching goes on to suggest that people were created by God as "spirit-beings." This doctrine has been taught in many Christian circles, and the conclusion that a human being is "a spirit" has profound implications, most of which are wrong.

Of course, people need to be taught about the spiritual side to their existence. People today are often so materially and naturally conscious that they ignore the role that the spirit within them plays. However, to call a person a spirit-being is biblically wrong. Please let me explain.

Look carefully at the three points made in the argument above. The first statement, "God is a spirit," is not in the Bible. The King James Version of John 4:24 words it this way, but in the original Greek in which the New Testament was written, there are no indefinite articles. This means that the letter "a", preceding the word "spirit" was added by the Bible translators of the King James Version. If you have a King James Bible, you will be helped in your understanding if you cross out the indefinite article and read our Lord's words as, *"God is spirit."* This is how most other Bible translations read, giving us a truer interpretation of the original meaning.[2] This change may seem insignificant to you at first,

---

2 The seriousness of this error can be seen more clearly if I point out a similar error made by the translators of the *New World Translation*, which is the official Bible of the Jehovah Witnesses. In John 1:1 they added the indefinite article "a" before the word "God." As a consequence, they teach that Jesus was "a god," rather than God. I point this out to show you how the insertion of one letter, "a," can lead to tremendous error. Although we may not like to admit to such an error in a Bible translation such as the King James Version, which has been so widely used by Christians, it is true and it should be recognized.

but the fact that God is spirit, rather than a spirit, changes much in our understanding.

The word "spirit" is translated from the Greek word *pneuma*, and it can be used in several different ways. For example, *pneuma* can refer to the spirit part of a person, or to the Holy Spirit, or to the breath or to the nature of the spiritual world. It is this last meaning that we see being used in the context of John 4:24. In that passage, Jesus was discussing with a Samaritan woman about worshiping God. The woman was asking the Lord on which mountain people should worship (John 4:20). She was focused on natural forms of worship and was asking "where" people should worship. In answer to that question, Jesus pointed out that God did not care where a person worshiped because He is not physical in nature. God is spirit, meaning He exists in the spiritual dimension.

The Bible clearly tells us in other passages that God is not just "a spirit." In several verses we are told that God has both a soul and a spirit. Both the soul and the spirit are spiritual in nature because we can neither see nor physically touch them, but we must know that there is more to God than just a spirit. Read God's own words as recorded in Hebrews 10:38, concerning His own soul.

> *But My righteous one shall live by faith;*
> *And if he shrinks back, My soul has no pleasure in him.*

God states here that He has a soul in addition to a spirit. In the Old Testament we see similar declarations. For example, when God was speaking about releasing blessings on His people, He said:

> *"Moreover, I will make My dwelling among you,*
> *and My soul will not reject you."*
>
> (Lev. 26:11)

Using the same reference to His own soul, God spoke about the curses He would release.

"...My soul shall abhor you."

(Lev. 26:30)

In I Samuel 2:35, we read God's words:

"But I will raise up for Myself a faithful priest who will do according to what is in My heart and in My soul...."

Throughout the Bible, God Himself speaks about His own soul.

Note in the above verses that God speaks of His soul as the core of His own being, from which He makes decisions of acceptance or rejection. Consider what this implies when we talk about a person being created in the image of God. God is not "a spirit." Therefore, man is not "a spirit," nor is he "a spirit being." If people are created in the image of God, then they consist of at least a soul and a spirit. More than that, their entire being is created in the image of God. The body was designed by the same Maker as the spirit/soul. The body is simply the natural expression of a person's invisible existence. We are created in God's image—spirit/soul/body.

Furthermore, the soul (not the spirit) plays the predominant role within our being.

This is in agreement with the rest of the Bible. Nowhere in the Bible are people called spirits or spirit beings. In fact, we are told specifically that Adam was created a *"living soul"* (Gen. 2:7). When the Bible speaks of individuals referring to one part of their beings, their souls are the focal point. For example, in Acts 2:41 we are told that 3,000 souls were added to the Church on Pentecost Day. In the Bible people are pictured not as spirits but as three-part beings, with their souls playing the predominant role.

Why am I making such a point of this? Because the doctrine which views a person as "a spirit" or a "spirit being" only adds to the dualist's deceptions. The Christian man who truly believes that he is a spirit, rather than a whole person, ends up denying a part of his own nature. If a man thinks he is a spirit-being, he is going to try to live as a spirit-being. This is dualism at its worst!

Let's contrast the nature of humanity with the nature of true spirit-beings. Demons, for example, do not have a physical body. They exist in the spiritual realm. In order to influence this natural world, they may seek a human vessel through whom to work. We are shown in the Bible that they even try to inhabit human beings. It is in this sense that they are different from us. They are, indeed, spirit-beings, created different from human beings.

Consider again the words exchanged when the disciples first saw Jesus after His resurrection. They *"thought that they were seeing a spirit"* (Luke 24:37). Jesus corrected their thinking, saying:

> *"See My hands and My feet, that it is I Myself; touch Me and see, for a spirit does not have flesh and bones as you see that I have."*
> (Luke 24:39)

Jesus took on our nature, hence, He is not a spirit. Although His body is now glorified, He took on a three-part nature, the same as you and I have.

This may seem very simplistic to you, but let me state it as clearly as I can: You are not a spirit-being; you are a human being.

I am not trying to lower in your mind the grandeur in which God created people. Unlike the animals, we were created in the very image of God. Furthermore, as Christians, we are human beings in whom God dwells. We are partakers of divine nature. The life of God flows through us. However, we have three parts to our nature. We are human. This is the biblical view.

In over-emphasizing the spirit of a person, dualists will sometimes summarize their doctrines by saying that every person is a spirit-being, and that a person's nature should be arranged in a hierarchy, with the spirit as the master, the soul as the servant and the body as the slave.

Dualistic Error Concerning the Hierarchy of Man's Nature

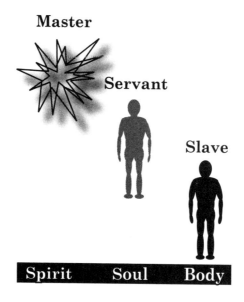

Is this hierarchy biblical? No. The Bible does not give us any hierarchy concerning our three-part nature. Furthermore, many Scriptures contradict the dualist's doctrine of ultimate authority in the spirit of a person.

For example, I Corinthians 14:32 tells us that *"the spirits of prophets are subject to prophets."* You cannot "subject the spirit" and at the same time have it as the ultimate authority in your being.

Furthermore, Proverbs tells us:

He who is slow to anger is better than the mighty,
And he who rules his spirit, than he who captures a city.
(Prov. 16:32)

Like a city that is broken into and without walls
Is a man who has no control over his spirit.
(Prov. 25:28)

The Bible is very clear concerning a person—including the Christian—ruling over, controlling and subjecting his spirit.

The idea of subjecting the soul and the body to the spirit stems from the dualistic view that the soul and body are evil. That contradicts a main point I have tried to make throughout this section: the victorious Christian life is one of redemption—including the redemption of the soul and body. To ask the question, "What should be the final authority in a person's being?" is to misunderstand how God created us. The will of a person is not limited to just the spirit, just the soul, nor just the human body. As I explained (chapter 15) the will of a person permeates his entire being—spirit, soul and body.

Hence, the Christian life is not meant to be one of denying, rejecting or subjecting one part over the others. Paul prayed that we may be sanctified throughout our being—spirit, soul and body (I Thess. 5:23). As we are sanctified, our spirit becomes one with God's Spirit; the desires of our soul come into alignment with God's desires; and the desires of our body conform to His will. Our entire being then comes into conformity to God's will.

I can make an analogy by talking about the relationship between your heart, brain and lungs. Your heart pumps blood to your brain and lungs. Your lungs draw in oxygen and transfer it to the blood, while at the same time taking carbon dioxide out of your blood. Your brain sends messages to both your heart and your lungs. But no one part is made to dominate any other part. They are made to be interdependent while working in unison and cooperation.

In similar fashion, we are not made to have one part of our being fighting nor dominating any other part. Rather, we are to be filled with the Holy Spirit throughout our being so that everything within us is in harmony and submission to God.

A Christian Sanctified Spirit, Soul and Body

Spirit   Soul   Body

206

Conclusion

In this section I attempted to lay out a biblically accurate view of our nature and how we relate to both the natural and spiritual worlds. In doing this, I have challenged and uprooted some misconceptions to which many Christians in the past have held. I trust that you have been able to see the significance of these, and, hence, escape any dualistic tendencies within your own life.

Still there is a warning that I must include before closing this section. In an attempt to escape dualism some may go to the other extreme and misjudge Christians who are in some unique situations of life. Please allow me to explain.

Consider Mary and Martha, two sisters about whom we read in Luke 10:38-42. In that passage, we see Mary sitting at the feet of Jesus and attentively listening to His words. At the same time, Martha was busy working to make arrangements for her guests. In the midst of this situation, Martha became frustrated with her inactive sister Mary, and she complained to Jesus. If we were to analyze Mary and Martha in light of dualism, we would note that Mary was detached from the natural world and acting irresponsibly. Yet Jesus commends Mary and corrects Martha for being so worried about natural affairs (Luke 10:41-42).

What are we supposed to do with this? Abandon our own responsibilities and go sit at the feet of Jesus for the rest of our days? Well, it is true that Mary had chosen that which pleased our Lord at that time. However, Mary was taking a moment to sit at our Lord's feet, not embracing a dualistic lifestyle. All Christians should take time when they sit at the feet of Jesus, captivated in the presence of God.

We can compare it with two young people falling in love. Young lovers may at times appear out of touch with the world around them. Sometimes they seem irresponsible in their natural affairs. However, the experience of falling in love is a precious, holy time of life. In the same way, it is healthy and normal for children of God to have periods in their lives when they are so enthralled with the Person of God that everything else fades in importance. This is not to condone dualism, but to recognize moments in our lives when we become captivated spiritually. These times should always be followed by a return to living out our Christianity in this natural world.

Having made these statements, we are now ready to go on. In this section I have attempted to impact upon your mind the fact that you are a human being. As a human, you have the residue of God's breath within you. Being a Christian means you also have the fresh breath of the Holy Spirit in you. These facts will enable you to live in this natural world, supernaturally. How this is done, I will continue discussing in the sections which follow.

Section 4

Powers and Activities of a Person's Spirit

The Christian faith declares that we have more to our beings than just physical bodies. There is an invisible, spiritual side to our natures. Although Christians accept this fact, few have dared to consider the implications. Let's be daring.

In section 2 we laid out the fundamentals of a person's nature. In addition to the physical body, we investigated the invisible side and discovered that it consists of two elements, a spirit and a soul.

A Person's Three-part Nature: Spirit, Soul and Body

Spirit   Soul   Body

We saw the soul as superimposed over the physical body, filling the body and having the same shape and size as the body. The spirit, we learned, is the flowing energy within. This energy sustains life within the soul and within the physical body (Job 34:14-15). It also acts as a light, quickening our thoughts and allowing us to think (I Cor. 2:11). The spirit of a person is the invisible energy circulating and flowing within, as a river from the heart.

The Spiritual Energy Flows from the Heart

Spirit/Soul/Body

Keep in mind that all human beings, Christians and non-Christians, have spiritual energy flowing within them. There is a difference, however, between the spirit of the Christian and the spirit of the non-Christian. When individuals place their faith in Jesus Christ, they receive a fresh injection of God's life. Jesus explained that the rivers flowing within the believer would be rivers of *"living"* water (John 7:37-39). Every human being has a spirit that sustains life and flows as energy, but only the believer has a spirit which has been made alive by a fresh injection of God's life (Rom. 8:10).

Proceeding from here, we will now study how the spirit of a person can reach beyond the physical body to touch and influence both the natural and the spiritual worlds.

Spiritual Presence

The spirit not only flows within a person, but it emanates beyond the confines of the human body. Consider how this works.

Spiritual energy manifests first upon the countenance of a person. The Bible refers to this in several passages, especially in the context of people focusing their attention upon God. For example in Psalms 34:5, we are told:

> *They looked to Him and were radiant,*
> *And their faces will never be ashamed.*

When Moses approached the people after talking with God, his face shone so brightly that he had to put a veil over it (II Cor. 3:13). Tradition tells us that in Old Testament times, the Jewish women were noted for their increased beauty as they came out from the presence of God. On the negative side, we can read how Cain's countenance had noticeably fallen when God did not accept his offering (Gen. 4:5-7).

When people are full of life, there is a spiritual brightness about them. When the channel of the soul is opened, the life-energy within a person flows out and becomes tangibly evident. Most people have observed this phenomenon in relation to the beauty of another individual. At times a person may exude an undeniable "glow." A loving husband may look at his wife and she appears to be "without spot or wrinkle." A new mother may be mesmerized by the beauty of her baby. An adoring fan may be captivated by the actor on stage. As two single people catch each other's eyes, they may feel an energy radiating between them. In such situations, we discover that beauty is not just a function of natural features, but also the result of spiritual dynamics between people.

The Spiritual Presence on a Person's Countenance

People involved in various occult and mystical groups have developed numerous teachings concerning this emanating energy. Typically, they talk about "auras" surrounding people and how various colors in people's auras mean certain things about their lives. As Bible-believing Christians we can see both positives and negatives in these teachings. Christians may hesitate in using terms such as "auras" which have been coined by those with occultic interests, but the Bible-believer need not deny the existence of this spiritual energy. God is the One who breathed spiritual substance into humanity. As for various colors in one's aura meaning certain things, we have no biblical evidence of this. It may be interesting for discussion purposes, but we would be wise to be sceptical.

This spiritual energy which emanates from individuals involves more than their countenances. It may envelop their entire being and become a spiritual presence which can be sensed by others.

The Spiritual Presence Surrounding a Person

You can identify this spiritual presence when someone sneaks up behind you. Sometimes you can "feel" them. A related phenomenon can be observed when a thief breaks into a person's home during the night, and the homeowner awakens with a feeling of fear or apprehension. Such experiences can be explained if we accept the spiritual dynamics occurring between people.

Even more amazing are the responses stimulated in people who are being watched. For example, think of two strangers sitting at different tables in a restaurant. If one stares at the other without the second knowing it, sooner or later the second is likely to turn to see who is looking. Most people have experienced such spiritual contact responses in some situation of their lives.

Spiritual Contact Between People

The spiritual presence surrounding and given off by a person is unique to that person and it influences other people in specific ways. For example, when a person is enraged, there may be a tangible energy given off that causes others to be cautious. At other times, a person may be emitting a flow of peace from a calm, gracious heart toward others. Even animals can sense this, as when a house cat crawls into the lap of a relaxed individual. The experienced hunter knows that if he takes on a peaceful and confident attitude, wild animals will be less likely to detect him.

People send out "vibes" to attract the type of relationships in which they are interested: be it a student seeking a teacher, a lonely man seeking female companionship or an empty-nest couple seeking children to help nurture. When a woman is in self-pity, others around may feel her trying to draw attention to herself. A man with an arrogant attitude may project spiritual energy that can make others feel inferior. Some people emit spiritual energy that brings joy and happiness.

The rivers of life flow from the heart of every person (Prov.

4:23), therefore, heartfelt motivations and desires powerfully influence the strength and character of that spiritual flow. The spiritual energy flows in the direction of a person's heart focus, and the strength of that flow is determined by decisions made deep within. The focus of one's entire being toward a specific goal with no confusion or indecision is vital to the power of that flow.

In earlier chapters, I discussed these and other characteristics which determine the strength of a person's spiritual flow. I prefer not to repeat those discussions here, but only to add the following determining factor. The *acceptance of personal responsibility* plays a major part in determining the flow of spiritual energy from a person. We can see this when we talk about the spiritual presence surrounding an individual. Every person develops a sense of ownership over the area just around them. If a stranger suddenly stepped two inches in front of your face, you probably would be offended, and you would be right in asking, "What are you doing in my space?" The truth is that you have accepted responsibility and demanded authority over the space right around your body. Different people establish different limits to their space. Even in different cultures of the world and in different socioeconomic classes, people are taught to claim a certain amount of area around themselves. That of which they take possession in their hearts becomes the area of their spiritual presence. A loved one may be allowed to step inside, but others must be invited. It is a reality of how we are made and how we live.

In summary, I can say the individual's spiritual energy is determined by the orientation of his or her heart. This orientation includes the acceptance of personal responsibility. The energy which flows out reflects the emotional condition, personality, purpose and authority of the individual.

Beyond the Body

It is no more difficult for the spirit of a person to reach across town than it is for one's spirit to touch the person sitting close by. Compare this with natural vision. It is no harder to look at the stars in the sky than it is to look at the paper in front of you. You can turn your attention toward things far away as easily as you can focus upon something near. In similar fashion, the spirit of a person goes where the heart is pointed and it can reach to any distance without effort.

A Person's Spiritual Presence Emanates Outward

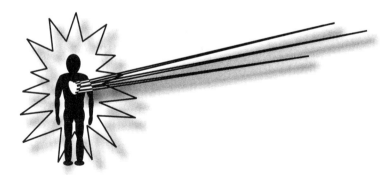

For evidence of this, consider what the Bible teaches us about our spiritual relationship to Jesus. Our Lord is sitting at the right hand of the Father in heaven. His glorified body is located there, and His soul is also there associated with His body positioned in heaven. It is His Spirit which extends from His being and reaches down to us: *"...God has sent forth the Spirit of His Son into our hearts..."* (Gal. 4:6).

In a similar manner, the Christian's spirit reaches out from his earthly vessel and into heaven. We know that our bodies and souls are located on Earth, but the Bible tells us that we are seated with Christ in the heavenly places (Eph. 2:6). It is the Christian's spirit which emanates out of his body and reaches even into the throne room of God.

In Colossians 2:5, the apostle Paul wrote to the early believers:

> *For even though I am absent in body, nevertheless I am with you in spirit....*

Paul referred to being physically in one location and spiritually in another. Are we to believe this verse literally? (See also I Cor. 5:3-4; I Thes. 2:17).

What we are about to discuss is difficult for many Christians to accept, especially those trained with a Western mind-set. Those programmed to the Western way of thinking tend to view life from a very natural perspective: natural things cause natural results. Christians with a mind fixated along natural lines tend to read verses such as Colossians 2:5 and just skip over them or excuse them as figures of speech. They have no place to put the idea that one's spirit could be located in a different place than one's body. Christians with a Western mind-set may firmly state that they believe the Bible, but in reality they consciously or unconsciously make excuses to explain away what the Bible actually states. The truth is that the people used by God to write the Bible were not confined to a Western mind-set (nor were they limited to an Eastern mind-set). If we want to understand what they wrote, we must open our minds to the whole realm of spiritual things. A Christian free of modern-day fixations is able to believe literally such Bible passages as Colossians 2:5 and, therefore, can begin to understand what Paul actually meant.

What, then, did Paul mean when he said he was absent bodily but with the Colossian Christians in spirit? Well, let's dare to take him literally. While Paul was writing those words, he was physically in one location, but his spirit was reaching out of his body and was present with the Christians in the city of Colossae.

We can read an even more revealing example of this phenomenon in II Kings 5. There we learn how the prophet Elisha was used by God to heal Naaman, the leper. Elisha would receive no gift for the blessing of healing, but afterward Elisha's servant, Gehazi, secretly went to Naaman to receive gifts for himself against his master's wishes. After Gehazi returned with the gifts, the prophet confronted him:

...Elisha said to him, "Where have you been, Gehazi?" And he said, "Your servant went nowhere." Then he said to him, "Did not my heart go with you, when the man turned from his chariot to meet you? Is it a time to receive money and to receive clothes and olive groves and vineyards and sheep and oxen and male and female servants?"
(II Kings 5:25-26)

The prophet knew what evil deed his servant had done. Without being present physically, he was still made aware spiritually. Elisha explained this by saying that his heart had gone with his servant.

We can understand such Bible passages only if we accept the truth that wherever a person's heart is pointed, that is where his spirit flows. Because the spirit exists in the spiritual dimension, it is limited neither in space nor by distance the way that natural things are limited in this natural world. Your spirit goes in the direction of your love, faith and hope. It extends over that for which you accept personal responsibility. The heart determines the extent and direction of your spiritual reach.

It is the spiritual substance—the energy, the divine breath, the residue of God's stuff in us—that reaches out of our body and goes where our heart is pointed. It is not the soul which emanates from the physical body. The soul can leave in other circumstances, and we will learn about those later, but here we are talking about the spiritual energy within people emanating out of their soul and out of their body, and then reaching to another place.

Also, for clarification, I need to point out that not all of one's spirit leaves the soul/body. If that happened, the person would die because there would not be enough spiritual energy left in the body or soul to maintain life (Job 34:14-15). Instead, think of the spiritual energy emanating outward and extending to the place to which it is directed.

Do not think of this as some mystical, rare experience. Your spirit is touching the people you love right now. A parent's spirit reaches out to his or her children. A married person is bonded spiritually to his or her spouse. The spirit of the pastor extends to his or her congregation. All Christians are joined together spiritually (I Cor. 12:12-13).

Whenever Christians pray earnestly for another person, their spirits literally reach out and touch the person for whom they are praying. If sister Suzie prays for her friend in a hospital across the country, Suzie's spirit may reach across the distance, and spiritual energy is imparted into that person. When we pray for our leaders, we literally release strength into them. When a father prays for his children, he increases the flow of his spirit to them.

It is helpful to distinguish between a person praying to God and a person directing his heart toward the person for whom he is praying. In our example of sister Suzie praying for her friend in a distant hospital, we could ask whether her spiritual energy is being directed upward toward God or laterally toward the hospital. The answer may be both...both can and do happen. Later we will address when such directional forces are used rightly, but here, recognize that both may be possible.

The human spirit (apart from the added strength of God) is limited. No woman can send her spirit over all the world or reach out to all people. Only to the degree that we love, accept responsibility and have faith can we extend our spiritual strength to others. This limited nature of our spirit has many consequences.

For example, Carl was working as a missionary for an extended period in Brazil. During that time, he bonded with the people with whom he was laboring. Carl's spirit abided with those people. When Carl left the mission field and returned to his homeland for a visit, his heart was still directed toward the people to whom he had been giving his life. He felt as if he was in one land physically while his spirit was reaching out to a distant location. This is similar to what Paul described (Col. 2:5).

I have worked with many missionaries who were in similar circumstances to Carl's. I have watched some become spiritually, emotionally and physically exhausted. I have come to understand this as result of not having enough spiritual substance left in their soul/body. As a result they sometimes become physically ill and mentally unable to make even simple decisions. Such symptoms are very common, and even the zealous Christian who goes overseas for a short missionary visit can experience a similar division of her spirit if she bonds with the people there. Typically, such a person will not be able to function at her peak back at home until a period of time has passed. The process can be accelerated by a conscious act of the person forcefully directing her heart to where she is located physically. Also, it helps to engage in activities which she thoroughly enjoys, hence captivating the heart and redirecting it.

Related problems are not restricted to the missionary. A military man may experience this phenomenon when he returns home from a tour of duty. The truck driver who loves being on the road gradually makes his home in his truck, and he extends his spirit wherever he goes. As a consequence, it is typical for truck drivers to have a difficult time ever being comfortable in one place or trying to settle down and change their lifestyles. Traveling salespeople, politicians campaigning on the road, businesspeople commuting internationally, etc., all experience similar problems.

Notice that it is not only the heart of love that extends a person's spirit outward, but also a heartfelt sense of responsibility. Paul wrote about his spiritual presence where he had sown the gospel and continued to hold influence. A pastor who accepts responsibility before God for his congregation will emit his spirit out to the sheep. The spirit of a responsible mother abides upon her children. A coach who accepts responsibility for his team will influence his players with his own spiritual energy. A businesswoman who accepts personal responsibility extends her spirit throughout her business. Every human being has a spirit that goes where his or her heart is directed.

33 The Emanating Spirit

The spiritual presence of a person extends not only over other people, but also over things, events and circumstances. When a couple purchase and claim responsibility for a new home, they cover that home spiritually. The teenage girl who claims her bedroom as her own places her spiritual impression upon that room. The artist who paints a picture imparts his own spirit into his paintings. A woman who takes great care and interest in organizing a large event involving thousands of people extends her spirit over the entire event. Anything for which a person takes responsibility and ownership will bear the spiritual imprint of that person.

As Abraham walked through the Promised Land, knowing in his heart that it belonged to his descendants, he literally was planting spiritual seeds and taking possession of it. As the Jews walked around Jericho they claimed the city as their own.

When a businesswoman buys a piece of land, she takes possession of it, not only physically (and legally) but spiritually as well. The act of giving one's money to purchase something releases one's own spirit to cover the object. Money that has been earned with personal sacrifice becomes an avenue through which a person extends his or her spirit. On the other hand, when some possession is obtained through thievery or is unearned (as a gift), it rarely is possessed spiritually, and, hence, will be lost in time. Whenever money is invested with thought and care, it carries with it the authority of the person.

A person's signature also carries the mark of his or her spirit. When a man signs his name with authority, he is revealing his heart. Depending on personal investment, he is—to various degrees—giving his commitment and making his intentions known. When a founding father signs a historical document, such as a Constitution of a country, which may be at the risk of his own life, that act may extend his authority for years or generations into the future. Every time a person signs his name with authority, he or she is leaving a deposit upon that which the signature represents.

Spoken words are also avenues through which people may release spiritual energy. There is a literal substance and force behind spoken words. The significance of spoken words is so important that I will discuss it further in chapter 35 and examine Bible verses which address the spiritual nature of spoken words.

Even our thoughts may release spiritual forces which influence the things around us. This concept, too, is so significant that I will take an entire chapter (37) to explain it in greater detail.

At this point, we need to identify how spiritual substance is released from individuals' hearts when they accept personal responsibility for their possessions, works of creativity, labors, money, signature, words or thoughts.

As you think of spiritual forces being released from a person, it is helpful to make several comparisons with light. Natural light consists of many different colors. If we pass sunlight through a glass prism the light will be divided into all the colors of the rainbow. Different colors of light have differing qualities of penetration. Because of these differing qualities water plants of various colors grow at different levels in the ocean. For example, green algae grow close to the surface of the ocean, while red algae grow at greater depths. The red algae can grow at those greater depths because the light which they absorb penetrates deeper into the water. Different colors of light penetrate in different ways.

In similar fashion, spiritual energy seems to flow out in different measures and strengths. Some spiritual energy seems to flow within the person, flooding the soul and quickening the thought processes. Spiritual energy also fills the physical body, making it alive and able to function. Another form of spiritual energy reaches beyond the individual, influencing the countenance or even encompassing the body, thus creating a unique presence. As I have been explaining, the human spirit also extends far beyond the physical location of the person, influencing things, circumstances and other people.

A Person's Spirit Flows as Light

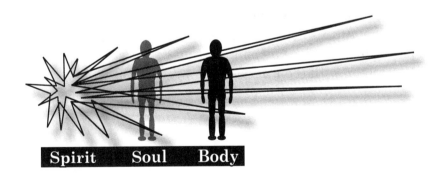

Spirit   Soul   Body

It is worth noting that the various flows of spiritual energy from within can act independently from one another. For example, the flow which produces a bright countenance upon a person may be very strong; at the same time the energy enveloping the rest of the person's body can be weak. One person may have a very strong presence and yet not have a spirit which emanates far beyond that. Another may not have enough spiritual life within to keep his body healthy, but he may have spiritual energy extending to a far distant place. These varying flows will become evident as we continue.

Let's conclude this chapter with a story of some native people who live in an undeveloped region of the world. They were on a long journey by foot and after several hours of walking they sat down for a rest. When asked by a foreigner why they were stopping, they responded, "To let our souls catch up with our bodies." If we were to look at the native hikers' words, we would err in trying to bring them into a Western understanding. However, as Christians we can fit them into our biblical standard of truth. Perhaps it would be better to say, "To let our souls be restored as our spiritual energy returns and mounts within us." Of course, we can also explain that they were waiting for their physical bodies to rest, and that would be a valid explanation. However, our whole view of humanity allows us to see that the entire person—spirit, soul and body—is involved, even in common activity such as walking. At this point my readers may want to pause before proceeding to the next chapter, to give their spirits a chance to catch up with their minds.

34 Spiritual Forces Acting on the Natural World

The spirit of a person carries with it the characteristics of that person: the personality, strength, faith, love, etc., of that individual. To the degree that the Christian is joined in heart to God, his or her spirit is one with the Holy Spirit, and, hence, the characteristics and energy of the Holy Spirit also flow out to those people or things which are touched. Demons can also add their influence to the spiritual flow of a person. At this point, I will not spend much time distinguishing good from evil; rather I will show the principle that whatever is in a person, good or bad, flows out to influence people, objects, circumstances and events.

To some degree, all people are subject, to the spiritual influences given off by others. At a sports event where everyone is excited, the newcomer easily is enveloped by the atmosphere. When a saleswoman is full of energy to sell, she may change your attitude toward her product. When someone is very angry, the energy in the air may set others on edge. At a funeral, where many people are mourning, there will be pressure even upon the unknown visitor to be sorrowful.

The spiritual forces are most powerful when emanating from people bonded together. For example, two close friends can be a tremendous influence upon each other. Married individuals may be sensitive to every feeling of their spouses.

When the people with whom you work have good thoughts toward you, you will find more spiritual energy available to you.

These spiritual forces are especially strong when coming from a person of authority, and, in particular, a person related directly to the recipient's life. A mother's care releases powerful blessings for her children. A father has great spiritual influence over his son. A grandmother can bless the children and grandchildren whose photos she keeps on her mantle. A political leader can impart spiritual influences into those over whom he has been given authority. Similarly, the boss at a business can release spiritual energy into his employees by the attitude he has toward them. All people can influence each other positively or negatively, but increased authority increases that influence.

We can see an extreme example of this in I Corinthians 5:15. In that passage, we read how the apostle Paul dealt with a man who was committing immoral acts. The local congregation would not deal with it, so Paul exercised his authority. He explained:

> *For I, on my part, though absent in body but present in spirit, have already judged him who has so committed this, as though I were present. In the name of our Lord Jesus, when you are assembled, and I with you in spirit, with the power of our Lord Jesus, I have decided to deliver such a one to Satan for the destruction of his flesh, that his spirit may be saved in the day of the Lord Jesus.*
>
> (I Cor. 5:3-5)

Many truths can be learned from these verses, but let me give a caution first. By quoting this passage, I am not giving credence to people releasing curses onto other people. Paul was exercising this authority in the name of Jesus with His power, and therefore, he was in God's will. Recognizing that, we can also note that Paul had authority from God in this church. He was their "father in the faith," having labored over them for years. He also had apostolic oversight of these people. Acknowledging that relationship, we can see the authority God had given Paul. He used that authority. He said, *"...being absent in body but present in spirit...I have decided to deliver such a one to Satan...."* Those words are sobering.[3]

In the realm of the spirit, authority is a very exacting, governing force. When a certain soldier came to Jesus, he said:

> *"Lord,...just say the word, and my servant will be healed. For I also am a man under authority, with soldiers under me; and I say to this one, 'Go!' and he goes, and to another, 'Come!' and he comes, and to my slave, 'Do this!' and he does it."*
>
> (Matt. 8:8b-9)

Authority is arranged in an ascending/descending pattern. Just as water runs downhill in the natural world, good and bad most easily run down the chain of command in the spiritual world.

For love, strength or other blessings to flow from one individual to another, some openness of heart is necessary. The apostle Paul wrote to the Corinthians, *"Make room for us in your hearts"* (II Cor. 7:2a). He went on to encourage them saying, *"You are in our hearts"* (II Cor. 7:3). To the Colossians the apostle Paul said he was *"with them in spirit."* This was stated to encourage them so they would take strength from his love and concern. Similarly, children can draw upon the

---

3 For further teaching on this refer to my book, *God's Leaders for Tomorrow's World.*

spiritual attributes of their parents, but their hearts must be open to receive. On the other hand, people may reject the spiritual influence of others by opposition within their own hearts toward those people.

Spiritual energy not only influences people but also things, events and circumstances. It does not matter whether that energy is released through spoken words, thoughts or the mere projection of a person's spirit. All things in this natural world are subject to energy from the spiritual world.

Consider the words of our Lord:

> *"Truly I say to you, whoever says to this mountain, 'Be taken up and cast into the sea,' and does not doubt in his heart, but believes what he says is going to happen, it will be granted him."*

> (Mark 11:23)

When a mountain is addressed in faith, that mountain will respond.

When God spoke, the world itself came into existence. Of course, God's faith was perfect and He has all authority, but we need to recognize the principle here. When faith releases that which is spiritual into the natural, the natural must respond, yield and change. When spiritual energy flows out of a person, it influences the natural world in accordance to what is within the heart. Whatever it is that the person believes, that very thing is projected wherever his spirit goes. The ideas, desires and goals of the individual influence the world accordingly. The greater the faith of the person, the greater will be that person's spiritual influence upon the natural world. Even objects are affected.

To understand this, we must recognize that when spiritual energy is released, it actually goes into the things toward which it is projected. As I mentioned earlier, the artist deposits a measure of his spirit in his work. The homeowner leaves spiritual energy upon her home. Spiritual impressions are left upon everything which has contact with a person's spirit.

This concept—that things can hold spiritual energy—is key. We read in the Book of Acts how handkerchiefs of Paul were carried to the sick and many were healed (Acts 19:12). The Jewish priests were not permitted to wear their clothing both in the presence of the Lord and in the midst of the people, lest they *"transmit holiness to the people with their garments"* (Ezek. 44:19). In II Kings 13:21, we are told the story of a dead man being thrown into Elisha's grave, and there was still enough power in Elisha's bones to raise the dead man to life. Several Bible passages talk about certain portions of land being holy, while others have been desecrated. I Timothy 4:4 tells us that all created things respond to spiritual input:

> *For everything created...is sanctified by means of the word of God and prayer.*

Here we are told that prayer and speaking the Word of God over things "sanctifies," that is, makes them holy.

Yes, sanctuaries where people worship God do become holy. The people of God in the Old Testament often built altars to God, and those locations became holy ground. Of course, God is spirit and our worship should never be restricted to a certain location (John 4:20-24), but there is also a reality to holiness literally being transmitted to natural things.

Furthermore, we can see how the "spiritual value" of things can change. On the negative side, we can talk about the evil release of power through objects. For example, one of the most common practices of witchcraft is to project spiritual energy through a "power object" or a "familiar object."

A witch may take a small object and secretly plant it at a location near the people whom she wants to influence. Then as the witch meditates upon that object and claims it as her possession, she may begin emitting from that object her own spiritual influence into the surroundings.

Some naturally-minded Christians mock the idea that evil people can exercise any such spiritual power. However, the Bible is very clear that such evil practices are real, and we are warned not to be involved (Deut. 18:10-12). The fact that the Bible tells us not to be involved implies that such things are real—evil, but real.

The list of examples of related present-day experiences could be extensive, but here I will mention just one. A few years ago a minister friend of mine was having great success in his church. People were being saved and great blessings were evident in his work. Then a woman in the congregation made a doily to be placed upon the pulpit in the sanctuary. She began making other items also and placing them around the building. It was not until later that the leaders came to understand the controlling forces within this woman's life. Shortly after she began "decorating" the church, the minister discovered tremendous forces against him as he tried to speak. It was as if a wall had been erected against him. It was only a short time before a multitude of problems erupted and the church collapsed.

Of course, we cannot blame all church problems on witchcraft. I do not believe that the enemy can overcome Christians unless those Christians have opened the door to evil in some fashion. However, we should recognize the reality of evil curses. There are evil people at work in the world.

We can learn from this that Christians should claim that which God has given to them. To give up responsibility is to release it to the enemy. To hold it is to take spiritual authority over it.

It is important to note that the battle between good and evil is in no way a fair war. Christians should realize that as they tap into God's power they are releasing the kingdom which is already victorious over Satan. Sometimes people misunderstand this and picture two opposing powers facing each other in some type of "star wars encounter." In reality, the battle between good and evil is not one of good and bad people shooting bolts of light toward each other. The proper perspective is more of a victorious kingdom being released through the Christian, and whenever it is released, victory is inevitable. Light overcomes and expels darkness. All that is required for the Christian to win is to act according to God's will.

When we release His will, we release His power. It is not only this good and evil struggle that we want to address. There is also a reality to the simple power of faith. When a woman holds responsibility for something, whether or not that woman is a Christian, her spiritual energy projects forth and influences those things: *"Be it done to you according to your faith."* Whatever is locked within the heart of the individual, spiritual energy will emanate to influence things accordingly. Spiritual energy literally flows out to bring things into alignment with the faith of the person whose spirit permeates them.

Just as objects and possessions may be influenced, so also are circumstances and events. People with a strong flow of spiritual energy find their paths being supernaturally established ahead of them. For reasons that cannot be explained naturally, a person with great authority will seem to meet the right person at the right time, be in the right place just when they are needed, have closed doors open before them and find key opportunities appearing at just the right moment.

Consider how God's Spirit was moving over the surface of

Earth before the six days of Creation (Gen. 1:2). The original language gives us the impression that God's Spirit was brooding over Earth like a hen broods over her eggs, preparing them for what is to come. In similar fashion, we can think of a person's spirit brooding over that which is encompassed by his heart. Being created in God's image human beings have spirits which have tangible effects upon that with which they have contact.

Power of the Spoken Word

As I promised earlier, I will now discuss how spiritual energy is released with the spoken word.

First consider God. When He spoke into existence this natural world, we recognize creative power within His words (e.g., Gen. 1:3). Hebrews 11:3 tells us that the entire world was brought into existence as God spoke.

Jesus testified to the spiritual nature of His own words when He said to His disciples, *"The words that I have spoken to you are spirit and are life"* (John 6:63b). Notice that the words themselves *"are spirit."* In another passage our Lord declared, *"Heaven and earth will pass away, but My words will not pass away"* (Matt. 24:35). Here we learn of the enduring—even eternal—quality of His words.

When we talk about the words spoken by common people, we must not assume or imply that people have the same power within their words that God does. However, we are identifying a biblical principle here. Words consist of more than sound vibrations moving through the atmosphere. Our words may not be as forceful as God's, but to some degree, they, too, carry spiritual substance with them.

The Bible explains that the power behind words is based on faith in the person's heart. Jesus said:

"Truly I say to you, whoever says to this mountain, 'Be taken up and cast into the sea,' and does not doubt in his heart, but believes that what he says is going to happen, it will be granted him."

(Mark 11:23)

The greater a person's faith—that is, his confidence in what he speaks—the greater will be the spiritual force behind those words. Paul exhorted every Christian to exercise his or her gifts according to the grace given, *"...if prophecy, according to the proportion of his faith"* (Rom. 12:6). Here we see again the role faith plays as a person speaks out. According to one's faith, the spiritual power flows out with the spoken word.

Spiritual Power Flows with Words of Faith

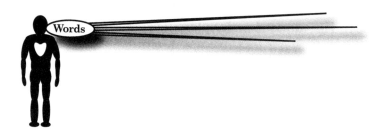

Let me offer and example from my own life revealing how words contain spiritual substance. Several years ago I was traveling home after speaking at a conference and my mind would not rest. My mind was reviewing over and over again every word I had spoken during the conference. Unable to sleep that night, I paced the floor of our living room, praying to God for peace. After some time passed, I remembered what God said about His Words not returning void (Isaiah 55:11, KJV). I sensed that God wanted me to take on this same stance of authority, so I stood in the middle of the room and with all the spiritual force and faith in my heart, I declared, "My words shall not return to me void!" I pushed the words out of my system and back to the people to whom I had spoken them. As soon as I had done this, peace came and I was able to rest.

What I have concluded is that words which are not received by the people to whom they are spoken may return to the source individual. It is not the sound waves in the air which return, but the spiritual substance of those words. That individual then makes a decision whether to defend those words or to receive them back. If he receives them back, they become void, of no effect, and the people who heard them forget or ignore the message. If, on the other hand, the speaker does not shrink back from that which he has spoken, the substance of those words remains out there accomplishing what they were sent out to do, according to the faith behind them.

Once I understood these principles, I discovered how easy it is to increase the authority of what I say. After a meeting I determine in my heart that I will not shrink back from believing the things I have taught.

I also find amazing strength in the support of someone I trust. For example, if my wife or a friend makes a reassuring comment to me after a meeting, such as, "You did good," I find an agreement that gives me strength. That agreement is not as powerful if it comes from someone who might be just trying to flatter me, but when it comes from someone who I know will be honest with me, I find that their simple reaffirming words enable me to stand free from "rebounding" words. More importantly, it seems to add authority to what I have said, making my words stay out there with greater power to accomplish what I have sent them to do.

Comprehending these principles shines light on why Jesus

instructed His disciples to brush the dust off their feet if people did not accept their message (Matt. 10:14). That act helped establish what they had said. It not only protected them from spiritual bombardment, but also kept their words from being erased in the minds of those who heard.

I use the terminology, "spiritual bombardment." This is what actually is happening. As the hearers reject the things spoken to them, the words go back to the speaker. It is not always a conscious rejection, but more a realignment of their own thoughts so that there is no resting place for the new ideas which were presented to them. Those dislodged words then return to the originator. The bombardment consists of spiritual substance, yet sometimes it may be physically felt, especially upon the forehead or face of the speaker, leaving them feeling as if they were beaten. For this reason God made the prophet's forehead harder than flint when he had to deliver a strong message to stubborn people (Ezek. 3:9).

Not all words carry the same weight or authority. The spiritual force is determined by that individual's faith, intensity of conviction, passion, agreement with others and depth of decision. When people with great authority speak, it impacts many lives. Another person could verbalize the same things and very few, if any, people would be influenced.

The greater the time and sacrifice invested in the formulation of a thought, the greater will be the force behind it. Usually, there is more authority in the written word than in everyday conversation because the writer has taken more time to think through exactly what he desires to say.

Some words carry authority that compel others to repeat them. For example, a certain speaker with much authority may speak a profound truth to one or two people. In such cases, it is as if that truth cannot be contained within just their spirits. The listeners will be compelled to repeat it again and again until the substance of those words has been distributed to however many people it takes to contain the related authority.

Not just truth contains authority, but all words have some level of substance to them. Enough thought may be put into a new idea, story or even a joke so that it bears repeating and sharing with others. Sometimes in telling a joke, people feel as if there were a little bit more "juice" in it, and so it may be told one more time. Eventually, however, the substance wears out and no one else will hear or receive it, unless someone adds their own spiritual substance in telling the story. People experience these forces in their daily lives all the time, but they rarely identify from where they come.

The more personal responsibility people accept for their own words, the more authority that accompanies them. When a person accepts responsibility for many lives or for the distant future, the spiritual substance within her words increases in a corresponding fashion. Words or messages also have authority even when they did not originate with the speaker, but rather were taken from the beliefs of a larger group of people. As the spiritual substance is drawn within a person, that person may pass it on and, hence, transmit the authority of others.

Communication between two people is both a spiritual and natural process. We are aware of the sound waves which carry our words from one to another, but we can also identify the spiritual transmission that takes place. I dare say that the spiritual transmission is more important than the natural. In many cases, people communicate without actually speaking vocally. It is common for people who are bonded together in spirit to know to some degree what the other is thinking. Of course, effective communication typically requires that sound waves actually travel from one individual to the ears of another, but there also must be a transmission of spiritual energy.

Since words carry spiritual substance, people must receive that substance if they are truly to hear and be changed by those words. Unless there is some kind of open door in the spirit between two people, they will be unable to communicate effectively. This open door can be either through a spiritual bonding between the two individuals or it can be through the yielding of one person's heart to receive from the other.

Paul described this openness of heart to the Corinthians:

> *Our mouth has spoken freely to you, O Corinthians, our heart is open wide..in a like exchange—I speak as to children—open wide to us also.*
>
> (II Cor. 6:11-13)

The apostle John wrote in his first letter about one area in which a spiritual union must exist between two people before they can communicate. He wrote:

> *We are from God; he who knows God listens to us; he who is not from God does not listen to us.*
>
> (I John 4:6a)

Jesus stated this same principle to the Pharisees, saying:

> *"He who is of God hears the words of God; for this reason you do not hear them, because you are not of God."*
>
> (John 8:47)

In these passages we see how people's spiritual condition determines whether or not they will be able to communicate.

These principles are applicable whether or not a person is a Christian. The depth of spiritual union between two people determines their ability to communicate. Any two people can talk about superficial things, but the deeper the content, the deeper the spiritual interaction involved. When two people's hearts are directed in different directions, they will have a difficult time communicating.

The experienced public speaker realizes that before he can communicate effectively, he must have access to the people's hearts. Telling a joke often opens the hearts of the listeners. As does sharing personal experiences and shared feelings.

The anointing of God upon a minister's life also opens hearts. It causes the spirits of the listeners to "hear" the words. King David praised God, *"Who subdues my people under me"* (Ps. 144:2d). There must be either a bonding in spirit or a yielding of the listener to the speaker before there can be effective communication. With the anointing, God causes the people to yield. His presence in some way manifests, and in His presence every knee bows and every person bows in spirit.

As the Spirit of God abides upon a group of people, communication is very easy. On Pentecost Day we even see the disciples speaking in tongues and the people hearing it in their own languages. In contrast, when demonic influence or closed hearts are present, two people can sit side-by-side and completely misinterpret what the other is saying.

It is easy to determine whether or not other people are receptive to what you are saying. You can sense when their hearts are directed toward you. You can be standing in a store at the checkout counter and "feel" a person standing next to you who wants to talk. On the other hand, you may stand in front of a large group and sense their resistance. Your child, your spouse, your brother, your neighbor, all people, open or close the doors of their heart. Every person is aware of these principles to one degree or another.

Words have an almost mysterious way of finding people

who are bonded to the speaker. The hearers do not even have to be present when the speaker speaks to hear his words. For example, one Sunday morning pastor Josh spoke a powerful message from the depth of his heart to his congregation. Ivan loves pastor Josh, but Ivan was unable to attend the meeting that morning because he was home sick in bed. Two days later Carol, who was in the meeting, saw Ivan, and in a short time she was stirred within to share some of the key points which pastor Josh spoke. Even though Ivan was not present, the words his pastor spoke eventually reached his ears.

Another example of this phenomenon is seen in the ministry of Sheri. She was a missionary to India for 20 years before she returned home. She loved the people of India and those people loved her deeply. She was not able to go back to the mission field but occasionally she shared in churches about her experiences during those years. One day she was speaking in a certain church, and the Holy Spirit came upon her very powerfully to share her love for those people with whom she had labored. Sitting in the congregation was a young boy who eventually grew up and went to the very same mission field. Something seemed to impact his spirit that day, and he eventually carried the words of Sheri back to the same people.

Words can travel even beyond the limits I have mentioned thus far. For example, a preacher may stand before a congregation of a hundred people, but his heart is extending toward thousands or even an entire nation. Because of that, his words will have more force behind them than that which can be contained by those people present. Many of them may be compelled to go out and share with others. Someone eventually may get on the radio and pass on some of that spiritual substance. The message may come across in a different form, perhaps even years later, but it will come forth. The number of people impacted by a speaker is not limited by the immediate audience, but by the number of people he loves and by the extent of his spiritual authority.

Picture this force when we talk about the words of our Lord. He said, *"My sheep hear My voice."* His sheep are those whose hearts are pointed toward Him. The words of our Lord find people in whatever country or generation they live. Having perfect faith, Jesus had the audacity to declare that His words would never pass away.

We can also talk about negative words reaching certain people. For example, Bill was gossiping about Sheryl. Three days later, the words Bill spoke were reported back to Sheryl who was devastated. They were not the exact words, because gossip often changes as it passes from one person to another. However, the negative substance of the gossip was carried until it reached Sheryl.

Ecclesiastes 10:20 teaches us that negative words spoken in secret will fly like a bird to the ears of kings, leaders and wealthy people. Notice the association with authority that words follow. When something negative is said about a person of authority, those words tend to reach his or her ears sooner or later.

Yes, words carry spiritual substance with them. That substance dissipates according to the faith behind those words. The greater the authority, heart conviction and responsibility accepted by the speaker, the more enduring will be the substance of those words.

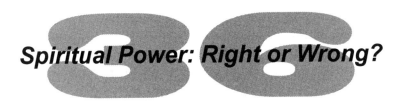

Spiritual Power: Right or Wrong?

Every human being uses the spiritual abilities I have been discussing whether or not they realize it. Even people who think only in terms of natural forces have a spirit which extends beyond their physical bodies. Every human being to some degree releases spiritual substance with their words. Every person exerts unseen forces upon the people and things around them. All of us were created with a spirit, and that spirit has influence upon both the spiritual and natural worlds 24 hours each day.

When is it appropriate to use these spiritual abilities? When should a Christian apply these principles by a conscious decision? We should be especially interested in a person taking the initiative in these things. What can we initiate ourselves, and what should we wait for God to sovereignly inspire us to do?

To answer these questions, I must introduce another biblical concept. In several places in the original Greek Bible the word *metron* is used. In English it is usually translated "measure." We are told in Romans 12:3 that to every person is given a measure of faith. In II Corinthians 10:13, Paul wrote:

But we will not boast beyond our measure, but

within the measure of the sphere which God apportioned to us as a measure, to reach even as far as you.

Paul explained that he would not go beyond his own God given sphere of influence or beyond his own metron. In passages such as these, "metron" refers to the level of faith, sphere of influence or the spiritual authority which God has given a person.

Each person, Christian or non-Christian, has a specific metron. It includes everything over which a person has responsibility. A parent's metron includes his or her children. A businesswoman's metron is over her business. A policeman has a metron which includes the responsibilities given to him. A woman who owns her own home has God-given authority to do what she wants with her home. A teacher has a metron over a classroom and the students. All authority ultimately comes from God, and whether that authority is over natural or spiritual things, one's metron encompasses it.

Every Person Has a Metron

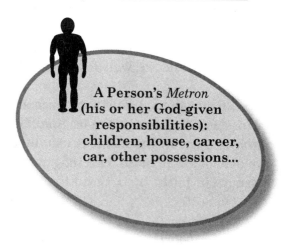

A Person's *Metron* (his or her God-given responsibilities): children, house, career, car, other possessions...

Only Jesus has an unlimited metron. John 3:34-35 tells us that He has the Spirit without measure, that is, without limits to His metron. There are no boundaries to His metron, and the Spirit flows out of Him to whatever extent He chooses.

We have limits to our metrons. Our authority is related to what God has presently entrusted to us. Paul wrote that for his own life he would not go beyond his sphere of influence (II Cor. 10:13). He knew the limits of his God-given authority. We as Christians have authority in both the natural and the spiritual realms, but we must understand the limits of our own metrons.

Some Christians may have a difficult time understanding this "limited authority," because the emphasis in their teaching has been that we, as believers, can do *all* things through Christ Jesus, and that we have been seated with our Lord in heavenly places far above all rule and authority. Their theology dictates a belief that Christians already have all authority. It is true that we have all things in Christ, but there is also a reality to our growing into them. God deals with us as His children. As we prove faithful, He releases to us that which He has promised.

This relationship between the authority promised to us and the authority we actually experience is parallel to how the Hebrew people took the Promised Land. It was all given to them by God. The land was theirs by promise. However, after they crossed the Jordan River and entered the land of promise, they could not possess it when or how they chose. God instructed them to take the cities in the specific order He would indicate to them. God also warned them that if they attempted to take cities into which He was not leading them, they would be defeated (Ex. 23:20-30; Deut. 7:22). Even though the whole land was theirs by promise, they could only occupy it as they obeyed God and progressively filled what they had already taken. In similar fashion, the fullness of God's power and authority has been promised to the believer. However, our experience of it is progressive as we step out, faithfully doing what God leads each step of the way.

Jesus said, *"For whoever has, to him more shall be given"* (Mark 4:25a). "To have" something in this sense is to accept the responsibilities which God has delegated to us. As we fulfill our present responsibilities, God increases our authority or in other words, He increases our metron.

Within a person's present metron, he has authority. This means that a person has the right to do what he desires to do. I am not saying that you can do whatever you want and get away with it. No. God will hold you accountable for everything you do. What I am saying here is that you have the "right" to do what you want to do within your metron because God has given you the authority to do it. Of course, you should endeavor to accomplish the will of God within all that He has assigned to you. But God gives you the authority to work within your metron.

Because you have authority, you can take the initiative. That is what authority means. It is in your hands. You decide. For example, if you are a homeowner, you have the right to decide what color you want to paint your house. If you have children, God expects you to take the initiative to provide for them and to raise them. It is your job to take whatever initiative is necessary to do what needs to be done within your metron.

The anointing of God provides the wisdom and the direction of God for a person to know how to manage everything within his God-given metron. I John 2:27 tells us:

> *As for you, the anointing which you received from Him abides in you, and you have no need for anyone to teach you; but as His anointing teaches you*

about all things, and is true and is not a lie, and
just as it has taught you, you abide in Him.

The believer has within himself the "knowing" concerning how and when he is supposed to act within his God-given authority. God's understanding already has been deposited there. The anointing "teaches." It supernaturally guides a person concerning when and how to act.

In the area of one's anointing, the Christian does not need God to visit supernaturally to tell him what to do every step of the way. God has already given him the wisdom. It resides within him. Just as a child matures and no longer needs parents to tell him what clothes to wear, so also a believer should not expect God to speak to him supernaturally and tell him what to do when the anointing already is directing him. The Christian is wrong in waiting around for God's additional external direction when he already has the internal anointing guiding in the area of his metron.

To understand these principles, look at some biblical examples. In the life of the priest, Eli, we can see how God expected him to take the initiative to exercise his own authority. Eli's metron included both his sons and the temple worship. Those were his God-given responsibilities but he failed, and his own sons began committing evil acts in the temple (I Sam. 2:12-17). We are told that Eli sinned by not stopping his sons (I Sam. 3:13). God did not have to come down sovereignly upon Eli and motivate him to fulfill his responsibilities. It was Eli's job to motivate himself. He was supposed to take the initiative, because God already had delegated the authority to him.

Look at Moses. It was in his heart to set the Hebrew people free from their captivity; however, as a young man he was unable to do so and he left Egypt defeated, running from Pharaoh. At that point in his life, he had no God-given authority to set the Hebrews free. Later in his life, he received a call from God to return to Egypt and deliver the people. When God gave Moses the authority, Moses had power to release amazing signs and wonders to carry out the will of God.

An interesting event occurred as Moses led the Hebrews out of Egypt to the edge of the Red Sea. It was there that Moses desperately cried out to God to help them. God's response to Moses in that situation is eye opening. He said:

> *"Why are you crying out to Me? Tell the sons of Israel to go forward."*
>
> (Ex. 14:15b)

God rebuked Moses. Why? Because Moses already had the authority to bring the people out of captivity. Moses was waiting for God to do something, while God was waiting for Moses to do something. Moses did not need to look to God for the directive to divide the sea. He needed to go forward; it was his responsibility. Even though spiritual power was required, Moses was supposed to take the initiative because God already had commissioned him and given him the related authority.

God intervenes supernaturally when He wants us to go beyond our present metron. That is, when He speaks and empowers us in additional ways. He has the authority to tell us to do whatever He desires. For us to rightfully go beyond our metron requires that He impart new authority into us. Only then can we effectively accomplish His will. Those steps beyond our present authority must be initiated by God. He has to tell us when to take the related steps. We do not have the authority to initiate such steps because they are not within our present metron.

See how this applies to our lives? Pastor Mark, who has oversight of a flock, does not need a visitation from God to tell him everything he must do. He already has the anointing within him to do what needs to be done. He has the tools, the wisdom and the guidance of his own God-given anointing to enable him. However, if Pastor Mark desires to minister outside of his congregation, he should seek the additional guidance and direction of God to proceed.

Going Beyond Our Metron When God Initiates It

GOD

A Person's *Metron* (his or her God-given responsibilities): children, house, career, car, other possessions...

The apostle Paul exercised authority over those who were within his metron. However, it would have been wrong for Paul to extend his spiritual influence to a people over whom God had not given him authority.

Whenever people today extend their spirits beyond the limits of their God-given authority, they are *usurping authority*. They may, whether or not they realize it, release evil spiritual influences. God's power works within God-given authority. If a person, therefore, extends his spirit to other people wrongly, those people may come under demonic attack. If he releases spiritual substance through his words upon things which are not under his authority, evil energies may be activated.

It is in this fashion that all the gifts, empowerings and spiritual authorities work. When we are confronted with things requiring more authority than we presently possess, we need the Holy Spirit to come upon us and impart the additional authority needed. The first time God is moving someone into a new realm, God must initiate it. If He only wants to use that person in that area one time, then He will not impart the ongoing authority. The only time a person may rightfully take the initiative to operate in some level of the spirit is if, indeed, God has given him the "abiding authority" and the corresponding anointing which will "abide" within him. Once God has given a person the authority, there will be an inner knowing and an inner guidance system to lead him as to when and how to establish the will of God within his expanded metron. If God has given someone specific authority to accomplish some task, then it is that person's responsibility: "Of him who has much, much will be required." It is, then, the individual's responsibility to take the necessary initiative.

As we continue, I will discuss sensing things in the spiritual realm, influencing angels and demons, out-of-body experiences, looking into the future, interpreting dreams, etc. All of these discussions must be understood in terms of God-given authority.

It is with this understanding that we can see the fundamental evil involved in witchcraft, occult practices, New Age exercises, astrology, certain experiments in parapsychology, etc. Christians need not deny the reality of these forms of spiritual activities. What we renounce is the usurping of spiritual authority. When a witch releases spiritual power upon another person, she is exercising authority which God has not given to her. When a student of transcendental meditation projects his spirit to another place, he is violating spiritual rights. When a woman uses extrasensory perception (ESP), to discover information which is outside of her metron, she is opening her spirit to receive things which are not within her God-given rights. When a medium calls a departed soul back from the dead, he is exercising authority which God forbids (Deut. 18:10-11). When New Agers meditate on worldwide peace and try to loose it into this realm, they may have well-meaning goals, but unless God initiates such worldwide releasing of energy, it may activate demonic influences. Any attempt by people to go beyond their God-given authority is evil.

These principles are vital for the Christian's life. When Christians go beyond their present level of authority, they expose themselves to demonic attack. God warned the Hebrews that they must take the Promised Land only in the timing that He ordained, or the enemies would become too numerous for them and they would be consumed (Ex. 23:20-30). In similar fashion, Christians who step beyond their metrons often experience undue pain and heartache (explained in the next chapter).

Some people, as they read these pages, may be wondering how to apply all the spiritual principles that I have been discussing throughout this book. It is precisely at this point of God-given authority that you must begin. For what has God actually given you responsibility? That is what you must embrace and toward which you must direct your energy. Do not try to change the whole world if you have not established the peace of Jesus Christ in your own life. Work on your home and your relationships. Spend time with your children. Get your finances in order before you try to exert authority over society. Release the presence of God into that which is immediately around you, and let God exalt you one step at a time. Begin right where you are presently.

Manipulations of the Mind

It is important to identify the relationship between people's thinking processes and the emanation of their spirits. As a woman focuses her heart and thoughts, spiritual energy may be projected accordingly. That spiritual flow may influence her own being, the natural world and the spiritual world. It is helpful to recognize all three of these areas and how they are influenced.

First, as Christians focus their minds upon the Word of God, they release the blessings of God into their own lives. Romans 12:2 exhorts us to *"be transformed by the renewing of your mind...."* The Christian is wise to meditate upon the Word of God continually. As one does, one's being will be brought more into alignment with the will of God.

Second, spiritual energy emanates out to conform the natural world to God's will. The kingdom of God is released as faith works in the heart of the believer.

Third, the spiritual world is influenced by our thoughts. Every time Christians reject temptation, in some way they are frustrating the plans of Satan. Every time believers obey the biblical mandate to think on that which is pure and holy (Phil. 4:8), they are releasing God's will.

Every human being is influencing the spiritual world every day, whether or not they realize it. At times, people even exert major influence upon spiritual entities. In the Book of Daniel we read about a struggle that went on in the spiritual dimension while Daniel fasted and prayed for 21 days (Dan. 10:1-14). As Daniel prayed, an angel advanced toward Daniel but was withstood by the *"prince of the kingdom of Persia."* Finally, the angel succeeded and Daniel received the answer he was seeking. There was a real relationship between Daniel's prayer and the battle in the spirit world.

It is not only Christians who have this authority to affect the spiritual world. As I have explained, non-Christians also have the power to bind or loose, but not in relation to the kingdom of God. In verse 8 of Jude we read about the activity of evil people who challenge spirit beings in the spiritual world:

> *Yet in the same way these men, also by dreaming, defile the flesh, and reject authority, and revile angelic majesties.*

Notice the mechanism by which these people do their evil deeds: *"by dreaming."* Dreaming in this context is not talking about the visions we receive while asleep. It refers here to the manipulation of the thoughts within one's own mind. When people, Christians or non-Christians, consciously alter the thoughts they have within themselves, they are, at times, exerting authority over the spiritual realm.

It is this "manipulation of the mind" that we need to examine further. When Yogis and New Agers talk about meditation, they usually are referring to actively conforming the visions and ideas in their minds to their desired goals. They will set aside time to sit and think along certain lines. It is believed that such time spent forming one's thought patterns will produce that which is envisioned.

When is this according to God's will and when is this power

used wrongly? To answer this, we must bring in our understanding of metron and God-given authority. Though we last quoted a Bible passage referring to an evil exercising of power, do not lose sight of our goal of discovering when the Christian should use such authority. This authority should be exercised in line with an individual's metron.

For example, think about a Christian named Frank who had a terrible inferiority complex. Because of his past experiences and conditioning, Frank had a difficult time holding down a job or even communicating with other people. Frank went to counseling and over the course of two years, Frank's pastor helped him to develop new thought patterns. Whenever Frank faces a challenging situation today, he meditates on the promises of God and such Bible verses as, *"I can do all things through Him who strengthens me"* (Phil. 4:13). Frank is now living a productive life and he no longer struggles with thoughts of inferiority, as he did during his earlier years. Frank has succeeded at manipulating the visions and thoughts in his mind.

Is this according to God's will? Of course it is. God gave Frank authority over his own life, and he should do what is necessary to succeed. It is important to note that Frank was dealing within his own metron, and he was bringing his thoughts into conformity with God's will. The apostle Paul exhorted Christians to take *"every thought captive to the obedience of Christ"* (II Cor. 10:5). Frank was doing what the Bible tells us to do.

If, however, people—Christians or non-Christian—manipulate the visions in their minds beyond their metrons or contrary to the will of God, then evil spiritual exercises may be employed. For example, if a woman envisions herself dominating other people, greedily accumulating wealth, conquering her opponents, ruling over her employer, etc., the issue of usurping authority is raised. Some of the positive-thinking techniques being taught today cross over into evil exercises of spiritual authority. Even Christians sometimes are guilty of wrongly manipulating their own thoughts while they are "praying." Wherever people actively alter the thought patterns in their own minds, they may release spiritual energies. Those energies will be evil if and when the person has no God-given authority in the related area. What I am saying is that we need to be careful with some of the aggressive battles which we wage in our minds.

The ministries today which are referred to as "inner healing" or "healing of the memories" should be considered here. The standard procedure in such ministries is first of all to help individuals remember bad experiences in the past, and then to help them walk through those times in their thought-life, all in an effort to let God heal them. Typically, individuals receiving ministry are asked to envision Jesus walking into their lives at the moments of crises, comforting them and helping them through whatever the trials were. One of the works accomplished through such inner healing ministries is that the people receiving ministry change their perceptions of experiences in the past and, hence, act differently in the present.

Now, some Christians have categorically condemned all such activities as evil. That is not my intent here. In fact, I clearly acknowledge that millions of people have been healed emotionally and set free by sincere, valid ministries using these methods. The time they are in violation of God's authority is either when they are applied as mechanistic techniques without the leading of the Holy Spirit or when the visions formed in the mind of the individual are not in line with God's will. Understanding this caution, we need to bless and encourage ministries which, indeed, are helping others think God's thoughts and clean up the wounds and bad memories of the past.

This subject of controlling thoughts has implications beyond one's own personhood or success. There are thought patterns related to other people that also should be taken captive. For example, if a mother has thoughts about her child being physically hurt, she should do in the natural what she can to assure her child's safety, but she should also cast those thoughts out of her mind. If she continues to focus on her child being harmed, she may actually start believing in her heart that it will happen and, to some degree, release spiritual forces to allow it. Remember what Jesus taught us— that which we loose is loosed. There may be times when the mother in our example is unable to rid herself of the negative thoughts. In such cases, she should become more forceful, using the Name of Jesus to bind the work of the enemy. It may also be helpful to enlist the support of another Christian, who, by agreeing in prayer, can more powerfully diffuse the strategies of Satan. By aggressively rejecting evil thoughts, the mother will bring peace of mind to herself and bind evil from coming upon her child.

Similarly, a person will release blessings upon other people by simply believing the best about them. If negative thoughts about other people are constantly rising, then a person may have to assertively and aggressively reject those impressions. The apostle Paul explained that he chose to recognize no person according to the flesh but to see them as God sees them (II Cor. 5:16). I am not talking about being naive or blinding ourselves to the evils of other people, but I am simply teaching the biblical principle of controlling our own thoughts toward others.

These truths also have implications for the whole world of the spirit. As I mentioned earlier, people can influence the activities of spirit-beings by manipulating the visions within their minds. Sometimes long seasons of prayer accompanied by fasting can release tremendous forces in the spiritual realm to accomplish that which is fixed in the mind. However, not all such exercises are in line with God's will. This issue is so important, I will address it more clearly in chapter 38, when we talk about out-of-body experiences.

The truth is this: by manipulating the visions in our mind and authoritatively rejecting certain thoughts, we are exercising spiritual authority. That should be encouraged when a person is moving within his or her own metron. However, it is wrong if a person extends his or her spirit beyond that which God has ordained for his or her life at the present.

There are some non-Christian teachings today which take the principles of thought manipulation so far as to claim that a person can "create their own reality." By this, they mean that a man who carefully controls his every thought and only thinks upon what he desires in life, literally will change the world around him to conform to his images. A woman who is living in a home where her husband physically and emotionally abuses her may be told to create her own reality with her thoughts. She may be taught that if she sees her husband as loving and gentle, he will eventually become what she believes. Another example is of the man who is in serious financial trouble, and he is taught to think of himself as wealthy and having no difficulties.

Again, I emphasize that our thoughts influence the emanation of our spirits, and that our spiritual energies influence this world. However, it is wrong and dangerous to go so far as to say that we can "create our own reality" simply by thinking a certain way. There are many people in mental institutions today who think they are something which they are not. The insane man who jumps off a roof will crash to the ground, no matter how much he envisions himself flying. Likewise, the woman who is trapped in an abusive home should try to keep a positive attitude, but she also needs to face reality and get practical help. The man in financial trouble must not be allowed to deny his difficulties. That is not faith. That is not Christian. Certainly, he should be encouraged to believe God and even to renew his mind to the fact that he can overcome his troubles, but he must not deny reality nor use positive thinking principles as an excuse to not work hard and pay off those bills.

Some Christians have misunderstood the principles of faith and gone so far as to live their lives denying reality. The Bible clearly tells us that faith without works is dead (James 2:26). We influence the world around us not merely by thinking but by determining God's will and then by acting in faith. Thoughts which hinder us from acting correctly should be cast down (yes, manipulated in our minds). Thoughts contrary to God's thoughts must be overcome. Then we will have the spiritual energy to act and change this natural world.

In all mind-renewing principles, we need to recognize where the power originates. Sometimes people think of any good result as coming from the mechanism itself. Of course, there is power in the human spirit itself, and controlling thoughts will release that power. However, Christians should be renewing their minds according to the Word of God. God's power abides within His words (Heb. 4:12; II Tim. 3:16-17; Rom. 1:16). When the Christian meditates on God's Word, God's blessings are released (Ps. 1:2-3).

There is substance within God's words. That substance contains the power of God. The words themselves are living and active and sharp (Heb. 4:12). Believers are not left with merely the power of the human spirit. They must ingest within their spirits the words of God. Then mind-renewing principles are divinely powerful (II Cor. 10:3-5).

Allow me to summarize by saying that Christians should bring their own thoughts in line with God's Word. Sometimes this even requires an assertive stance in the spirit, whereby contrary thoughts are forcefully rejected. This authority should be exercised over everything pertaining to an individual's own metron. Christians should think positively about the future. They should reject thoughts of condemnation, negativity and failure. They should also think positively about other people and the world around them. When Christians assert authority in this fashion over the thoughts within their own minds, they release the spiritual energy within according to the will of God. When meditating upon the words of God, God's power flows out accordingly.

Out-of-body Experiences

As I mentioned earlier, it is from the Bible that we get the terminology out-of-body experience. It was the apostle Paul who explained that he was taken up into heaven, *"whether in the body or out of the body,"* he was not sure (II Cor. 12:23). Of course, there are many such phenomena reported in the non-Christian context today, and I am not giving credence to all of them. We need to determine what is true and what is false, what is right and what is wrong.

Witches are often pictured as riding on a broom, which is a symbol of their practice of sending their spirits to another location. The medicine men of certain tribal groups and those steeped in black magic are said to be able to send their spirits into other places, and then watch what is going on at those locations. There has been all kinds of folklore developed around the mystical stories of medicine men, witches and warlocks. We would be naive to believe most of it, but it is worth considering what they can and cannot do.

What they can actually do is clouded by the fact that things in the spiritual realm are not perceived by people as logical, accurate information. As I explained in chapter 2, the spirit perceives things in the forms of impulses, words, visions, impressions, etc. When a witch, therefore, sends her spirit to another place, that which is perceived does not come to her in clear thought patterns, as we typically understand them. Her mind is in an altered state of consciousness. All impressions received must be interpreted, and images are only partial, at best. Stories that have developed from the evil use of this power are exaggerated very easily. In addition, because the witch is often exercising authority beyond that which God has given her, demonic activity may be involved. Satan, who is the father of lies (John 8:44), distorts visions and spiritual reality any way he can for his own purposes. Witches and others who attempt to operate in the spiritual realm typically are very deceived about what they are perceiving and accomplishing.

Another form of spirit emanation being used today is called *transcendental meditation* (or TM). Some advocates have tried to remove the magical, mystical elements and present TM under the guise of scientific investigation. The related techniques are being taught in some universities and high schools as a part of normal classroom activity.

It is helpful to identify what is actually happening in such spiritual exercises. First, we should ask, "What leaves the physical body in these experiences? Is it the spirit or the soul?" When people without a biblical worldview try to address this question they offer many confusing answers because they do not even understand the difference between the spirit and the soul. They sometimes refer to their practices as soul travel, when they are really engaged in spirit emanation. Having no biblical basis to understand the nature of a person, they rarely know what takes place during such experiences.

In preceding chapters, I have been discussing various emanations of a person's spirit, that is, the spiritual energy within a person reaching out of their soul and body, to touch other people, places or things. This is common to every human being.

It is also possible for a person's soul to be in a different location than the body. These experiences are not as common. When Paul was taken up into Paradise, he was not sure whether he was in the body or out of the body. Such terminology implies that he himself, spirit and soul (maybe even bodily), was lifted into the throne room of God. When a person's soul is taken to another location, he will experience that new location to some degree, as if actually present in that place. He will see it or touch it or experience it in some tangible way. On the other hand, if only his spirit is reaching out, he will typically have a mere intuitive feeling concerning what is happening in that other location or with the people there.

Another point for our understanding concerns the dimension in which a person's spirit or soul travels. Non-Christians involved in projecting their spirits and/or souls often describe their activities as *astral projection*. By this terminology, they are referring to a person sending his spirit or soul out of his body through a spiritual dimension, to which they refer as an *astral plane*. This terminology is deceiving. When they use the phrase *astral plane*, they are implying that there is a spiritual dimension out there which is much the same as a road on which we could drive our cars. It is true that the spiritual dimension is real, but we must not see it as neutral grounds on which people can travel safely.

As a Bible-believing Christian, I would rather refer to that spiritual dimension as the "second heaven." We understand that the third heaven is the throne room of God where He Himself dwells (II Cor. 12:2-4). In contrast, the first heaven is the natural realm above us, including the sky, the clouds, the stars and everything you can see as you look up at night or during the day. If you stepped outside and looked up, we could say you are looking at the first heaven. It is the "second heaven" which we understand as the spiritual dimension encompassing and superimposed upon this natural world. It is in the second heaven that angels and demons interact. It is not up in the highest realm where God dwells in unapproachable light. Nor is it the natural sky or region of the stars, but it is in the spiritual world corresponding to the natural world in which we live.

Most of the spiritual activity about which we have been talking occurs neither in the third heaven nor in the natural heavens. When a woman projects her spirit and/or soul, she is projecting it through the second heaven. When people project their spirits and/or souls, they are not traveling a neutral, abandoned astral plane. They are sending a part of themselves into a world in which spirit-beings act, a world where definite territories and authority structures exist. Demons are active there, and God's angels are also at work in that realm.

When people let their spirits flow out over their own God-given metron, they are not violating authority. However, when people project their spirits beyond their metrons into the second heaven, they may be crossing authority lines. It is dangerous. Demonic powers have the authority to hurt people there. And they do.

It is not only demons which may be encountered there. God has spirit-beings which also deserve respect. When Elisha's servant had his eyes opened, he saw into the spiritual realm and beheld the mountains around filled with horses and chariots of fire (II Kings 6:17). For another example, look at what Ezekiel saw: four living beings in the middle of spinning wheels with fire and lightning flashing forth (Ezek. 1:1-14). The wheels, we are told, extend all the way from the surface of Earth to the throne room of God above. A terrifying sight it was to Ezekiel. It was just as terrifying for the apostle John to see in the spiritual realm some of the beings which serve God, as he recorded in the book of Revelation.

When people extend their spirits and/or souls into the second heaven, they may be crossing established authority structures and may be violating those authority lines.

An example of such violations can be seen in the passage we read earlier from the book of Jude:

> *And angels who did not keep their own domain... as Sodom and Gomorrah and the cities around them...in the same way these men, also by dreaming, defile the flesh, and reject authority, and revile angelic majesties.*
>
> (Jude vs. 6-8)

These evil men were going beyond their authority, as angels who do not *"keep their own domain."* By dreaming, in the sense of manipulating the visions within their own minds, they were challenging spirit entities. This passage is primarily referring to evil people who envision themselves as conquering kingdoms, oppressing other peoples and dominating areas which God has not given to them. As people manipulate the visions in their minds in such fashion, they actually may exert forces upon established authorities, either angels or demons.

Similar violations can happen by well-meaning Christians. For example, if an intercessory team begins praying against some spiritual force, they may begin to see visions of certain evil spirit-beings bow to them; at that time, they may actually be exerting forces upon demons which exist in the second heaven. Those demons may indeed bow, especially if there is unity among the intercessors and they have united their hearts through intense fasting and extended periods of prayer. I am not condemning all such intercessory prayer. What I am doing is teaching how to stay within the limits of God-given authority. Prayer warriors should boldly take and

267

hold the spiritual territory which God already has given to them. They also should move into new areas as they sense the Holy Spirit leading them. However, it is the overzealous, even arrogant challenges against the devil which we must warn Christians to avoid. It is wrong and dangerous.

Jude went on to explain:

> But Michael the archangel, when he disputed with the devil and argued about the body of Moses, did not dare pronounce against him a railing judgment, but said, "The Lord rebuke you!" But these men revile the things which they do not understand; and the things which they know by instinct, like unreasoning animals, by these things they are destroyed. Woe to them!
>
> (Jude vs. 6-11a)

Notice that the people who engage in such spiritual violations of authority may even be *"destroyed"* by those spirit-beings whom they revile.

We can see this truth in operation in the world today. When people project their spirits into the second heaven where they have no authority, wicked demonic encounters can occur. Demons may come to use a person for their own benefit or they simply may come to steal, kill and destroy. Deception often creeps in. Thought patterns frequently become twisted. The spirit of the person may be projected to such a great extent that the spiritual energy left in his mind is diminished, and rational thought is no longer possible. Bizarre behavior patterns sometimes become established in those involved in such activities. There are people in mental institutions today as a result of such encounters. Sometimes a person's spirit will leave his body to such a degree that there is no longer enough spiritual energy resident within the body to maintain physical and/or mental health. Those stepping into Satan's territory are open targets for his wicked schemes.

Even evil people who teach others how to project their spirits and/or souls are aware of some of the related dangers. Witches are known to experience sudden attacks of illness and emotional torment. People involved in transcendental meditation commonly go through periods of depression, collapse of relationships and financial disaster. There are several books written by New Age advocates giving testimonies of people who have suffered tremendously after going too far in such spiritual exercises. Although these groups do not stop their evil activities, they are somewhat aware of the dangers and sometimes even warn their own trainees to beware.

If the heathens who do not know God are cautious, how much more should Christians who believe the Bible be wise to these truths? As people exalt themselves beyond their metrons, they extend themselves beyond God's protection and, therefore, open themselves to demonic activity. This warning is for the Christian and the non-Christian.

On the other hand, God sometimes will carry a person through the second heaven. He has authority to do so. When the Holy Spirit initiates it, the person is safe. To be in God's will is to be within His protection.

There are many examples in the Bible of second heaven experiences. Thumb through the pages of the Old Testament prophets and pick out phrases that talk about visions or of being taken to another place. For example Ezekiel wrote:

In the visions of God He brought me into the land of Israel and set me on a very high mountain....
(Ezek. 40:2)

Then he brought me to the porch of the temple....
(Ezek. 40:48)

269

The hand of the Lord was upon me, and He brought me out by the Spirit of the Lord and set me down in the middle of the valley....

(Ezek. 37:1)

There are several similar accounts in the New Testament of second-heaven experiences (e.g., Acts 10:37; 10:9-20; 16:9).

Understanding that it is only within God's authority that we act, Christians should be open to second-heaven experiences. When Christians yield to the Holy Spirit, they may find themselves being taken to another place spiritually. As I mentioned earlier, intercessors extend their spiritual influences to those for whom they pray, but they may also go a step further and actually be taken to another location in their spirit and/or soul. Many believers have also been carried to other locations while worshiping God.

Such experiences are true and should not be rejected. They should be judged as all revelations and spiritual phenomena should be judged (I Cor. 14:29-32). But we, as Bible-believing people, must be open to all the works of God. God is the God of the second heaven, and individuals who take it upon themselves to travel there are stepping beyond personal authority. However, if God's Spirit takes a Christian through such an experience, let God be God.

A final point worth mentioning is that people often project their spirits into forbidden areas of the spirit world unconsciously. Many have pierced the heavens through intense meditation. Others have lost touch with this world by slipping into their own imaginations. Still others end up drifting into the spirit as a result of sudden breaks in relationships with other people. For example, a woman who is bonded closely in marriage or to a certain group of individuals may at some time experience complete rejection. As a consequence, her own spirit may lose contact with those people. Then if bitterness or anger sets in, she may turn her heart with such force that her spirit is carried away as a kite on the wind. Of course, I am speaking only in terms of comparisons here, but we need to understand that many people, perhaps most, who experience destructive second-heaven encounters, enter without realizing what they are doing.

Proverbs 25:28 tells us:

Like a city that is broken into and without walls
Is a man who has no control over his own spirit.

People who project their spirits out into the spiritual world, and let their spirits wander out there, are as an unprotected city. They are unclothed. They are naked and open for attack. Don't allow that to happen in your life.

Through Space and Time

Now we will investigate how things may be experienced at a distance as one's spirit and/or soul touches the related locations. First, we will consider the experiences through space and then through time.

I have made a distinction between spirit emanation and soul travel. Both entail a portion of a person's being leaving the physical body and reaching to another location. I will not make that distinction in the following discussion; however, keep in mind that if one's soul touches another location, it will be a much fuller experience. When one's spirit reaches out, the individual usually is not aware of what is occurring but on occasion may have an intuitive impression concerning that other place. We can compare the spirit of a person with a film projector which projects images and spiritual impressions upon the screen of the person's soul. The soul is conscious of that with which the spirit has contact, if it is focused and receptive to the spirit. Those impressions are vague and may never be noticed. However, if the entire soul of an individual leaves the body, it will be a much more impacting and memorable experience.

In the Bible, we can read of several amazing incidents of people perceiving things at a location removed from their physical body. We already looked at II Kings 5, where the prophet Elisha confronted his servant Gehazi after Gehazi left the prophet and committed an evil deed. The prophet said to Gehazi upon his return:

"Did not my heart go with you, when the man turned from his chariot to meet you?"

(II Kings 5:26)

The eyes of the prophet's heart "watched" what happened. His spirit literally went out with the servant, and Elisha, who was located physically in another place, became conscious of his servant's act.

The prophet Daniel had many such experiences. One of several recorded in the Book of Daniel reads:

I looked in the vision, and while I was looking I was in the citadel of Susa, which is in the province of Elam; and I looked in the vision and I myself was beside the Ulai Canal.

(Dan. 8:2)

Daniel had been taken by the Spirit of God to a distant location, and he saw as if he actually were present there. Ezekiel, similarly, tells of such experiences:

And the Spirit lifted me up and brought me in a vision by the Spirit of God to the exiles in Chaldea.

(Ezek. 11:24a)

In the New Testament, we can read about the apostle Peter being told by the Holy Spirit that there were three men looking for him and he was supposed to go to them (Acts 10:19-20).

Jesus demonstrated this perception at a distance in several

instances. One example is given in John 1:46-50, where we read about our Lord meeting Nathanael for the first time. As Nathanael came to greet Jesus, our Lord declared a characteristic of Nathanael's life. When Nathanael inquired of Jesus how He knew these things, Jesus said:

> *"Before Philip called you, when you were under the fig tree, I saw you."*

> (John 1:48b)

Jesus said that He *"saw"* Nathanael, even though he was at a distant location.

Each of these examples from the Bible, as well as many present-day experiences, could be explained as a sovereign work of the Holy Spirit, and we, as Christians, could understand that in each incident the Holy Spirit is simply coming upon a person and revealing that which He wants them to know. It is good to give credit to the Spirit of God in such cases, and He often does intervene sovereignly in the affairs of humanity to reveal that which cannot be known through natural means.

However, the biblical understanding we have been developing points to the fact that the spirit of a person has the ability to perceive things. We discover these abilities at work in both the Christian and non-Christian. These spiritual senses do not open only by the sovereign work of the Holy Spirit. The individual's spirit can simply sense things. Of course, we should recognize a sovereign God who is at work within us and outside of us. But believers should understand that God has given them a spirit, just as He has given them a physical body. The spirit has senses just as does the body. The spirit itself can hear, see and perceive things. That is how God created us.

Remember that every human being has a spirit which is

not limited to the confines of the body. Every human being has a spirit which emanates from the heart. A businesswoman who accepts responsibility for her business is sending out her spirit all the time. The pastor who cares for his sheep is bathing those people in the realm of the spirit. Every time people talk with authority, they are emitting spiritual energy. All human beings sense things with which their spirits have contact.

For example, consider the mother who is asleep at home when her daughter gets in an automobile accident across town. Even though that daughter is miles away, the mother may be awakened suddenly, knowing something tragic has happened.

People often feel the pains and troubles of those to whom they are bonded spiritually, even when they are distant. The Bible tells us that when one part of the Body of Christ hurts, we all hurt (I Cor. 12:26). Married couples often sense what their mates are experiencing before anything has been communicated in the natural. People sense things about their children, even if those loved ones are miles away. It is common for people to react and respond to others spiritually before they do naturally.

Many individuals have experienced a "knowing" concerning others, especially if those other people have their hearts turned toward them. For example, when the telephone rings, some individuals have an amazing ability to know who it is that is calling them. If someone is about to meet them unannounced, they will be thinking about that person immediately preceding the encounter. These types of spirit contacts are common, and all of us experience them to some degree.

Not only does the spirit sense at a distance things related to other people, but also to events, circumstances, dangers and opportunities. For example, a businessman who accepts responsibility for his business may have things about his business revealed to him by no naturally understood means. A real estate investor will have a "gut feeling" about an impending investment. An administrator organizing a huge event may experience an uneasiness concerning that which needs more attention. A mother may feel her children, left in another room of the house, making a complete mess of things. People regularly base decisions on what often is called intuition. Many such sensings are real impressions which a person's spirit is perceiving at a distance. This is not evil. It is how God created us.

A very common experience shared by many people is how they perceive things with their spirits as they drive their automobiles. People who do much long-distance driving tend to relax and confidently sit back while they are traveling down the road. In such a posture of soul, their spirits may reach out ahead of them. The spirit then becomes involved in the driving process in such a way that if a car suddenly stops ahead or danger appears on the road, their spirits sense it before their eyes do and they are alerted spiritually. In many such incidents, people are brought to attention just before it is too late. The danger initially was perceived by the spirit.

The spirits of individuals will also reach out and fill their metrons, if they accept responsibility for them. Their spirits then are going to have contact with their areas of God-given authority. Of course, God is the only One who can delegate true authority, but when God delegates to individuals certain metrons, those individuals will have the spiritual abilities to manage them. Their spirits will emanate outward and project back to their conscious minds that which is perceived. All people know things about their own metrons through their spirits.

Such experiences of sensing things at a distance are not necessarily demonic in nature. Of course, there are evil men and women practicing spiritual sensings forbidden by God.

Many of them are assisted in their endeavors by demons who are very willing to become involved in such spiritual exercises. I am not giving approval to any such practices, and I warn all Christians to stay away from such activities.

However, we should recognize that the human spirit which God put within us is capable of sensing things at a distance. That is how God made us. All people are influenced and directed, to some extent, by that which their spirits are receiving. It is foolish and contrary to biblical truth to categorize all spiritual sensings as evil.

I have heard stories of Christians who have experienced some supernatural phenomena, and when they tried to share the experience with some person in their churches whom they respect, they were told to never talk about it so that it never would happen again. For example, Don, a Christian man, told me that years earlier he saw a vision of a person stranded on a snowmobile near his snow-laden home. He went to investigate. Sure enough, he found an individual in desperate need and he was able to help. When Don told the leaders of his church what had happened, they told him that it was a demon communicating to him. He spent the next several years feeling guilty and trying to deny his experience. That was, of course, until he met me.

Obviously, you have figured out by now that I am presenting a new look at the spiritual realm. At this point you either must be upset with me or you are rejoicing to hear these truths. I trust the second is your response.

We can take one step further into these truths by saying that a person's spirit may also touch things belonging to another time period. The most obvious examples are of the prophets in the Bible seeing the future. When prophets such as Jeremiah, Ezekiel, Daniel and Isaiah prophesied, they would often describe visions that they were seeing, and their words were stated as if they were watching the future as it happened.

For example, they described the birth of Jesus hundreds of years before it actually occurred.

It is unclear whether such prophetic experiences were the result of the prophet's spirit reaching into the future or of God's Spirit bringing a vision of the future into their spirit. Either way, the results are identical: the spirit of the prophet is receiving information belonging to another time.

In the Book of Acts, we read about the prophet Agabus perceiving the future on two different occasions. In Acts 11:27-28, he foretold a coming famine. In Acts 21:10-14, Agabus told Paul about the imprisonment awaiting him in Jerusalem. Paul said:

> *"And now, behold, bound by the Spirit, I am on my way to Jerusalem, not knowing what will happen to me there, except that the Holy Spirit solemnly testifies to me in every city, saying that bonds and afflictions await me."*
>
> (Acts 20:22-23)

Notice that the apostle mentioned how *"in every city"* the Holy Spirit would warn him about the future. It was, therefore, a fairly common experience for Paul to have some inclination about what was ahead of him. In Paul's experiences and the two recorded of Agabus, the Holy Spirit is given credit for revealing the future events.

The whole topic of transcending time is taboo in many Christian circles today. This is partly due to the evil, occultic exercises in this area and partly because of a fear which keeps Christians from actually looking in the Bible to see if these things are true. I am declaring to you that such experiences are true and not automatically evil.

For example, sometimes Christians who are deeply involved in a church know in advance what that group of

Christians will be doing next. Often before a church service, a faithful woman of the church will be reading her Bible and then when she arrives at church, she discovers that the pastor is going to preach on the very Bible passages she was led to read earlier. We can explain this phenomenon as the Christian becoming one with the Holy Spirit who is guiding that group of Christians.

In some inner healing ministries, the minister will be praying for the counselee, and she will begin to see visions of what happened in the past. The Holy Spirit may reveal how the person was hurt emotionally or perhaps rejected years earlier. These are true words of knowledge given by the Holy Spirit.

Another example of experiencing future events is when God reveals to a person something about to happen. John Alexander Dowie was a famous minister in the United States around the turn of the nineteenth century. He had several thousand people looking to him for leadership; he also had some enemies. On one occasion, while he was sleeping, he had a vision of a bomb going off in his office. Later he went to his office, but left early believing that God had warned him. Sure enough, the explosion would have killed him had he not heeded the vision.

There are many, many accounts of missionaries who have been warned of some impending danger through visions. If we were to compile some of the stories, we could fill several books.

There are also experiences of the future outside the Christian context, which we should not consider evil. Here I am not talking about a palmreader's attempt at reading someone's future, nor the astrologer's endeavor to perceive the future by gazing into the stars. Those activities are undoubtedly evil and condemned in the Bible (Deut. 18:10-12). Please do not think I am giving credence to any such practices.

Consider the engineer who designs and oversees the construction of a huge bridge. If he has a premonition of that bridge collapsing, we need not jump to the conclusion that he is having problems with demons. Perhaps a demon is involved and is just trying to discourage him. In such cases, those thoughts should be rejected aggressively. But it also may be true that his human spirit is simply sensing a danger. He would be wise, in that case, to investigate and see if, indeed, a genuine problem has been perceived spiritually.

Many people also have had experiences of knowing the future in very small practical ways. An example is when a woman sets the alarm clock to awaken at a time different than her regularly scheduled time. In the morning, one instant before the alarm sounds, she wakes up to turn it off. Her spirit sensed what was about to happen.

Many people have had the experience which we call "deja vu." A person will be performing their normal activities and suddenly feel as if they have already experienced everything around them. It is as if they are reliving that exact time period. It is possible that the person's spirit at an earlier time reached into the future and "tasted of the things to come." This is not a conscious endeavor, but it simply happens because our spirit has this ability.

Such spiritual sensing of the future or past are not always evil. They can be. Of course, the devil at times may be involved. I am suspicious of any such exercises done by a person with known occultic involvement. A person with past experiences in evil spiritual exercises or drugs can have demonically inspired visions for years afterward. We must discern and judge all things (I Thess. 5:21). However, we must not reject them all categorically. It is by God's design that people were created with a spirit. That spirit is assigned to a time, but on occasion it may sense something in the past or future.

40 Understanding Dreams

With the understanding that we have developed concerning the human spirit, I now can explain the function and role that dreams can play. I do not intend to discuss everything involved in dreams in this chapter. That would be as foolish as trying to explain in just a few pages everything which the human body does. At this point, simply a basic understanding will help us.

The spirit of a person does not sleep. The spirit is always willing, even though the flesh is weak (Matt. 26:41). While the body rests, the spirit remains active. During sleep, a person receives information from everything with which his or her spirit is having contact. Even though the mind is detached from the natural world, the spirit continues to flow outward. That which the spirit contacts is projected back to the soul and often appears as images upon the mind. This causes many different visual experiences.

At times, the images seem entirely disjointed and meaningless, but they are not. While we dream, our spirits draw in all sorts of information. We could compare it with how our natural senses would perceive many things if we were standing high on top of a mountain surveying the countryside. A difference, though, is that our spirits draw in information from both the natural and spiritual worlds.

From the spiritual realm, sleeping people often perceive things related to angelic or demonic activity. If an evil presence passes through a home, a sleeping person may sense it. More than once I have been asked to pray over a person's home because they were having bad dreams. In one of the worst cases, the woman of the house was waking up night after night screaming. It was no surprise when we learned that the person who had lived in the house prior to them had committed suicide. After praying and taking authority over the situation, the home was cleaned out and dreams became peaceful. Pure and holy dreams typically are prevalent in a godly atmosphere.

It is also common for people to know some of the activities going on around them in the natural world, even if they are asleep. For example, sleeping people may incorporate into their dreams activities going on around them, such as a dog walking through the house, or a burglar breaking in, or a television show that is playing beyond hearing distance at the other end of the house. Such experiences reveal to us how the spirit is in touch with the natural world in ways that even our natural senses never are.

Dreams are also very much influenced by the people with whom our spirits have contact. For example, family members, friends, coworkers and the people to whom we are bonded spiritually are likely to appear in our dreams. It is common for a child's dreams to correspond to their parents' spiritual condition. It is also true that if a person with great authority is sleeping nearby, say in the motel room next to yours, you may find yourself receiving images which that person's spirit is giving off. Whether people are tied together spiritually or by proximity, their spirits influence each other during the night.

Often visions of the night reflect events that happened throughout the person's daily activities. One's spirit is still in touch with those things. Especially stressful events will hold the person's spiritual attention longer. Images of the people involved in those various events may appear throughout the night.

One of the processes happening while people are receiving images during their sleep is that their spirits are resolving problems related to those images. We can see this if we add to our understanding how the authority of individuals emanates from their spirits. When God spoke over humanity, *"Fill the earth and subdue it,"* He imparted into people the authority to manage the affairs of their lives. Because of this abiding authority, the spirit of a person constantly is arising from within, helping that person have dominion in all the areas of life.

When a problem during the day has not been resolved, the spirit within a person will continue to flow through his mind in an attempt to develop the needed answers. An individual may dream a certain dream for several nights or even weeks in a row, until the spirit within has enough strength to give the person the related authority.

For example, a woman who is starting a new job at a factory may have dreams about her work for several nights in a row. Not understanding what is happening, she may become frustrated and try harder to sleep without being bothered by those dreams. In reality, those night visions are for her benefit. The spirit within her is rising, and it is trying to take dominion of the new tasks she is facing. She may have several nights during which she seems to fail miserably in her dreams. Then, after a season of those dreams, she will find herself more efficient and successful on the job. Because the spirit within her has had enough time to rise, she can function better. Her body works better. She thinks more clearly. She has strength to last through the day.

People often find themselves able to handle new responsibilities after they have finished dreaming about them. Once they have succeeded in their dreams, those dreams no longer occur. The spirit within them has then finished doing the necessary work. New avenues of spiritual energy are flowing through the person and the person's spirit is flowing out to influence the circumstances, events and people involved.

For similar reasons, a person who is trying to learn a foreign language may dream in that language. When language fluency is experienced in a dream it is evidence that the language has been mastered in the natural.

The spirit of a man constantly is rising within him, releasing life energies to keep him healthy, strong, thinking right and effective in this world. Often the problems being resolved through dreams may deal with difficulties which arose years earlier. For example, a certain woman may have undergone a terrible relationship problem when she was a young girl. Such events can be so devastating that she is unable to deal with the hurt, rejection and misunderstandings. Her spirit, therefore, may bury the related thoughts until a later time when she is mature and strong enough to handle them. Then when she is old enough to deal with the past, her spirit may bring it back to her in dreams. Her spirit then will be able to begin resolving the related issues, reevaluate what actually happened and align thoughts and feelings in ways that can be incorporated into her whole system of thought.

As the spirit within a person flows freely during sleep, it searches through the mind and bathes the memories and thought patterns. This performs an important function. Since the spirit provides the energy which allows people to think, it is essential that new energy be supplied to the mind on an ongoing basis. The spirit "searches" the mind: *"For who among men knows the thoughts of a man except the spirit of the man which is within him"* (I Cor. 2:11a). As it searches and scans through the mind, the spirit reenergizes thoughts and memories which are still important and believed by that individual. However, if information is no longer needed or certain ways of thinking have changed, the related thoughts are released, that is, allowed to diminish in strength. Thoughts that are not touched by the spirit of a person from time to time will disappear completely. So we see that one of the functions of dreaming is to bathe the mind and reorient its patterns of thought according to present beliefs.

For this reason, a woman who is undergoing major changes in life will experience an acceleration in dream activities. Thoughts will seem to flood through her mind at an amazing rate when she is in transition or is being exposed to new ways of thinking. Often thoughts will be linked one to another for future reference, or various forms of "revelation" will come alive. It is the function of the spirit to help us cope and adapt with such changes we all experience.

Another major role played by dreams is related to the function of the human spirit in healing a person within. The spirit and soul may need to be healed of wounds resulting from rejection, abuse, errors made in the past, etc. People can also be wounded within as they watch violent or scary movies. Any stressful experience can hurt people leaving them in need of healing. That healing may come immediately, or it may take years until the spirit within is able to rise with enough force to expel the negative effects.

In this sense, dreams can fulfill the same role for the soul/mind as the human kidney does for the physical body, expelling impurities and cleansing the system. In this process, wounds and difficult memories may surface years after they were inflicted. As these things arise, they can appear upon the screen of the mind in the night. Some people, not understanding how this operates, become very concerned and even plagued with guilt when they themselves are going through such "a cleansing season" in their lives. They wrongly consider such dreams as signs of present evil, rather than past wounds being healed.

It is important to note here that all these activities of the spirit in the night deal with spiritual impressions, not natural ones. This means they cannot be taken literally according to logical thought patterns. For example, an adult man who starts dreaming that he was abused by his father years ago should not conclude that he was, indeed, beaten or in any other way physically abused. The spirit projects out the intensity of the wound, not the literal accuracy. As a child, the man may have been verbally abused by his father, and the damage resulting from that verbal abuse may be equivalent to being stabbed with a knife. If, however, this child grows up and later dreams that his father stabbed him, we should not conclude that the event actually occurred physically. What is important is that with dreams we are dealing with impressions of equivalent intensity left upon the spirit and soul of the individual.

It is normal and healthy for the rivers of life to be flowing constantly out of a person's innermost being. When a woman is under spiritual attack, or she is depleted of spiritual strength, she may find her dreamlife influenced accordingly. When she does not have enough spiritual energy within to maintain healthy thought patterns, errors of the past can flood her mind. Without spiritual energy a person is defenseless. Problems and the intensity of the battle are compounded by demonic activity which often come to condemn and accuse a person. A healthy individual is able to admit to mistakes and then move on in life. A person depleted of spiritual strength is not.

Therefore, if an individual is drained of his own spiritual energy, he may find in the night terrible thoughts flowing through his mind related to unworthiness and shortcomings.

The wise person learns to identify such negative thought patterns as indicators pointing to the need for rest and rejuvenation.

We should add to our understanding of dreamlife by pointing out that the spirit is still in touch with the physical body of the person, healing, helping and bathing it. Therefore, a woman who is sick may dream about her illness. When health is seen in dreams, it is a good sign that the body is on the way to recovery.

So, also, the spirit may accommodate certain needs of the physical body. For example, a young man may have sexually stimulating thoughts while asleep. Those thoughts may be the result of bad images he has put within his mind during the day, but they may also be formed by his spirit in order to cause his physical body to release sexual passions. Most young men experience what sometimes is called a "wet dream," where they become so sexually aroused that their body emits seminal fluid. A person need not feel guilty for such experiences. Of course, I am not making excuses for constant or prolonged sexual dreaming, but some such images are normal and even necessary for the development and maintenance of one's body.

What people eat before going to bed also influences their thoughts at night. Fatty substances seem to cause people to act more authoritatively while they sleep. Certain foods seem to keep people from going into as deep a sleep as they normally should. Spicy foods often activate the mind so that more is experienced and remembered. Cheese is high in the amino acid which intensifies color and imagery. Because of such influences of food, some people have used the terminology "pizza dream" to refer to the thoughts which race rapidly in the night after a meal of pizza.

This phenomenon is another example of how our spirit, soul and body influence each other. Throughout these writings I have been trying to portray the spirit, soul and body of a person as completely engaged. As three gears engage one with another so that the teeth perfectly intermesh, so also the spirit, soul and body are engaged so that whatever happens to one part influences the others.

This intermeshing of spirit, soul and body has some profound implications when talking about dreams. We can consider how the physical body may be changed in subtle or even dramatic ways by the ongoing influence of dreams. One's faith orients one's heart. From the heart flows the spiritual energy within. Therefore, as a person dreams, she may be altering the actual structure and makeup of her physical body. Concerning this, we gave the example of how a sexual dream may activate sexual organs. We could also consider how a dream inducing fear could accelerate one's heart and stimulate the secretion of certain hormones. Similarly, the spirit of a person may form countless variations of images, each of which triggers different physical responses. The spirit, therefore, plays a significant role in adjusting chemical balances in the body, immune system responses, metabolism and numerous other physical processes.

It is with this perspective that we view dreams. We must realize the incredible intricacy and far-reaching effects which they have. They are spiritual functions which adjust the soul and body of a person and also cause the spiritual energy to flow out of each individual in ways that allow him or her to be more successful in life.

There is yet another key role which dreams play. Since the spirit is the *"lamp of the Lord"* (Prov. 20:27), God may intervene in the flow of spiritual impressions to communicate with people. There are many examples in the Bible, but one of the clearest explanations concerning dreams was given to Job by Elihu. Job had three counselors who gave him questionable advice, but the fourth, Elihu, was inspired by God when he said:

> *"Indeed God speaks once,*
> *Or twice, yet no one notices it.*
> *In a dream, a vision of the night,*
> *When sound sleep falls on men,*
> *While they slumber in their beds,*
> *Then He opens the ears of men,*
> *And seals their instruction"*
>
> (Job 33:14-16)

When God speaks, our spirit responds. Often we have no consciousness that it is Him talking. Other times, our spirit is troubled because of a dream (Dan. 2:1). Or a certain dream will return to us because God speaks *"once, or twice."*

Since God gives instructions to people while they sleep, we need to heed what He is saying. It is not the pizza dream to which we should listen. It is not the mass of spiritual information flowing in every night that needs our attention. Nor is it the ongoing bathing of our thought processes. It is when God has intervened in those flowing spiritual impressions that we should pay attention.

The meaning of some dreams is very obvious. A woman may go to bed wondering how she is supposed to act in a certain situation, and then that night have a dream giving her the answer. Of course, we never should receive a dream that tells us to act contrary to God's nature or His Word. The devil can also influence our dreams. Visions of the night need to be discerned just as prophecies or any other spiritual messages.

Dreams whose meanings are not obvious need to be interpreted with spiritual understanding. We read in the Bible about Daniel interpreting the dreams of King Nebuchadnezzar and Joseph interpreting the dreams of Pharaoh and others.

Because we are dealing with spiritual impressions, logic or mechanical formulas of interpretation cannot be trusted. Sometimes people who do not understand the spiritual dimension try to develop "rules of interpretation," implying that a certain picture always means some specific thing. It doesn't. There may be some patterns that can be applied, but for the most part all formulas are faulty. Things which are spiritual only can be discerned spiritually (I Cor. 2:12-14).

We are told that Daniel could interpret dreams because:

> "...an extraordinary spirit, knowledge and insight, interpretation of dreams, explanation of enigmas and solving of difficult problems were found in this Daniel...."
>
> (Dan. 5:12; see also Dan. 1:17)

Similarly, Joseph had a gift from God enabling him to interpret dreams (Gen. 40:8-22).

I do not point out these truths to discourage Christians from trying to understand their own dreams. After all, God is communicating with people through dreams. He is not purposely making it hard for them to understand. I simply am emphasizing the need for spiritual rather than natural understanding. When God communicates to an individual through dreams, He breathes His Spirit into the heart of the person. As a consequence, images that are in the heart of the person come alive. For example, a boy who loves dogs may see in a dream a dog licking his face. Or a woman who is bonded in heart to a close friend may see that friend in her dream. Intimate, personal thoughts are brought to mind as God communicates Spirit to spirit.

Because dreams are so personal, only the dreamer is able to understand the true interpretation of a dream. Others may give their thoughts and ideas, but the individual who has the dream will always have the final understanding. God can even give an interpreter a clear interpretation, but still the dreamer is the one who will have the final revelation, because the message is always personal and direct.

I have learned through studying my own dreams that when God is communicating to me it is important to respond. The moment I awake from the dream, I have a choice to go back to sleep or arise and write the dream down. If I just go back to sleep, I usually will not remember in the morning what I dreamed that night. On the other hand, if I make myself get up and write the dream down immediately, then I am rewarded by God. As the Scriptures say, God rewards those who diligently seek Him (Heb. 11:6). If I get out of bed and record the dream on paper—motivated by the possibility that God may be speaking to me—I typically discover an interpretation coming to me almost immediately. Or if I mediate on the dream during the next day, I commonly find intimate, personal messages being spoken to me by God.

There are many books written on dreams and their interpretation. Although I do not recommend any of the non-Christian writings on such topics, the Church is becoming more open to the reality and significance of spiritual truths such as these. The Body of Christ should be at the forefront of understanding such spiritual realities. In the Bible, what made Joseph and Daniel stand out as God's men was the fact that they could interpret dreams better than the magicians and evil spiritists of the day. Similarly, as Christians we are the ones who should understand the spiritual realm most accurately.

Conclusion

We have discussed subjects such as the spiritual presence of a person, the emanation of the human spirit, the power behind spoken words, out-of-body experiences, how the spirit senses through space and time, and the function of dreams. These topics may seem too mystical for some people. In many Christian circles these topics are taboo, and others simply avoid speaking publicly about them because they stir up unwanted controversy. By God's grace, I trust that the biblical understanding which we have developed will benefit the Body of Christ.

At this time in history our discussion of these subjects is essential. The secular world is moving on with these things, with or without us. We cannot help them by ignoring the phenomena and shutting ourselves off from the subject of spiritual realities. God wants us to be at the forefront. He is raising the Church to a place of maturity and power. We are moving in a direction, and that direction is advancement.

Each time God advances His people in an area, He begins by inspiring related teachings. In the Book of Amos we are told:

> *Surely the Lord God does nothing*
> *Unless He reveals His secret counsel*
> *To His servants the prophets.*
>
> (Amos 3:7)

Before God acts in significant ways, He stirs the leaders of His people to begin teaching and speaking on the related subjects. As John the Baptist was sent to prepare the way of the Lord, God inspires various leaders to begin speaking out the plans of God, before He acts.

It is time for the Church to enter into a greater experience of God's power and provision. In the Bible we read about people seeing into the spiritual realm, having angelic visitations, perceiving the future, interpreting dreams, being led by the Holy Spirit and experiencing the glory of God. God desires to open His Church to greater dimensions of the spiritual realm. Therefore, we will continue advancing our studies in the pages which follow.

Section 5

Spiritual Dynamics
Between People

The spirit of every human being originated with the breath of God. This *God stuff* in each of us is the energy which circulates and flows, enabling us to live, think and influence the world around us. The spirit is not limited to the confines of the physical body, but is directed outward by the focus of our hearts. I established these truths in preceding sections.

Our focus in this section will be upon the dynamics and interaction between people's spirits. There are specific properties of the human spirit which we will identify and discuss. Understanding these properties will give great insights into human behavior and the spiritual dynamics that take place between people.

Bonding and Harmonizing

The apostle Paul warned Christians not to develop too close relationships with people of very different beliefs:

> *Do not be bound together with unbelievers...What harmony has Christ with Belial, or what has a believer in common with an unbeliever?*
>
> (II Cor. 6:14-15)

Paul warned them not to be *bound together* and not to be in *harmony* with unbelievers. Notice these two aspects of a relationship: bonding and harmony. Let's examine these more carefully.

First, consider the *bonding* which happens in many different situations of life. The Bible tells us about the marriage relationship in which *"two become one."* Parents and children also bond with one another. Co-workers unite in heart and, therefore, spiritually as well. Whenever any two people open their hearts one to another, they bond together and those associations are real spiritual ties knitting their souls together.

Consider I Samuel 18:1 where we are told that *"...the soul of Jonathan was knit to the soul of David, and Jonathan loved him as himself."* Some Christians call such relationships "soul ties." Earlier I explained how the term "soul tie" can be misleading because the soul of one person does not literally reach out across space and touch the soul of the other. The soul is limited to the confines of the body (except at death and in certain cases discussed in section 4). It is more accurate to see these bonds as spiritual energy emanating from the soul and touching the soul of another. It is spiritual substance which ties the soul of one to the soul of another.

Two People Bonded Together

Bonding can occur not only between two people, but also with an entire group. The Bible tells us that believers are submerged by the Holy Spirit into one Body (I Cor. 12:12-13). We are united in the spiritual dimension. When one part hurts, we all hurt; as one is blessed, we are all partakers of that blessing (I Cor. 12:26). Our spirits are bonded in such a fashion that they influence each other, both positively and negatively. This is the way God made us.

In order to embrace this truth, we must envision the human spirit as having the ability to merge with the spirits of others. This is more than just a mixing of two people's spiritual energies. The spiritual energy of one actually merges (in the sense of becoming one) with the spiritual substance of others. Only if we accept this property of the human spirit can we understand the spiritual dynamics we observe in life and in the Bible. We are not just talking about joining or adding, but a supernatural—spiritual—merging.

It is in this fashion that all spiritual bonding takes place.

The apostle Paul explained: *"But the one who joins himself to the Lord is one spirit with Him"* (I Cor. 6:17). In chapter 18, I gave an example of how in a certain tribe husbands and wives express their love for one another, not by kissing, but by inhaling each other's breath. That is a beautiful picture of the spirits of two people intermingling and being taken within. Similarly, when Christians are united with God, their spirits are one with God's.

The extent of merging between two people is determined by the depth of heart commitment. As they work together, they increase their unity. As they go through trials and difficulties, their hearts must become more fixed. Each time a problem arises, they must make a decision whether to remain together or split and go their independent ways. Therefore, every project, trial or stress is an opportunity to deepen the spiritual bonding between them.

Bonding Deepens with Commitment

In addition to bonding, the human spirit can *harmonize* with others. Paul warned Christians not to harmonize with unbelievers (II Cor. 6:15) but certain Bible passages talk about harmonizing in a positive sense. Jesus explained how two or more believers can come into agreement with each other (Matt. 18:19). The Greek word which has been interpreted "agreement," is *sumphoneo*, from which we get the word "symphony." In some Bible passages this Greek word is translated "harmony." In the book of Acts, the disciples became of one accord (e.g., Acts 4:24; 5:12). They had their hearts oriented toward God and each other to such an extent that they were willing to sell their personal properties and hold all possessions in common (e.g., Acts 2:44-45; 4:32). Both their desires and their actions were in agreement.

To develop a helpful picture of what is taking place spiritually as two people come into harmony, envision two similar musical tuning forks. If one is struck it vibrates and gives off a specific tone. If the second tuning fork is moved close to the vibrating one, it too will begin vibrating at the same frequency.

Two Coming into Harmony

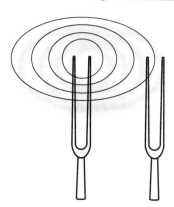

In similar fashion, the human spirit has the ability to harmonize with the spirits of those around. To borrow from the vocabulary of sound production, they become of the same frequency or get on the same wavelength. I will use all the terms—harmony, agreement or one accord—to refer to the characteristic of a relationship wherein people come into wholehearted unity.

The orientation of the heart determines with whom a person will come into harmony. As Proverbs 4:23 tells us, from the heart flow all the issues of life. Because the heart is the core from which our spiritual life flows, it determines with whom we will be in tune. As people orient their hearts in unison, they come into harmony.

People Coming into Harmony

This harmony is different than bonding. Bonding refers to the depth of commitment and the resulting forces which hold people together. Some people may be bonded, yet not be in harmony with each other. A married couple may be committed to stay together, but they may not be experiencing harmony at any one moment in time. Bonding results from commitment and harmony results from people orienting their hearts in the same direction. These are two distinct characteristics of every relationship.[4]

As we become comfortable with these concepts of bonding

---

4 For further teaching on bonding and harmonizing refer to my book on marriage entitled, *Two Become One.*

and harmony, we can more easily understand many of the spiritual dynamics which occur between people.

Transference of Spiritual Substance

Not only is it possible for people to bond and come into harmony with others, but there is also the possibility for a *transference of spiritual energy* from one person to another.

In the Bible, a woman with a hemorrhage pressed through a crowd in order to touch the hem of Jesus' garment. Our Lord turned and asked who had touched Him, for He was aware that power or virtue had flowed out of Him (Luke 8:43-48).

Consider also how Elijah's spirit was transmitted to his disciple Elisha (II Kings 2:7-25). Before Elijah was taken up into heaven, Elisha asked him, *"Please, let a double portion of your spirit be upon me"* (II Kings 2:9). Elijah responded by saying that Elisha would have his request if he saw him being taken up into heaven. After Elijah was taken from Earth, the other prophets noted, *"The spirit of Elijah rests on Elisha"* (II Kings 2:15).

What was actually being transferred? Was it the Holy Spirit or was it the human spirit? In the example of Elijah and Elisha, the Bible tells us that it was the *"spirit of Elijah"* which came upon Elisha (II Kings 2:15). Those who saw the resulting transformation in Elisha's life said, *"The spirit of Elijah rests on Elisha."* (I Kings 2:15b). Yet, God's Spirit was also upon Elijah. As explained earlier, God's Spirit and the human spirit become one when a person's heart is one with

God's. Therefore, the spiritual substance which flowed out of Elijah and into Elisha was Elijah's spirit along with the Spirit of God.

For further clarification we can distinguish between the spirit and the soul of Elijah. It was not the soul which was transferred to Elisha. Otherwise we would be giving credence to a form of reincarnation—which I definitely am not doing. It was the spirit which was in Elijah that was passed on to Elisha.

A Spiritual Transfer Between People

In the following examples, I will not spend much time discerning what spirit—Holy Spirit, human spirit, good or bad—is being transferred. Here I simply want to establish the principle of how the spiritual life-energies resident within a person can be drawn out and deposited in another individual. Whatever spiritual energy is within a person, good or bad, it can be passed to another person.

The most dramatic exchange occurs within marriage. Not only do a man and a woman bond and harmonize, but the life-energies in each actually go into the other. The more time two people spend with one another, opening up their hearts to each other, the greater this transfer of life will be.

Similarly, in the family, children draw upon the spiritual

energies of their parents. In a church, the preacher influences his congregation not only with his teaching, but also with the spirit flowing through him. Every leader transmits spiritual substance to his followers. The coach transmits his energy to his team. As a famous singer pours out her voice to her fans, she is releasing her spirit along with her voice, and people receive her spiritual energy as they are bathed with her music. Any person with authority emanates spiritual energy, and others who submit to it may actually receive it within themselves.

As the spiritual substance of one person is incorporated into the life of another, the second person will take on certain characteristics of the first. Their thoughts and desires will become similar. Jesus said that a pupil becomes as his teacher (Luke 6:40). Followers receive the nature of those they admire.

Sometimes this spiritual transfer has a negative influence in the life of the receiver. For example, parents have watched their children make dramatic shifts in their personality and behavior after attending a distasteful music concert. A teenage boy may be doing well in school and living in harmony at home, but after attending a huge concert, he becomes rebellious toward authority. His priorities and attitudes change. He no longer enjoys school and he craves more exposure to the same negative crowd of people. We can explain such radical changes as we recognize the spiritual principles involved. Spiritual transmissions can occur easily as a young person idolizes, submits to and longs for whatever he sees in the new-found idol.

In the Bible, we are told that *"bad company corrupts good morals"* (I Cor. 15:33). To see how such corruption can be the result of spiritual transfers, read II Corinthians 6:14-7:1. In chapter 7, verse 1, Paul told the Christians to cleanse themselves from all *"defilement of flesh and spirit."* The five preceding verses reveal how such defilement can happen through our bonding with people who worship idols, commit fornication or give themselves to other sins. Similarly, we can read in I Corinthians 5:1-6 where Paul explained how the evil influence of a sexually perverted man could spread to everyone bonded to him, in the same fashion that yeast spreads and leavens a whole lump of dough. From such passages, we can recognize how the transfer of spiritual substance can influence the thoughts, desires and behaviors of those who receive it.

Spiritual Transfers May Cause Changes in Nature

Likewise, we should recognize the good transfers of spiritual energy. For example, when a young boy admires and associates with his godly father, there are forces activated which mold that son's character. When a daughter spends quality time with her mother, she is being bonded to her mother and molded to her image.

Not only are the thoughts and desires of a person changed through such transfers, but authority, wisdom, healing power and blessings can also be transferred. There are many examples of healings in the Bible, but consider also how Elisha received an anointing and empowering upon his life similar to what Elijah had. God told Moses to lay his hands upon Joshua so that his authority would be transferred (Num. 27:20). Amazingly, Joshua received not only authority from Moses but also wisdom (Deut 34:9). It was a common practice in Bible times for a person of stature to lay his hands upon others, especially his own children, to pass blessings on to them. This truth—that spiritual substance can carry with it some measure of power, authority, wisdom, healing and blessing—is eye-opening, challenging, exciting, hope creating!

When such a transference is made, we use the term *impartation*. An impartation is a transference in which some measure of power, authority, wisdom and/or blessing moves with the spiritual substance between people.

We can also identify how people actually draw out spiritual substance from another person. The woman who touched the hem of Jesus' garment was believing, submissive and longing. Similarly, a person must submit to or "get under" their leader if they hope to receive that leader's spiritual strength, authority or wisdom. It is as if they are tipping a glass of water to flow downward toward them. They must have an openness and desire to receive that which is pouring forth.

People posture themselves in different ways to receive different things. A daughter finds a specific manner in which to draw upon her father's love. A wife discovers a different place from which she relates to her husband. An employee approaches his boss in one way, and he will speak to his fellow workers in another manner. Friends posture themselves in specific ways toward each other, and those manners may change from time to time.

Of course, there are some people who posture themselves wrongly. A certain woman may try to intimidate everyone around by taking on a domineering, threatening posture. A lonely man may posture himself to draw upon the sexual desires of unknown women. A salesman may manipulate his customers by pulling on the strings of their hearts. Individuals raised in an environment with very little affection may constantly yearn for the acceptance of others.

Self-pity is a negative force in these respects. Through self-pity a person wrongfully draws on the spiritual energy of those around. Self-pity is the positioning of one's heart in a selfish manner, which draws in—or steals—the energy of other people. It is a form of lust for or coveting of other people's strength and love. Some people develop a lifestyle of self-pity, and they drain the energy of everyone who comes around them. Of course, there are needy people to whom we must give special attention, but the pattern of life which wrongly pulls on the spiritual energy of other people should not be encouraged.

In coming pages, we will see many more situations in which spiritual transfers are made. At this point, recognize that transfers take place as people bond and harmonize with each other and as individuals longingly look up to some leader. The more people open their hearts and receive, the more they are changed by the resulting transfer of spiritual energy.

Although we are not always aware of these spiritual dynamics, they are evident in the world around us. Many of us are consciously or subconsciously aware of energy moving between us, but we seldom have the opportunity to discuss these realities. More importantly, we Christians have not been taught a biblical basis for understanding these spiritual dynamics. As a result, we rarely talk about them, even though the transfer of spiritual life between us is real and experienced every day of our lives.

43

The Giver of Spiritual Substance

We have studied how spiritual substance can be transferred from one person to another and how that will result in a change in the recipient. Now, let's turn our attention to the giver and see what effect there is upon his mind, emotions and behavior.

As spiritual energy flows from a person's heart, that energy influences his entire being. Remember that the spirit of a person reveals the thoughts of that person. As the spiritual energy flows, it stimulates certain thoughts, emotions, desires and strengths. Even the physical body of a person may be energized. Therefore, as followers believe in and pull on their leader in a healthy way, the resulting increased flow of energy through him may energize his soul and body in varied ways.

Because of these dynamics, the football hero performs his best when the crowds cheer. A businesswoman is more efficient and effective if her staff respects her. The pastor knows the direction of God for his congregation as the hearts of the people look to him for guidance. It is easier for the army general to make brilliant decisions if his subordinates believe in him. The president is more effective if his country supports him. The foreman on a construction site will have more energy and creative ideas if the people working for him respect him and his position.

Public figures who often appear before large crowds become sensitive to these principles. They may not understand that it is spiritual energy being released, but they commonly realize that the audience must draw upon them before they can function at their best. Actors and public speakers know that they cannot communicate effectively until the listeners are waiting expectantly for them to speak. A hostile or bored crowd is a difficult group before whom to perform; a great output of inner energy is demanded. A minister typically finds it much easier to bring forth his message in front of an eager congregation. The hunger and desire of the people draw the spiritual energy out of the person at the front. As the energy flows through the leader, it is easier for him to think, act in boldness and speak with authority.

That which is pulled from a leader is a specific flow of spiritual energy. A stream flows out from the person and quickens their thoughts in the related area. That area may be knowledge for a specific endeavor or strength to accomplish some task. Sometimes Christian leaders find themselves receiving incredible revelation, that is, inspired understanding, as they stand before expectant people. Comedians depend upon a specific stream being pulled out of them—a stream that quickens their own thoughts, giving them cute things to say, fast responses and unusual ways of looking at life. In my own work as an author, I find that I cannot write effectively unless I expose myself to the people for whom I am writing and keep them in mind and heart as I write. Similarly, inventors, scientists and people doing research in various areas are very often dependent upon the needs of those around them to draw out of them the spiritual energy they need to formulate answers. In all such cases, it is a specific stream of spiritual energy being pulled out of their innermost beings and through their minds.

The flow of spiritual energy through a person or into a person is normally healthy and feels good. The mother holding her child senses the love flowing out of her, and this creates a sense of warmth and significance. When a daughter acts cute for her father, both are usually enjoying the interaction. As a young man and woman look romantically into each other's eyes, there is a pleasurable sensation that we call "falling in love." As people pull on the athlete to perform, she feels energized and powerful. The strong leader directing a large crowd is aware of confidence and energy stirring within. He may feel a rush of energy through his entire being. Some actors and musicians are even known to get "addicted to the rush." Having other people pull on one's spirit can be a very rewarding and pleasurable experience.

Sometimes, however, people can pull energy out of an individual wrongfully, resulting in harmful effects. Just as the physical body can become exhausted, so also can the spirit of a person. Several Bible verses talk about the spirit of a person being depleted, crushed or oppressed (e.g., I Sam 1:15; Ps. 142:3; Prov. 15:4). In some cases, this may be the result of negative interactions between people. People can be so longing for the direction and strength of their leader that they drain their leader's spiritual energy. This can happen just as easily in the life of the minister as it can with the mother who cares for her children. Because the human spirit can be drained away and weakened in this way, wise leaders consciously keep enough energy in reserve to maintain themselves and stay strong.

Some givers are not aware of these dynamics, and they allow others to take too much of their spiritual energy. They can become so depleted that they do not have enough energy left within themselves to maintain their own well-being. Physical illness can result. It may become difficult for them to keep healthy thought patterns, and they may lose all motivation to live. Often, Christians fall into this condition because, in their earnestness to do good, they force themselves to help others beyond what is healthy. Guilt, too, can become a trap holding or causing people to drain themselves on behalf of others.

When a young man looks longingly at a beautiful woman, he may draw upon her spiritual energy. If she is uninterested in him, she may have a true sensation that he is stealing from her. If, however, she desires a relationship with him, she will find his glance appealing and pleasurable. What makes the experience pleasurable or not for her depends upon her heart and whether or not she desires his attention.

Spiritual energy has an incredible living, reproductive nature. Remember, it originated with God. It is not natural in its essence, but is from the very breath of God. Realizing this, we can more easily understand its properties within people. When it is stolen, that is, when a person's heart is not directed toward the taker, the person's spiritual energy will be depleted. If, however, the person wants to give, the spiritual energy reproduces itself. The more that is given, the more that grows. An amount may be released from a certain person, and yet the same amount or more remains in that person. Spiritual energy is creative in this sense, and when it is allowed to flow in the direction of one's heart, it reproduces itself in the receiver and in the giver.

Allow me to summarize. We have identified specific spiritual dynamics between people and several properties of the human spirit.

Spiritual Dynamics Between People
1. Bonding,
2. Harmonizing,
3. Transference of spiritual substance.

Properties of the Human Spirit
1. Bonds and harmonizes with people,
2. Merges with other people's spirits,
3. Reproduces when given willingly.

Conditions for Spiritual Exchanges

Now, let's discuss the conditions under which spiritual dynamics between people occur. Remember that the heart is the fountainhead of a person's being (Prov. 4:23). Therefore, when people expose their hearts to each other, they are opening the doorways of their spirits for bonding, harmonizing and spiritual transfers.

Heart-to-heart, open communication is a spiritual exercise. When a husband and wife share their deepest feelings with each other, they are harmonizing. When two friends meet for a cup of coffee and a chat, they are exchanging more than stories with each other. When a public speaker exposes her heart, everyone who is listening will be influenced by her spirit.

If people hold up the walls of their hearts against each other, then transfers and bonding are hindered. However, as individuals relax and allow themselves to trust each other, the pathways for transfers are opened.

Eating with another person increases spiritual exchanges. There is something about eating which relaxes people—not a formal meal, but a less tense time when people enjoy each other's company and communicate openly. They typically let down their guards and expose themselves more freely.

Laughter can further crumble the walls that divide. Every

public speaker knows that she will be able to communicate more effectively with an audience if she can loosen up the crowd with a joke or two. College roommates who find themselves laughing together uncontrollably will be bonded for life. Consciously or subconsciously, people sense that they are bonding every time they laugh unhindered with others.

It is not only laughing, but losing control that opens the door for transfers. When individuals release their inhibitions, they are usually lowering their inner walls. Because of this, people who drink alcohol together often bond with each other. People who smoke marijuana or experiment with hallucinogenic drugs together typically form deep bonds.

Of course, the walls can be erected back up even higher after an individual sobers up or comes down from a drug-induced experience. Bonding that has been forced or is unnatural often leads to a ripping away at a later time.

Losing control happens in numerous other, more acceptable situations of life. For example, when two men are watching a football game, they may become so absorbed in the excitement and intensity that they shout, laugh and abandon all restraint. When a woman cries at the theater, she is losing control and may be yielding her heart to the person with her. When a father and son wrestle playfully in the living room, they may be having such fun that the walls completely fall.

Similarly, the sight of something beautiful can cause a person to lose control. For example, when a woman and a man gaze at a sunset together, they may be releasing strong forces which are harmonizing them as one. As a man is captivated by the beauty of his wife, his spirit is harmonizing with hers.

Notice again the difference between bonding and harmonizing. Bonding develops slowly and endures. Harmonizing is a much more immediate process resulting from hearts oriented the same. Therefore, a married couple may be bonded because of years together. However, they may find themselves not in harmony with one another because their hearts have been oriented differently. Perhaps his heart has been oriented toward his work and she has been focused on her own career or their children. Because of this, they may be out of sync or on two different wavelengths. When they come together they may find it difficult to communicate with each other. They love each other and have years of bonding, yet the condition of harmonizing is a much more immediate, short-term condition.

A husband and wife who find themselves out of sync with each other can get back on the same wavelength by orienting their hearts in the same direction. The best thing for them to do is avoid arguing about problems. First, they need to get on the same wavelength by re-orienting their hearts in the same direction. Talk about the children whom they both love. Do things together such as enjoy a relaxed meal, go to a movie or sit on the porch and look at the stars. Any time two or more people point their affections and attention toward the same focal point, strong forces are activated to bring them into harmony.

Parents who understand these principles can more effectively reach a child who seems distant or estranged. The way to reach that child is not to attack or forcefully demand that they fall into submission. Instead, wise parents can determine where their child's heart is pointed and allow the child to talk about that interest.

Christian parents often have difficulty with this, because their estranged daughter may have her heart directed toward something of which they disapprove. However, by allowing her to talk about her heart's desire, they are opening their hearts to harmonize. On the other hand, by forbidding their daughter to talk about that which has seized her heart, they are isolating her.

Similarly, a woman who is trying to win the love of her husband can determine where his heart is pointed and then take steps to orient her heart in the same direction. A man who desires to get on the same wavelength as his wife needs to allow her to talk about the concerns of her heart.

The forces of bonding and harmonizing are especially powerful when two people forget their personal problems, relax and become still in each other's presence. Therefore, when two people are gazing silently at a sunset, tremendous forces may be working between them.

As a family takes a vacation together, they may first have several days of being extremely busy and rushing from place to place. But later they may stop, sit quietly next to each other and say nothing. At that moment there are forces at work bonding and harmonizing them as one. The individual orientations of their lives is ceasing. Energy is being exchanged and thoughts are being aligned. At such moments individual lives may be readjusted and set on common paths.

Similarly, when two people sleep in the same location together, there is typically a bonding and harmonizing that takes place. During sleep people relax and an exchange seems to happen comparable with osmosis.

Sexual intercourse activates even more powerful forces. As two people's passions are aroused, the longing within their hearts draws the nature of one into the other. Intercourse is, as I mentioned in chapter 4, both a physical and a spiritual experience. In the act, two people detach from the natural realm and focus their affections upon each other. As such, they are open channels to receive the spiritual energy of the other person within themselves.

To various degrees, people become bonded to each other simply by having relationships with one another. Friends become spiritually linked. The apostle Paul wrote of how he was of kindred soul (in Greek: *iso pseuche*; Phil. 2:20) with Timothy. The depth and strength of such bonds vary from one relationship to another.

Authority plays a significant role in forming such bonds. Whenever someone yields to another's authority, he may come under that person's spiritual influence. For example, if a police officer rescues a lady in distress, that lady may find herself dreaming about her hero for some time afterward. A husband who provides security for his family will have greater influence in their lives. A pastor who is bold will have a strong influence in the lives of his congregation.

Similarly, the receiving of gifts from another person can be accompanied by the reception of spiritual substance. When money is received as a gift, spiritual strings may be tied to it. In some cases, when you eat a well-prepared meal, you are yielding to the love, care and influence of the cook and provider. When people admire the beauty or skill of some person, they may also come under his or her spiritual influence. Therefore, the singer may sway or influence the crowd not only with her music, but also with her beliefs. An artist may make an impact upon the spirit of the viewer. A gifted writer may draw the reader into a story that captivates the heart and, hence, brings the reader into a new belief system.

Now, all this is not said to put fear into people's lives. I am not pointing out these conditions for transmissions so that the reader will avoid contact with those around them. Contact with the world around us is inevitable, just as is breathing the same air. There is nothing wrong with enjoying the skills and talents of other people. The time we must exercise caution is when evil people are using their gifts and talents to extend their evil purposes.

A time when people are especially receptive to transfers is when they have a spiritual void within them. For example, when a loved one has died, the person left alone may easily reach for a spiritual replacement. Similarly, if a man has gone through the rejection of a close friend, he may be left especially vulnerable. When people in crisis situations reach out in desperation, there may be increased opportunities for transfers. Car accidents, hospital emergencies and other life-threatening situations may put individuals in positions where they reach out for help and, hence, embrace the spiritual touch of another.

There are also certain rhythmic activities which open people spiritually. As I discussed in chapter 4, rhythmic music can open people spiritually. Even more powerful is dancing together. So also, when an army marches hour after hour in unison, they are being made to bond and harmonize as one. When two people walk side by side they may bond—whether it is a man and woman, a father and son, a teacher and disciple or any other two people. The nature of humanity is designed in such a manner that when people engage in regular, repeated motion together, they tend to blend as one.

Whenever two or more people go into the realm of the spirit together, spiritual transmissions may occur spontaneously. I explained in chapters 3 and 4 that going into the spiritual realm entails detaching from the natural affairs of life and focusing one's entire attention on something in the spiritual world. Whenever people do this jointly, their spirits are open to receive spiritual substance from each other.

For this reason, bonding occurs when a group of Christians have a worship service during which they all direct their hearts toward God. You may observe evidence of such bonding by watching a group of Christians after a church service. They will tend to hang around and fellowship a long time after a service when the worship time has been especially captivating and powerful. On the other hand, if God's presence is not evident during the service, people are more likely to leave quickly after the service. For similar reasons, it is difficult for Christians to move away from a city and leave their church if that church regularly has intense times of worship together. The exchange of spiritual life has bonded the people as one.

The environment of worship is very similar to the environment of romance between a man and woman. As they gaze into each other's eyes over a romantic candlelight dinner, they forget their natural concerns and focus their affections upon each other. In that condition, spiritual bonding and harmonizing easily occurs.

In a worship service where God's presence manifests, not only are transmissions among people common, but also spiritual impartations. In particular, the anointing of the leaders may "leap off them" and be deposited in those who are open to receive. A good example of this is from the Old Testament, where Moses and the 70 elders were enveloped by the presence of God (Num. 11:25). In that presence, the anointing which was upon Moses was transferred to the 70 elders.

I was once in a church meeting where the minister was laying hands on people for powerful divine healings to take place. At the height of the service, the minister's eyes caught mine, and in an instant I felt a power emanating from him and into myself. For several weeks after that I experienced increased authority to lay hands on people and see them healed. Similar impartations commonly occur when people of great anointing minister under the manifesting presence of God.

The last example I gave you brings up the interesting point concerning how eyes may be paths through which spiritual energy flows. Proverbs 20:8 tells us how the ruler can disperse evil with the glance of his eyes. Similarly, a mother may bring her child under her reign with eye contact. John G. Lake, one of the most famous healing ministers of the twentieth century, used to explain how he liked to get eyeball-to-eyeball with a person from whom he was casting out a demon. Through such eye contact, authority may be exercised and power released.

Hands are also points of contact for spiritual impartations and transferences. In the Old Testament times, the men of God would often lay their hands upon their children as they imparted specific blessings into their lives. This was a common practice in the early Church as well. Not only was the Holy Spirit imparted with the laying on of hands (e.g., Acts 8:17), but specific spiritual gifts were imparted (e.g., I Tim 4:14). The practice of laying on of hands implies that spiritual substance actually flows through the hands of people. When Israel laid his hands upon the heads of his grandchildren, Manasseh and Ephraim, a big issue was made concerning which child would have Israel's right hand upon him (Gen. 48:13-19). The point was that more authority flowed through Israel's right hand than through his left.

There seems to be differing points on the human body which have various values in serving as transmission points. There also seem to be specific places on the human body which are more receptive to spiritual substances. For example, hands are laid upon the head to impart spiritual authority and blessings. Hands may be laid on an area of sickness to dispel that sickness from that location. Hands placed upon the shoulder of another person join the two in courage and faith. Feet may be blessed to add strength on a person's journey. The tongue may be touched to sanctify that which is spoken. Hands may be laid upon the temples of a man's head in order to help him change the visions in his mind. And hands may be placed upon the cheeks and upper neck of a woman to guard her emotions.

Of course, in pointing to these truths, I am not giving credence to inappropriate behavior related to "touch therapy" or practices involving immodest contact between people. I am simply noting how God made us, and that different points of our physical body are more sensitive to spiritual transmissions.

The apostle Paul warned Timothy not to lay hands on anyone too hastily (I Tim. 5:22). Spiritual impartations are real, and we must be wise in how we become involved.

A final, yet powerful condition for transmission is the sharing of a "secret place." In this context, a secret place refers to the conditions in which a person places himself to find a complete state of rest. For example, a young man may have a place on a mountainside, in a forest or by the sea where he goes to pray, to find peace or simply to quiet himself. Another's secret places may be in a flowerbed or sitting at a table with a cup of coffee when no one else is present. The secret place may not necessarily be a physical location, but rather a meditative condition in which an individual completely relaxes. It can be a place inside of oneself, where an individual turns his attention to block out the activities of the world and find complete solace. It can also be a memory that fixates one's attention because of its significance in establishing one's own life. A secret place is where a person anchors and finds himself.

When one individual allows another to go to a secret place with him, he is giving an invitation to touch his spirit. For this reason, a woman who desires the heart of a man may long to discover him in that state. Powerful bonding takes place when two people recall and discuss memories of past events which determined who they are and what they think. A disciple may be changed radically the instant he experiences with his teacher such an open, unhindered condition. A hypnotist knows that if he can get the subject to relax to that state, he will have access to influence the subject with spoken words. Once two people experience a secret place together, they have made a spiritual bond that links them and, hence, gives them ongoing access into each other's lives.

People Functioning as a Unit

Spiritual dynamics influence who you are and how you act. Especially powerful are the expectations of the people around you. The more closely you are bonded to them, the greater will be the forces they exert upon your life.

Especially influential are the initial impressions people form of you. How you enter into a relationship determines to a large extent how people will continue to treat you in the future. If a woman confidently introduces herself to others and continues to emanate confidence during the beginning of a relationship, people will expect her to always be self-assured. Another individual who acts as a comedian in front of others will be expected to be funny in the future. For a similar reason, parents who nurture and care for their children will always tend to look at their offspring as "their children," regardless of their ages.

Such expectations release spiritual forces which form the lives of others. As planets in orbit within a solar system, so people are linked in relationships. Each planet moves and revolves in its own course, yet powerful gravitational forces act upon each one. In similar fashion, people have their own destinies and paths to walk, yet the spiritual dynamics occurring between us influence who we are, what we do and what we think.

These spiritual dynamics can be both positive and negative. On the positive side, it is comforting to know how you stand with friends and family. We can relax in the presence of people with whom we already know how to act. In addition, the expectations of others can add strength to our lives, so we continue to act as consistent, stable people.

On the negative side, the forces released by others' expectations can hold us in a type of prison. If we desire to change ourselves, it requires not only the energy to alter our own behavior, but also the inner strength to break and then remold the expectations of others.

The longer two or more people relate to each other, the greater will be the spiritual forces between them. These bonds can be so intense that their lives not only influence but actually depend upon each other. In the Bible, we read of Jacob who so loved his son, Benjamin, that it was said, *"...his life is bound up in the lad's life"* (Gen. 44:30). In another passage, it is said that if Benjamin left his father, *"...his father would die"* (Gen. 44:22). We have observed similar dynamics in long-standing, close marriages where a spouse dies and a short time later the other also passes away.

Furthermore, two people may be bonded so closely that they feel the same hurts and pains. When one is sick, the other feels weak. A mother may be so bonded to her newborn that when the baby has a restless night, the mother tosses with every move of the child. An even more obvious proof of these spiritual bonds is the case where a grown child far away from home gets into trouble—perhaps a car wreck— and the parents are disturbed until they find out what happened. Many people have experienced such bonding with others, especially their own children.

It is interesting to note how pain, burdens or sorrow may be relieved in a person when shared by another. For example, when people visit a sick loved one, they may leave feeling some discomfort, but the sick person may feel a little better. Expressions of concern may do more than merely exchange words; they may actually orient the hearts of people so that some measure of pain is relieved in the hurting person. There are also times when pain seems to be relieved in a person through the touch of a loving friend. Can it be that spiritual substance is exchanged and strength is given to the sick person while some measure of pain may be transferred back to the healthy person? Yes, God has created us to share one another's burdens.

It is more than emotions, pain, sorrow or intangible feelings that can be transmitted. People who have sympathy pains for another individual may actually develop the related illnesses. Yes, the physical body may change as bonding takes place or as spiritual substance is shared.

Studies done on women in the military who live, work and march together day after day reveal how their physical bodies may change to the extent that they all experience their menstrual cycles at the same time.

Among people closely bonded, we also see certain characteristics and habit patterns develop. For example, young boys in a street gang may talk and dress alike. Medical personnel who work closely with one another tend to share similar values and develop the same sense of humor. Even people who all attend the same church begin to laugh the same, dress alike and view life from the same perspective. I am not implying that they become as clones of each other, but they do develop tendencies toward similar behaviors and characteristics.

Not only do bonded people tend to think alike, but they begin acting as if they share a common mind. One seems to know what the other is thinking. Amazingly, they function as a unit, working together with very little verbal communication. It is as if they all are plugged into the same computer, aware of each other's needs and desires. Invisible lines of communication seem to exist between them, directing their desires, thoughts and actions.

Bonding Creates a Shared Mind

These group dynamics are real and can be observed in many situations of life, yet the concept of a common mind may seem a bit mystical for some readers. Since the Bible is our final authority on such subjects, let's look there for evidence. When the Holy Spirit filled the early believers, they *"...were of one heart and soul"* (Acts 4:32). The Holy Spirit was enveloping and bathing them. In that atmosphere they, indeed, did share a unity of thoughts and desires. In the Old Testament, the Jewish people on several occasions were molded together to act as *"one man"* (e.g., II Chron. 5:13, 30:12; Ezra 3:1).

Not only does the Bible declare that people can share a common mind, but we see evidence of this in many situations of life, especially where people must work together and depend upon each other. For example, individuals in war, police officers, firemen, paramedics, emergency workers and others in life-threatening situations may learn to depend upon each other so intensely that when one needs the other, they automatically fill in the required roles. Similarly, in team sports the individual members may bond so closely that they can work together and perform as if they are a unit. They may not even need to communicate with each other, but they simply "know" and move into the right positions at the right times.

One result of this common mind is a shared sense of responsibility. All the members of a team work toward the same goal, however, they each do not carry out the same tasks. Instead, responsibilities are distributed among them, so that they can work together, each fulfilling their individual role in the total purpose of the group.

Bonding Produces Shared Responsibilities

As any one person in a united group accepts responsibility for some area, it tends to decrease the sense of responsibility upon the others in that same area. Often, nothing needs to be communicated verbally. A spiritual dynamic is established wherein united people can act corporately and, hence, accomplish much more together than those working individually. God created people with this ability to work with others.

It is amazing to see how responsibilities can be shifted from one person to another in bonded relationships. A personal example I can give is from the time when I pastored a church. During the early years the church was small and, as the pastor, I had to oversee every area of the ministry, both natural and spiritual. Therefore, during the Sunday morning service I was thinking not only of the message to deliver, but also if the chairs were in place, the P.A. system was functioning correctly, the heat was adjusted appropriately, new people greeted, etc. After training several individuals to help with the ministry, I found that they could not fully accept the related responsibilities until I gave up those responsibilities. One Sunday morning this was particularly evident. In the middle of the church service, I found myself consumed with thoughts concerning the practical functioning of the church service—in particular, I was concerned that the room in which we were meeting was getting much too warm. As I thought about this, I became upset about why one of my helpers was not aware of the problem and adjusting the heat. Rather than fix the problem myself or say anything, I decided to force myself to stop thinking about the heat. I knew I would be unable to bring forth an anointed message if my mind was consumed with thoughts about the physical comfort of the people. So I forcefully ejected any more thoughts concerning the heat. The instant I pushed the related concerns out of my mind, one of my helpers standing nearby walked to the room thermostat and solved the problem. It was amazing how quickly the sense of responsibility switched from me to him.

In a well-functioning family, the parents normally carry the sense of responsibility for the welfare of the children. If, however, the parents are unable or are negligent toward the care of their children, often one of the children, usually the oldest, will arise and carry many of the family responsibilities to the best of his or her ability.

In a marriage relationship, one person may be irresponsible financially, which leads the other to be overly responsible, perhaps even obsessed with money concerns.

People exert spiritual pressure on others to such an extent that it molds their character. A girl forced to carry too much responsibility may pursue a career as an adult where great expectations are placed upon her, and she may only feel good about herself when such pressures continue to be placed upon her by others. On the other hand, a child who has received too much care (sheltered to an extreme) may grow up unable to deal with common stresses and trials, often leading to escape mechanisms such as alcoholism or drug abuse.

Because of these dynamics, a mother who worries too much about her children actually may be damaging them. The conscious or unconscious act of worry is often the acceptance of personal responsibility for the actions and welfare of another person to such an extent that the person becomes irresponsible. Such worry often is hidden in the life of a Christian parent behind prayers. Some parents think they are praying for their child, but actually they are accepting so much responsibility for their child that they are stealing the weight of responsibility that should rest upon that child. Such "prayer" is destructive. The more they pray in this fashion, the more they are releasing forces which make their own child irresponsible.

We are instructed to cast all of our cares upon the Lord (I Peter 5:7), praying until the peace of God which surpasses all comprehension guards our hearts and minds (Phil. 4:6-7). Such a transference of a burden to the Lord creates a dynamic where God can lay the weight of responsibility upon the appropriate individual. This is effective prayer.

Learning how to relinquish certain responsibilities, either to God or others, is key. A father who carries too much may hinder his children. A businessman who constantly worries about his employees will keep them dependent upon him and unable to think for themselves. A pastor who wants to control every aspect of his church will hold his congregation in a state of immaturity.

Often the giving of responsibility to another person requires dying to vision. To die in this sense means to abandon all efforts of fulfilling a certain vision. This is often necessary because a vision-driven person may be so obsessed with the vision that no one else has "room" to help carry the load. Only if the vision is abandoned—that is the ownership is relinquished and shared with others—will those others actually help carry it.

Jesus explained:

> *"Truly, truly, I say to you, unless a grain of wheat falls into the earth and dies, it remains alone; but if it dies, it bears much fruit."*
>
> (John 12:24)

Relate the grain of wheat in this parable to a God-inspired vision in a believer's heart. Jesus taught that unless the seed dies *"it remains alone."* When a woman is consumed with a vision, even a God-inspired vision, she will remain alone— other people may help, but they must depend upon the constant energy input of the visionary. The visionary, indeed, may have enough energy to inspire everyone around, but immediately when that visionary is not around, the energy wanes in all who are involved. The visionary remains alone in carrying that vision.

However, if the seed dies, *"it bears much fruit."* When the visionary arrives at the point where her own hopes of ever accomplishing the desired goal are dead, the energy to fulfill that vision will be planted in the hearts of those to whom she is bonded. To die, in this context, means to relax in the passion and zeal of that vision, even to relinquish the vision to such an extent that it is entrusted back to God. When a person yields her own desires in this way, a vision may be planted in the hearts of those around. Through such an impartation, visions may be shared and many people energized to carry out the related goals. Often a visionary will be required to die to his own vision repeatedly before the spiritual energy is released or passed on to others. If it dies it will *"bear much fruit."* This is another way in which people can be influenced to act as a unit.

Through all the means we have studied, bonded individuals will come to a point of unity where they share a common mind, desires and responsibilities. In addition, they can share a vision which unites them in deep ways so that they may function together as a unit.

In today's world, psychologists have studied such group dynamics. Referring to the common mind they sometimes use the terminology "group consciousness." Accepting these social dynamics, I have tried to look deeper and explain the spiritual dynamics behind this phenomenon. Every person has a spirit/soul which exists in the spiritual world. That spirit/soul has the ability to bond with others. Spiritual energy is the light which illuminates minds, enabling people to think. The reason people seem to act as if they are united is because they are united. There is, indeed, a group consciousness among people who are bonded together.

The Human Spirit and Authority

How does the human spirit respond to authority?

Picture a group of people who are all seated in a classroom facing the front. If someone with great authority walks through the door at the back of the room, many of those seated will turn to see who walked into the room. On the other hand, if a person with very little spiritual presence walks in, almost no one will turn to see who entered the room. Such a phenomenon can be explained when we recognize that authority can be sensed spiritually by others.

Not only can people sense authority, but their spirits actually yield to it; in a sense, they bow to a person of greater authority. The Bible gives us an example of this when the Queen of Sheba met King Solomon. After the King showed her all his wealth, the Bible says that *"there was no more spirit in her"* (I Kings 10:5). The Queen was left speechless, awed by the blessings of God upon Solomon's life. Her spirit was left without strength in the presence of Solomon's grandeur.

We see a similar reaction when a person encounters God. For example, when the glory of God manifested in the Jewish temple, the priests were unable to stand. John fell as a dead man when Jesus appeared before him (Rev. 1:17). Isaiah had a similar experience, as he was undone before the throne of our Lord (Is. 6:1-5). All the soldiers who came to take Jesus

335

from the Garden of Gethsemane fell back when Jesus declared who He was (John 18:6).

In some churches today we see people being "slain in the spirit." There are false encounters of this phenomenon, but in true experiences, the person's spirit is bowing to the presence of God to such a degree that his body no longer has strength within it to continue standing.

Of course, authority encounters don't happen just in religious contexts, but in our everyday lives. An employee may be intimidated by her boss, which we understand is the result of her spirit yielding to that boss. For the same reason, a timid boy may have to summon all his energy to talk to adults. Some people find themselves speechless in the presence of famous individuals. They cannot think as clearly, and their physical body can actually lose its strength as the spirit within is pulling back.

We should not put all forms of authority in the same category. Obviously, authority can be used either for God's glory or for evil purposes. I am not trying to make a distinction at this point, but I am merely explaining how authority influences the human spirit. What we discover is that the human spirit is very responsive to the authority which abides in others.

The Human Spirit Responds to Authority

Where does authority originate? Romans 13:1 tells us, *"... there is no authority except from God, and those which exist are established by God."* This is true whether the authority is used for good or evil. God is the ultimate source of all authority. When He spoke over Adam and Eve, *"...fill the earth and subdue it,"* He instilled in the nature of humanity the authority to manage this world (Gen. 1:28). God has given each and every human being some measure of authority. We decide whether to use that authority for good or evil.

An individual's authority grows as he accepts the related responsibility. Jesus said, *"For whoever has, to him more shall be given"* (Mark 4:25a). Our Lord went on in the same Bible passage to say: *"and whoever does not have, even what he has shall be taken away from him"* (Mark 4:25b). As we apply this truth to authority, we can say that individuals will lose their authority if they do not embrace and use it.

The authority of individuals also increases as they make deep heart decisions within themselves. For example, a young woman may make a decision to escape the lifestyle of poverty in which she was raised and, hence, become a financial success. The strength of her decision will increase her authority to accomplish her goals.

Many times the decisions that are made are destructive, and they have negative effects upon others. For example, if a woman is deeply hurt in a relationship with a man, she may consciously or unconsciously make a firm decision to never again expose her heart to another man. As she makes that decision, she is exercising the authority she has over her own being, yet it will affect many other people throughout her life, and the depth of her decision will determine the strength of her authority in the related areas.

A man who repeatedly gives himself to the abuse of alcohol can yield to the temptation so many times that he will lose his authority to control himself, while at the same time making deep decisions such as, "I will do anything for another drink." That lifestyle will diminish his authority over his self-discipline, yet it may give him authority to obtain more alcohol. Hence, alcoholics have an uncanny ability to find their next drink.

Authority is especially increased as people pay a high price for the decisions they have made. When people sacrifice or stand against tremendous opposition, persecution or trials, their heart-commitment deepens. As a person's heart is pointed more and more firmly in a specific direction for long periods, it releases powerful spiritual forces which flow in the corresponding direction.

Authority Increases with Commitment

Similarly, authority grows as people invest more time and energy in a project, profession or other endeavor. People with years of experience in a certain area develop confidence in themselves and, hence, authority in their work.

Authority can also be obtained from another person. We saw this earlier as we discussed how Moses laid his hands upon Joshua and imparted some of his authority. In similar fashion, parents, teachers or leaders can impart some of their authority to those under their care. Again we can note our Lord's words that a pupil will become as his teacher (Luke 6:40). A student who invests years at school draws upon the strengths of his instructors. Similarly, an individual who develops close relationships with others in authority obtains authority. Married people typically share authority. In fact, if a weak, timid woman marries a man with great authority, in time she may begin to speak and act with more authority. The opposite may also happen if the weaker person yields in the sense of becoming more and more irresponsible.

There is also a corporate authority which results from two or more people taking their individual authorities and orienting them toward the same goals. Their corporate authority is greater than the sum of their individual authorities and is the result of deep heart-commitments. This dynamic of corporate authority is so significant, I will discuss it in pages which follow.

Corporate Authority in the Family

Once a group of people have bonded, they can fulfill a corporate function greater than their individual elements. As I already explained, a corporate mind develops and people share responsibilities in an uncanny sense. They can work together and accomplish great tasks. Not only is work easier, but the authority upon them is greater. This authority flows out of the united group as if a spiritual stream were established in the spiritual realm. In this chapter, we will examine how this authority functions in the family unit.

When a husband and wife join themselves together, they form a team to work united in this life. If they are in agreement, then together they have more authority than each has separately. This authority is evident in the family atmosphere where children are raised. A husband and wife united in heart are able to create an environment where children grow feeling secure and loved.

The spiritual influence which emanates from parents has a real effect upon the thoughts and decisions of their children. It is not forced upon their children, nor automatically deposited within the children's spirits. Envision the stream as a wind of influence gently blowing over the mind and heart of each young one. The children open or close their own hearts to receive or reject their parents' influence.

When a husband and wife realize they have the ability to form a spiritual stream for their descendants, they no longer limit their thinking to just themselves or their children. A marriage is, in fact, the merging of two streams. As two family lines are joined in marriage, a new entity is created. A stream of blessings and/or curses is released upon those who follow.

Two Family Lines Merge into One

In Western society, we tend not to think in these terms. We are focused more upon present relationships than family lines. In Bible times, people thought much more generationally. For this reason, family lineages are emphasized in the Scriptures, and for them it was important to know who was a descendant of whom. People today who do not think generationally are missing profound truths.

Now as I discuss this, I am not denying the freedom which we find in Jesus Christ. We are taught in the Bible that Christians have been spiritually grafted into the family lineage of God. As such, we can escape, to some degree, the negative influences which may flow through our natural family lines. As we grow in our walk with God, we draw strength from our lineage in Him. However, we must not ignore the natural family forces which continue to act upon us. These spiritual streams are real. Every one of us is influenced by them. In our natural family, there are forces acting upon our thoughts, emotions and behavior. This brings us back to the sense of responsibility we should have in developing healthy family relationships.

Of greatest importance is how the strength of the bond between a father and mother determines the strength of the spiritual flow through their lives. A husband and wife with no sense of commitment to each other are not providing a spiritual base upon which their descendants may stand. Their children will suffer for it. They will be tossed by other winds throughout their lives until they find strength elsewhere; they will tend to become a part of other groups which provide them a spiritual base.

In contrast, a husband and wife deeply committed to one another establish strong forces in the spiritual realm in which their descendants can grow. Trials that come against that man and woman can be the means by which their authority increases. Sickness, lack of finances, personal struggles, etc., each demand that the husband and wife orient their hearts more wholly toward each other. That deepening commitment increases the spiritual flow through them. The longer they stay together and the more deeply they cling to each other, the greater will be their authority in this world.

That authority is not just for the present. The spiritual stream they create through their covenant and bonding moves down the family line. It goes wherever their hearts are pointed. If they believe for their children, grandchildren and beyond, then they will establish spiritual blessings in which the generations to follow will bathe.

An amazing example of this continued stream of blessing can be seen in the life of Jonathan and Sarah Edwards, ministers who stood together faithfully believing God in the midst of incredible trials during the 1700's. A study of 1,400 of their descendants revealed that the family produced 13 college presidents, 65 professors, 100 lawyers, 30 judges, 66 physicians, three senators, three governors and one vice president of the United States.

In contrast, we can see negative effects coming upon generations when there are violations of the marriage covenant. Recall King David's sin when he committed adultery with Bathsheba (II Sam. 12:10-11). Even though David repented and God forgave him, God told David that his nation would suffer through inner turmoils and wars for many years to follow. Indeed, we see his sons deceptively fighting one another until the nation of Israel was divided. David had authority over the nation and, therefore, the entire nation was affected when his heart was divided.

Consider where parents separate through divorce. The family authority has been divided, and the spiritual influence, therefore, will be divided. Let's say the husband, Doug, has the children visit him on weekends, and the mother, Nancy, has the children on weekdays. While the children are with Nancy, she influences them according to her thoughts and desires. As long as the children's hearts are pointed toward their mother, she is able to direct them easily. Then on weekends when the children visit their father, he takes over the spiritual headship. At first, Doug finds the children moving in their daily lives contrary to his desires. But after a day or two, their hearts start pointing toward him, and he has greater influence on their thoughts and actions. When it is time for the children to return to the care of their mother, Nancy finds the children going in a direction different than when she left them. She feels as if she must take the first two days just to get them back on track with her goals and plans. The pattern continues week after week. When the children's hearts are directed toward their mother, they respond to her, and then when they turn their hearts back to their father, they come under his influence.

What we see are two different authority lines, as two streams, flowing from the separated parents. The children submit to and draw upon the stream to which their hearts are pointed. Their thoughts and desires align with the father or mother as they yield to the authority of each. When there is a divorce, there is not only the separation of two people, but also the division of a spiritual stream.

One Spiritual Stream Divided into Two

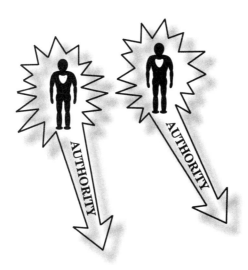

Of course, divorces are common today, and we do not want to condemn those who have suffered through the related difficulties. God does heal. He does forgive. However, seeing divorce from the spiritual dimension helps us realize how divorce divides the spiritual stream intended to bathe a family line.

48 Authority Streams Throughout Society

The spiritual dynamics in family units involving corporate authority, a common mind and shared responsibilities, operate similarly in many other groups in which people work together. Consider a local church. When a group of church elders commit to working together, they develop an authority greater than can any single individual. The longer they work together, the greater their unity. Each time they face a problem, they will decide to continue working together or separate and go their individual ways. As they stick it out and work through their differences, they are entering deeper and deeper into relationships with each other. The more they invest in each other and in a common goal, the greater will be their corporate authority.

When we talk about this corporate authority in the Church, we also should mention corporate anointing, because the word "anointing" refers to the flow of the Holy Spirit. As Christians become of one heart and mind, the presence of God manifests. The Holy Spirit and the believers' spirits become one. Therefore, the resulting authority has the added dimension of the flowing Holy Spirit.

The congregation benefits wondrously through this corporate anointing. The blessings of God flow. The people bathe in the love and security produced. Their thoughts and desires melt together. As they yield to and enter the spiritual stream, they form a united, loving body.

Consider, however, what will happen if there is a tragic split among the church leadership. Let's say some of the elders go one way and the others go another. What will happen to the people? What will they do?

Many congregational members will feel as though they have to choose between one set of elders or the other. When they visit with the first set of elders and listen to their side of the issues, they will see things similarly. Then as they visit the other elders, they may switch position to the opposing view. There may not even be any conversation related to the church split, but because spiritual streams are determined by heart-bonding, church members will start to think along the lines of the leaders whom their hearts are pointed toward.

Spiritual streams exist not only in churches and families, but all human beings have spiritual energy flowing out of them. Whenever people bond together, a *corporate stream* is established. Strong streams are evident in businesses, big corporations, clubs, political associations, schools, sports teams, musical groups, street gangs, etc. In every situation of life where people make commitments to each other, the spiritual energy from within them flows together. That spiritual energy can and does influence people's thoughts.

When I talk about these streams, I am not saying that people's thoughts are determined 100% by the outside spiritual influences acting upon them. Rather, I am pointing out streams that influence thought patterns. People still have authority over their own minds, and individually they are responsible for themselves.

We can compare the influence of spiritual streams with the influence a big city has upon a small-town person. When a person lives for an extended time in an isolated area with very few people around, there is a tendency to slow down and simplify one's lifestyle. However, when that person drives into a metropolitan area, everything seems to be moving quickly. In a short time, the small-town dweller will find himself speeding up to the pace of those around.

Similar dynamics are evident in an institution of higher learning. A mature, well-trained professor can exert tremendous pressure upon the thoughts of a young student. How much greater is the authority of the whole institution backed by hundreds of teachers, millions of dollars and years of labor? A student enrolling in such an institution should expect powerful forces to begin molding her thought patterns accordingly.

Consider a large mass of people united around a specific religious belief. If a man who is not strong in his own beliefs visits a Muslim country where thousands of Muslims chant five times a day while facing Mecca, there will be a lasting impact upon his mind. His weak thought patterns may even "bow," and as a result, he may no longer remember what he used to believe or why.

From these examples, we can see the forces of spiritual streams reaching beyond immediate organizations or groups and flowing out to influence large regions of the world. Such forces are evident within every nation. As people work and play together, the corporate authority of a country develops. National activities such as elections, the death of a leader and sports events cause the people to orient their hearts in the same direction.

Perhaps the greatest forces are established for a nation as they go through a war. In such conditions, the leaders must unite their people for the common defense. The resulting commitments among citizens can be intense. Soldiers bond under life-and-death situations. Loved ones at home direct their hope, faith and tears toward a common goal. Sacrifices are made, and some of the deepest bonds possible are formed with the yielding of blood. Such covenants produce spiritual forces. When tens of thousands of people in a country have their hearts oriented along a common path, there are consequences in the spiritual realm. After a war is finished, the energy does not shut down quickly. Hate, fear, love and passion are powerful forces orienting the hearts of people. Such forces help establish a nation's identity and culture. Future generations will have similar thoughts for years to come.

The resulting spiritual streams move through time. Remember that spiritual substance is not limited to the time restrictions which we know in the natural world. The spiritual breath which God breathed into Adam is still sustaining life generations later. So, also, spiritual substance released through human beings today influences people who will live years from now.

We are all influenced by the streams acting upon us. People like to think that they are logical, independent thinkers. In reality, every one of us orient our hearts down certain paths and toward certain people. We then align our thoughts according to where our hearts are pointed. We choose the facts that reinforce what we already believe. We subconsciously make excuses for our heroes' mistakes. Even the most logical among us progressively build their thought patterns along the well-worn paths of those who have gone ahead of us.

Changing or Escaping a Spiritual Stream

We live in a world flooded with the thoughts and currents of other men and women—not just from those around us, but also from people who have gone on ahead of us, especially where corporate authority streams have been established. The apostle Paul cautioned us not to be *"tossed here and there by waves and carried about by every wind of doctrine..."* (Eph. 4:14). Even when we think we are being progressively logical, we simply may be riding on the thought patterns established by others.

This raises questions concerning how we can think freely today. Can we ever get a perspective from above the streams which tend to influence us? Can we undo some of the negative consequences of our foreparents? And is it possible to change the flow which goes beyond us to those who follow in our footsteps? The answer is, "Yes," to all three questions.

First, we may undo the wrong decisions made by those preceding us. An example is when hate and bitterness have released forces which split a family in two, and later forgiveness heals and removes from the spiritual dimension the energy which stirred negative feelings.

To see an example of such a powerful undoing of evil, read in the Old Testament about the covenant which the Jews made with the Gibeonites. One day the Gibeonites disguised themselves and tricked the Jewish people into promising them that they would never hurt anyone of their people (Joshua 9). That covenant established forces in the spiritual dimension that influenced people for years afterward. In II Samuel 21, we read how King Saul did not honor the covenant made by his forefathers and this resulted in a famine in the nation of Israel. God held the Jews accountable to fulfill the covenants of their forefathers. When they did not, there were serious consequences. King David, however, sought the Lord to find out how he could end the resulting famine. God told David exactly what to do, and after he obeyed, the famine ended (II Sam. 21).

Another example of a man undoing the consequences of evil can be found in the Book of Daniel. At that time the Jewish people had been in captivity for their sins for 70 years. Daniel began fasting and praying for God to forgive their sins. He interceded, asking God to forgive the people; at times he prayed as if he were accepting personal responsibility for the sins of his foreparents (Dan. 9:1-19). God answered and, indeed, the Jews were set free.

Apply these principles to what happened through the Protestant Reformation. We can study Church history and learn of the great split between Protestants and Roman Catholics during the 1500's. Tremendous spiritual forces were established at that point in history. Thousands of people died for their faith—on both sides. Hate, fear and faith directed the hearts of millions. The consequences of those forces are still in the world today, influencing thoughts and directing people's lives.

Can we escape those forces and get a perspective from above those streams? Yes. Repentance for the sins of our forefathers is necessary, and lifting ourselves above the spiritual influences is also key. In addition, God may guide individuals in unique steps of obedience.

Stepping above a certain spiritual stream usually requires a re-identification of oneself. For example, I do not like to consider myself a Protestant anymore, because the name *Protestant* comes from *Protesting One.* Personally, I am not protesting. That is not the core of my Christianity today. Abandoning a label is a step to rise above the resulting spiritual forces.

See this principle in Paul's writings to the early believers. In I Corinthians, chapter 3, Paul corrected the Christians for aligning their thoughts and allegiance either to himself or to another leader named Apollos. He explained that when one group claimed to be "of Apollos," while others claimed to be "of Paul," they were thinking as immature babies. The lesson is that we should not limit ourselves to the influence of any one leader, but instead, we should all be "of Christ."

It is through such a position of maturity that we can rise above the spiritual influences acting upon us. When we place our allegiance in the One who sits on the throne of God, we lift ourselves higher in the spiritual dimension. To help us in this, we have an anchor which is the revealed Word of God. We cannot remove ourselves completely from the spiritual ocean around us, but we can do our best to keep our hearts in a stream that glorifies God and exalts Jesus as Lord.

The last question I want to address here is, "How can a person change the stream which flows to those who come in later generations?" It is not only ourselves who need to be freed. Those who may follow in our footsteps should not be hindered by our errors. In fact, we want our influence to bless them.

It is possible to stop negative influences from being passed to one's descendants. Even if a woman has had to battle for years against negative pressures from her forefathers, it is her personal resistance which stops the flow. She is fighting for her generational line when she battles against temptation. Only then can she say with authority, "The curse stops here!"

Even more inspiring is how individuals may bring positive strengths and new spiritual blessings into their authority line and pass it on to those who follow. An example is Abraham receiving the blessings of God. When God spoke to Abraham, He promised to bless him and his descendants:

> *"And I will make you a great nation,*
> *And I will bless you,*
> *And make your name great;*
> *And so you shall be a blessing...*
> *And in you all the families of the earth shall be*
>   *blessed."*
>
> (Gen. 12:2-3)

As Abraham received this blessing, it not only came upon him, but also became available to his descendants.

This blessing was first passed on to Isaac, Abraham's son. Later Isaac had two sons and it is enlightening to see how the blessing was released into their lives. The firstborn son was Esau and he was in line to receive the blessing. However, one day he traded his birthright to his brother, Jacob, for a single meal (Gen. 25:27-34; Heb. 12:16). The consequences affected not just the two brothers lives, but the blessing of God was actually transferred from Esau's line of descendants to Jacob's. Millions of people were removed from the blessing line, while others were brought into and under the blessings of God.

This transfer of spiritual blessing is another example of how spiritual impartations are not deposited automatically into certain individuals. Each person must accept or reject that which is offered to him or her. Once a spiritual stream has been established, it makes available to one's descendants the related benefits. However, people must choose whether or not to open their own hearts to receive.

Distinguish in your mind the difference between the words *importation* and *impartation*. *Importation* is used to identify the movement of new spiritual substance from out of the spiritual realm into a specific stream. *Impartation* is how that spiritual substance may move from one individual to others. An importation moved a blessing into the family line of Abraham, while that blessing was imparted to Abraham's descendants through Isaac and then Jacob.

We can see more examples of this in the Bible. Hannah, for example, was a woman who cried out to God for a child, and in those prayers she agreed to dedicate that child to the Lord's service (I Sam. 1:9-19). As a result, she imported into her family line a specific blessing from God. That blessing was imparted to her child Samuel, who became a powerful and influential prophet of God.

When a person is standing in God's presence, praying for some particular need, God sees not only the person, but also those to whom that individual is bonded. For example, a father is bonded to his children, and God can see those children linked with the father. God tells us in the Bible that He will bless the person who loves Him and those blessings will extend to generations after that person (e.g., Ex. 20:5-6). Parents who understand this principle realize that they can stand in the presence of God and receive blessings—not only for themselves, but also for their offspring. Those blessings are not forced upon their descendants but become available to those willing to receive.

Evil can also be imported into a family stream, and then, imparted to those who follow. The first example we have in the Bible is related to Adam's sin in the Garden of Eden. We are told that through Adam *"...sin entered the world, and death through sin, and so death spread to all men..."* (Rom 5:12). As noted earlier, Adam was the doorway for sin to enter into the world. Death then spread to all descendants of Adam as they opened themselves to evil and sin.

We see this principle working in many ways in our daily lives. A father who yields himself to anger may import the related forces into his family line. As a consequence, his children may have strong forces released upon them pushing them to give in to similar anger problems. Similarly, parents who repeatedly give in to sexual perversions may release like forces upon their own descendants. Some would prefer to accredit such evil forces to social and psychological tendencies learned from parents. Of course, many behaviors are learned from those by whom we have been reared. However, I also want to recognize the spiritual forces that can be released from parent to child.

It will be helpful to introduce one more term here, the word *porter*. I take this word from the service of a porter who assists us boarding a train or stands at the front door of a hotel assisting or forbidding certain people to enter. In similar fashion, any person can act as a porter, admitting or restricting spiritual influences that would enter any stream of which they are a part.

Every human being acts as a porter to some degree. Within a single family unit, each person can import spiritual substance positively or negatively. A parent's anger may bring the entire household under emotional stress. A son may import a bad attitude which he imparts to others. On the positive side, one person may develop a strong positive attitude and great faith, by which everyone is lifted and strengthened. Or a parent may recognize a negative influence trying to enter the family and by an assertive stance refuse to allow its entrance.

Spiritual transmissions from one to another tend to flow from a person of great authority to those with less authority. However, all people bonded together can and do influence each other to some degree. If the father comes home to his family one day with a bad attitude, he may unload on his wife, who takes it out on the children, who kick the dog. People bonded together influence each other, but the strongest tendencies flow downhill in respect to authority.

Let's end this chapter with a positive example of the principles I have been discussing. In a local church a certain leader may receive (import) some anointing, authority or other blessing from God. All the people under the care of that leader may eventually benefit from what has been imported. They will not receive the related blessings automatically; however, as they open themselves up to receive, they indeed may enter into the stream of blessing.

50 Pyramid Dyamics

We have seen where authority originates and how it affects people. Now, I want to use the figure of a pyramid to explain some authority principles.

Before I discuss the pyramid I need to set your mind at ease concerning this geometric figure. Many Christians associate the pyramid with evil spiritual practices. It is true that some occult practitioners use the pyramid in their evil works. However, the devil did not create the pyramid. It is a figure which is useful to explain all spiritual authority, whether good or evil. Please let me explain.

If plants or animals are allowed to reproduce with none of them dying, growth will be exponential. For example, one rabbit may produce five rabbits; then each of those five rabbits would produce five more rabbits giving us 25 more rabbits; and then each of those 25 rabbits would produce five more rabbits giving us 125 more rabbits. Such growth is exponential.

Our Lord taught several parables explaining how the kingdom of God grows in similar fashion. He compared the growth of the kingdom to yeast cells growing in dough; a yeast cell reproduces, first one cell, then two, then four, then eight, then sixteen, then thirty-two, etc. Jesus also described the kingdom growing like seeds, eventually yielding thirty, sixty and a hundredfold (Mark 4:8)—first the blade, then the head, then the mature grain in the head (Mark 4:28). Both the kingdom of God and all living things grow exponentially.

All Living Things Show Exponential Growth

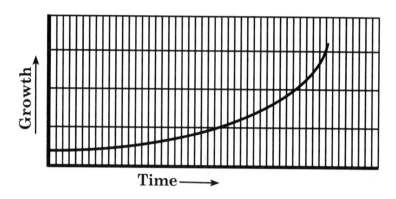

Exponential growth in geometric form or in three dimensions is represented by the pyramid.

Exponential Growth in Three Dimensions

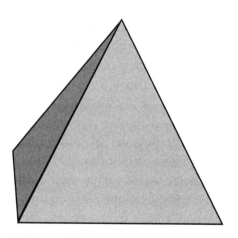

This pattern permeates authority structures.

Consider the relationships surrounding Jesus during His earthly ministry. There were three who had privileged access to Him: Peter, James and John. They alone saw Jesus revealed in glory on the Mount of Transfiguration and later, weeping in the Garden of Gethsemane. Those three were among the twelve apostles who all stayed close by His side. Next we see the 70 disciples who followed our Lord, and then there were crowds of 4,000-5,000 to whom Jesus fed the loaves and fish. Beyond these were the multitudes who heard His teachings and, of course, He blessed the entire world. If we arrange these numbers in a descending order of their closeness to Jesus, we have a pyramid.

The same pattern of relationships assembled under the ministry of Moses. He had three close to him—Aaron, Miriam and Joshua. Then he had the heads of the twelve tribes of Israel, and under those were the 70 elders. Below those in authority were the heads of the family units, and finally, all of the Hebrew people.

It is also interesting to note the numbers that appear in the Book of Revelation concerning those who assemble around the throne of our Lord. We do not have the complete picture, but we are told about the 24 elders and the 144,000 who were sealed and protected from judgment. It is interesting that archeologists tell us there are 144,000 stones in the perimeter of the bottom layer of the great pyramid in Egypt.

I am not saying that the Egyptian pyramids are of God. Nor am I teaching that everything with a pyramid on it is good. Rather, I am trying to break the thinking which some Christians have embraced toward this symbol. Only then can I explain its significance and why we see it appearing in authority relationships in the Bible.

The pyramid symbolizes spiritual dynamics that occur in relationships involving authority. People carrying authority are the top of the pyramid, and those below are the people under the established authority. As we study relationships in real-life situations, we typically see these dynamics taking shape. Whether we are studying governments, corporations, organizations, businesses or schools, there typically forms a structure of descending authority. These are the facts of life.

When the pyramid is used in relationship to authority, it is often drawn with an eye positioned on the top portion of the pyramid. The great pyramid in Egypt has the top peak left off. On the back of the American dollar bill, an eye is positioned very prominently at the top of a pyramid.

Again, I need to set at ease readers who have had unfounded suspicions towards the pyramid, and especially a pyramid with the all-seeing eye positioned at the top. Some who have negative views of the United States see the pyramid on the back of the American dollar bill as somehow associated with Satan's realm. In truth, the founders of the U.S. thought of the eye as the Providence of God, that is, the supernatural guidance of God in His working out of His sovereign plans.[5]

I explained earlier that authority is the result of people working together. Every single person represented in the pyramid adds to the whole authority structure. As people unite, they see the need to trust certain individuals with the oversight of what they hope to accomplish corporately. The eye pictured on top of the pyramid symbolizes the effects of the people's trust on those in leadership. Leaders receive the ability to lead. Their eyes are opened supernaturally to guide those under their charge. This is good. This is how God designed us to work together.

---

5 Some people with a negative view of the U.S. wrongly interpret the Latin words (*Annuit Coeptis Novus Ordo Seclorum*) on the back of the American dollar bill as: "Announcing a New World Order." In truth the Latin words are properly translated: "He has favored our undertakings. A new age now begins."

Consider some examples. In a family unit when all members of the family trust the father of that family, he will have more confidence to lead. As they trust their mother, she will be guided supernaturally. If one of the children falls into a dangerous situation, something within the father or mother will motivate them to check on that child. The incidents of such occurrences are common. The motivation parents receive is not always because they hear anything or see anything, but one or the other is motivated instinctively—spiritually—to go and correct the problem.

In a business, when the CEO, president, boss or others in charge are carrying the responsibility given to them, they will find themselves being supernaturally guided to fulfill their duties. If there is a financial difficulty, something inside the boss may nudge him to direct attention to the problem. If there is a certain employee causing difficulties, the boss is likely to discover it. That discovery may be the result of diligent oversight or it may be just a coincidence where the boss catches the problem out of the corner of his eye. Somehow everything under his charge will remain open to his oversight. The wise boss learns to trust his gut feeling in such cases.

The principle symbolized by the pyramid with its all-seeing eye is evident in all authority relationships. *"For there is no authority except from God, and those which exist are established by God"* (Rom. 13:1b). It is helpful to equate the eye with the providence of God as the founders of the United States did. This providence is not God's intimate intervention in the life of every individual. Instead, when we think of divine providence we envision God gently steering and guiding nations and other large blocks of humanity down His preordained paths. His divine guidance pours out over all of humanity as He works out His will in the world. We can think of it as rain falling from heaven or as the light of the sun shining upon all of humanity.

Guidance Flows from Above

Because of these dynamics, the president of a nation is more likely than the average citizen to sense a force guiding him or her down a specific path.

This does not mean that everything a leader does is divinely inspired. Though they may sense something guiding them they must discern good from evil. As we have discussed, the devil can add his temptations and "inspiration." The spiritual inspiration upon which a leader draws is determined by her heart. If her heart is oriented toward evil, the inspiration she receives will guide her and those who follow her down evil paths.

So also a leader can direct his heart toward a specific stream of authority already established in the realm of the spirit. For example, a leadership team may be committed in heart corporately to some university and its goals. As a result, those leaders will have their eyes opened as to how to further the goals of the university. Because their hearts are directed accordingly, the leaders will be spiritually guided down a specific path in line with the university's goals.

When leaders are simply trying to do what is right for the people under their charge, God gives those leaders wisdom—even if they are non-Christian leaders. When a nation walks in unity and peace, God helps the leadership. When a businesswoman rises up to govern her employees, God offers His help so He can bless society through her business. When a father accepts responsibility for his family, God gives wisdom. When brothers dwell together in unity, the anointing oil flows downward (Ps. 133:1-3).

It does not matter if people are Christians or non-Christians. God lets His light shine on the good and evil. He loves the world. Of course, not all authority figures want to receive God's guidance, but He is offering it. He wants to help humanity and one of His avenues of blessing this world is through establishing authority.

This principle is amplified for God's children. The Holy Spirit is being poured out freely for them and the spirit within them bears witness to the Holy Spirit. As John wrote the anointing is within believers and the *"...anointing teaches you..."* (I John 2:27).

Therefore, a pastor who accepts responsibility for his sheep will have divine inspiration on what to teach and where to guide his people. Many pastors have learned this principle and have learned to depend on its operation. For example, if a pastor does not know what to teach at an upcoming meeting, he can simply orient his heart toward the people and accept responsibility for them. As he is postured in that place between God's flowing authority and the needs of the people, spiritual energy flows from God and inspires in him the thoughts of God.

This is how God created us. Where there is unity and order, His grace and blessings flow. When people accept responsibility for the positions of authority which God has entrusted to them, their eyes supernaturally open.

Having said this, I do not mean to justify hierarchical relationships in which leaders see themselves domineering those under their charge. The Spirit that flows from God creates in leaders the characteristics of servanthood. The same Spirit that inspires wisdom is the same Spirit that reproduces the nature of Jesus in people. Hence, leaders receiving the breath of God become both divinely guided and divinely humble.

Unfortunately, people seem to over-emphasize one or the other, authority or servanthood. Some leaders demand submission of their followers and take advantage of those under their charge. Other Christians emphasize servanthood so much that they do not allow individuals to rise in authority and lead. Both extremes hinder the work of God. A leader whose heart is to dominate rather than serve will release evil forces into the world. People who misunderstand servanthood to the point of becoming doormats will not allow people to function together to accomplish much good for humanity.

The same Spirit which stirred in Peter to stand up and preach on the streets of Jerusalem on Pentecost day is the same Spirit which led Jesus to give His life on the cross. The same Spirit which led Jesus to wash His disciples' feet is the same Spirit that ascended our Lord far above all rule and authority.

Conclusion

Every human being, whether or not they realize it, experiences the spiritual dynamics which we have been discussing. Even people who think only in terms of natural forces have a spirit which sustains their lives and allows them to think and interact with those around them. All of us were created with a spirit and that spirit is influenced by unseen forces 24 hours of each day. These are facts of life.

Because we live in a world of interacting spiritual forces, peace and order result from a life of spiritual harmony with God and our neighbors. When a person finds peace with God and orients his heart toward Him, the force of God's blessings flow. As people keep their commitments to other people, such as honoring their marriage vows, paying their bills, forgiving those who offend them and obeying the laws of the land, spiritual authority will establish peace around them. On the other hand, when individuals violate established authorities or covenants, they cause turbulence in the spiritual dimension.

In this light, we also see the promises of God in operation. When people seek first the kingdom of God, forces are released to cause all good things to be added to their lives. As they prove faithful with what God has given to them, they will be exalted. As they delight in the Lord, He gives them the desires of their hearts.

In conclusion, make your life better by loving God with all of your heart and your neighbor as yourself. This is the path to spiritual power.

Other Books by Harold R. Eberle

Christianity Unshackled

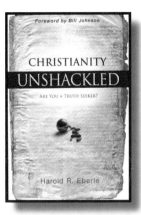

Most Christians in the Western world have no idea how profoundly their beliefs have been influenced by their culture. What would Christianity be like, if it was separated from Western thought? After untangling the Western traditions of the last 2,000 years of Church history, Harold R. Eberle offers a Christian worldview that is clear, concise, and liberating. This will shake you to the core and then leave you standing on a firm foundation!

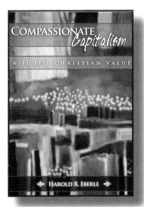

Compassionate Capitalism:
A Judeo-Christian Value

This book is a look into history to see where and how capitalism was born and developed through the centuries. As you read this book, you will learn how capitalism first developed as God worked among the Hebrew people in the Old Testament. The resulting economic principles then transformed Western society as they spread with Christianity. What remains is for us to apply the principles of capitalism with compassion.

Releasing Kings into the Marketplace for Ministry

By John Garfield and Harold R. Eberle

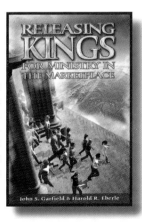

"Kings" is what we call Christian leaders who have embraced the call of God upon their life to work in the marketplace and from that position transform society. This book explains how marketplace ministry will operate in concert with local churches and pastors. It provides a Scriptural basis for the expansion of the Kingdom of God into all areas of society.

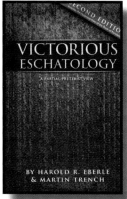

Victorious Eschatology

Co-authored by
Harold R. Eberle and Martin Trench

Here it is—a biblically-based, optimistic view of the future. Along with a historical perspective, this book offers a clear understanding of Matthew 24, the book of Revelation, and other key passages about the events to precede the return of Jesus Christ. Satan is not going to take over this world. Jesus Christ is Lord and He will reign until every enemy is put under His feet!

Jesus Came Out of the Tomb...So Can You!

A Brief Explanation of Resurrection-based Christianity

Forgiveness of sins is at the cross. Power over sin is in the resurrection and ascension. Unfortunately, too many Christians have only benefited from the death of Jesus and not His life. If God raised Jesus from the tomb in power and glory, then we can experience that resurrection power. If God raised Jesus into heaven, and us with Him, then we can live in His victory!

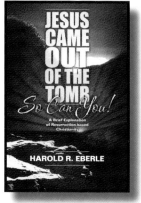

Developing a Prosperous Soul

Vol. I: How to Overcome a Poverty Mind-set
Vol. II: How to Move into God's Financial Blessings

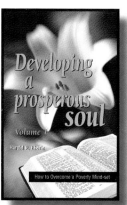

There are fundamental changes you can make in the way you think which will help you release God's blessings. This is a balanced look at the promises of God with practical steps you can take to move into financial freedom. It is time for Christians to re-capture the financial arena. These two volumes will inspire and create faith in you to fulfill God's purpose for your life.

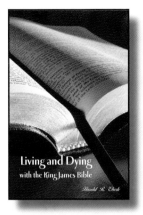

Living and Dying with the King James Bible

The King James Version (KJV) has been a gift of God to the Body of Christ. It has been the standard of truth and inspiration which has stabilized the Protestant Church and blessed millions of people. But someone needs to say it: the KJV is an inferior translation. In these pages, Harold R. Eberle clearly shows the errors and biases of the KJV, hoping you will consider the advantages of more modern Bible translations.

The Complete Wineskin
(Fourth edition)

The Body of Christ is in a reformation. God is pouring out His Holy Spirit and our wineskins must be changed to handle the new wine. Will the Church come together in unity? How does the anointing of God work and what is your role? What is the 5-fold ministry? How are apostles, prophets, evangelists, pastors, and teachers going to rise up and work together? Where do small group meetings fit in? This book puts into words what you have been sensing in your spirit. (Eberle's best seller, translated into many languages, distributed worldwide.)

God's Leaders for Tomorrow's World
(Revised/expanded edition)

You sense the call to leadership, but questions persist: "Does God want me to rise up? Do I truly know where to lead? Is this pride? How can I influence people?" Through an understanding of leadership dynamics, learn how to develop godly charisma. Confusion will melt into order when you see the God-ordained lines of authority. Fear of leadership will change to confidence as you learn to handle power struggles. It is time to move into your "metron," that is, your God-given sphere of authority.

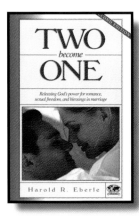

Two Become One
(Second edition)
Releasing God's Power for Romance, Sexual Freedom and Blessings in Marriage

The keys to a thrilling, passionate, and fulfilling marriage can be yours if you want them. Kindle afresh the "buzz of love." Find out how to make God's law of binding forces work for you rather than against you. This book is of great benefit to pastors, counselors, young singles, divorces, and especially married people. Couples are encouraged to read it together.

Grace...the Power to Reign
The Light Shining from Romans 5-8

We struggle against sin and yearn for God's highest. Yet, on a bad day it is as if we are fighting against gravity. Questions go unanswered:

- Where is the power to overcome temptations and trials?
- Is God really willing to breathe into us that these dry bones can live and we may stand strong?

For anyone who has ever struggled to live godly, here are the answers.

Who Is God?

Challenging the traditional Western view of God, Harold R. Eberle presents God as a Covenant-maker, Lover, and Father. Depending on Scripture, God is shown to be in a vulnerable, open, and cooperative relationship with His people. This book is both unsettling and enlightening—revolutionary to most readers—considered by many to be Harold's most important contribution to the Body of Christ.

To place an order or to check current prices
on these and other books, call:

1-800-308-5837 within the USA or
509-248-5837 from outside of the USA

Worldcast Publishing
P.O. Box 10653
Yakima, WA 98909-1653

E-mail: office@worldcastpublishing.com
Web Site: www.worldcastpublishing.com